17.50

Banking on the Poor

Banking on the Poor

The World Bank and World Poverty

Robert L. Ayres

The MIT Press
Cambridge, Massachusetts
London, England

str. 17.50 | 9.00 | 6/24/83

This book was set in Baskerville by The MIT Press Computergraphics Department and printed and bound by The Murray Printing Co. in the United States of America.

Library of Congress Cataloging in Publication Data

Ayres, Robert L.
Banking on the poor.

Bibliography: p.
Includes index.
1. World Bank. I. Title.
HG3881.5.W57A96 1983   332.1'532   82–17961
ISBN 0–262–01070–4

Banking on the Poor was prepared by its author at the Overseas Development Council (ODC) in Washington, D.C. The ODC is a private, nonprofit organization established in 1969 to increase American understanding of the economic and social problems confronting the developing countries and to promote awareness of the importance of these countries to the United States. In pursuing these goals, ODC functions as a center for policy-oriented study and analysis, a forum for the exchange of ideas, and a resource for public education.

To Kenneth and Rachel

Contents

9
The Politics of Poverty-Oriented Projects   *209*

10
The Bank after McNamara   *229*

Preface

My desire to explore the theme of this book—Robert S. McNamara's efforts to reorient the World Bank toward a more explicit concern with poverty alleviation in the world's poor countries—had its origins during my years in the political science department at the University of California in Berkeley. My principal field was Latin American politics, and in my research I was struck by two facts: the importance of external factors in political and economic developments there and the glaring features of poverty amid abundance that characterized the countries of the region. I was searching for a topic that would combine these twin preoccupations and found it when McNamara began the poverty-oriented redirections at the Bank. The Bank was an increasingly important actor in the development of Latin America. At the time I was conceptualizing this study it was on the verge of surpassing the Inter-American Development Bank as the largest official lender to the region. I also reasoned that the antipoverty orientation would be particularly interesting to explore in Latin America with its concentrated structure of landholding, notoriously inegalitarian income distribution, and manifold political obstacles to an equitable pattern of development.

Having written on some of these themes in an article which attracted considerable attention ("Development Policy and the Possibility of a 'Livable' Future for Latin America," *The American Political Science Review*, 92, June 1975, pp. 507–525), I drafted a research proposal and submitted it to the International Affairs Fellowship Program of the Council on Foreign Relations. The Council awarded me a fellowship for the 1975–76 academic year, and I left Berkeley to take up residence as a guest scholar at the Brookings Institution in Washington, D.C. While there I conducted the background research that has eventuated in the publication of the present study. I have worked on the study intermittently since 1976, with the bulk of the research being undertaken between 1978 and 1980 following my appointment to the position of senior fellow at the Overseas Development Council (ODC).

My initial inquiries at the Bank concerned its operations in Latin America, and I am grateful to Adalbert Krieger Vasena, former finance minister of Argentina and then the vice-president of the World Bank for Latin America and the Caribbean, and Barend de Vries, then the regional chief economist, for facilitating my first contacts with staff and officials of the institution. But it soon became apparent that the inquiry needed to be extended beyond simply Latin America to other regions where the Bank's poverty-oriented emphases were increasingly being put into practice. It also seemed necessary to expand the inquiry to explore a wide range of issues concerning the Bank, not only its recent antipoverty work. While Edward S. Mason and Robert E. Asher had published their monumental book on the Bank (*The World Bank Since Bretton Woods*) three years before my research commenced, the book had not dealt with the institutional implications of the Bank's poverty-oriented work for the simple reason that the work only began after their research had ended. The decision to write a somewhat broader book about the Bank than originally planned vastly increased the research demands of the enterprise and led to interview and documentary work at the Bank well beyond that envisioned at the outset of the study.

The turning point of the study took place in January 1978, when I joined the staff of the ODC. Its president, James P. Grant, who has since become the executive director of UNICEF, was intensely interested in the themes I was pursuing. So was ODC's vice-president, John W. Sewell, currently the organization's president. Both encouraged me to continue my research despite my other commitments involving ODC's many activities in the field of international development. ODC was a virtually unique base from which to pursue such a study. The range of its concerns with development issues and the breadth of its contacts with development policy makers within and without the World Bank provided me with the access and stimulation necessary to complete my work. While I must express my appreciation to many individuals and organizations, a special sense of appreciation is reserved for Jim Grant, John Sewell, and the Overseas Development Council. Its work on the most vital issues of contemporary international development continues to be of the utmost service to scholars, the Washington policy community, and the public concerned with development.

Those who assisted me at the Bank itself are far too numerous to mention and would in any event probably prefer anonymity. I must, however, register my particular indebtedness to John E. Merriam, the

Bank's director of information and public affairs throughout the course of this study. He facilitated my work at the Bank in countless ways. I thank all who assisted me at the Bank, ranging from project officers and country economists through division chiefs and department heads to vice-presidents. In the latter months of the study Bank Presidents McNamara and A. W. Clausen were themselves generous with their time and insights.

Crucial research assistance was provided by Philip C. Erquiaga. Philip pored over Bank documents, gathered data, systematized my notes on interviews, and checked the manuscript for any glaring inaccuracies. More than that, he was my main source of intellectual stimulation throughout much of the course of my research. "Research assistant" is inadequate to describe the role he played in this study.

A word of thanks is also due those who read the manuscript in one or another form and offered helpful comments and suggestions: Robert E. Asher, J. Burke Knapp (former senior vice-president for operations of the World Bank), and S. J. Burki, senior adviser to the Bank's vice-president for external relations.

At the time I began the study I did not realize how prominent and controversial the subject was destined to become. The poverty-oriented redirections of the Bank provoked adverse commentary from both left and right, and I was consistently pressed to "take a stand." The stand taken here is to reject the extremes and adopt a realist's defense of the Bank as a reformist institution. My defense of the Bank against rightist critics was contained in an article entitled "Breaking the Bank," which appeared in *Foreign Policy* (Summer 1981, pp. 104–120). Parts of chapters 1 and 10 represent a revised and expanded version of arguments contained in that article. A defense against leftist critics is contained in the present volume. I have found much to criticize but not enough to alter my view that the Bank functions in an effective manner in face of the severe national and international constraints under which it must operate. This conclusion will, I anticipate, be open to the same criticisms that the Bank itself has experienced from those searching for more definitive pronouncements.

In a personal sense the real contribution of the Bank has been to my own intellectual evolution and growth. I began the study with some degree of regional expertise on Latin America and with limited knowledge of what has come to be called "North–South relations." Intimate involvement with the Bank over the course of this study has opened windows on other regions of the developing world, issues confronting the international economic system, and the complex nature of the interdependence between the world's rich and poor countries.

In a very real sense, therefore, I am grateful to the officers and staff of the World Bank for much more than simply their contributions to this study. Like many of the written reports of the Bank itself, the process by which the study was conducted is perhaps as important to me in an ongoing sense as the substantive themes that it addresses.

A Note on Sources

The primary sources for the material contained in this study are documents, to which I was provided access by the Bank, and interviews with Bank staff and officials.

The World Bank is not a noticeably open institution. Nevertheless, after some period of time I was able to obtain access to a considerable number of internal documents that went beyond the Bank's country economic and project appraisal reports which, although labeled "confidential," are generally available through the office of the American Executive Director of the Bank. Among these were project supervision reports on projects under implementation, various intra-Bank memorandums of one sort or another, country programming papers which detail the Bank's anticipated lending program for the next five years in recipient countries, project performance audit reports which are Bank comprehensive audits on all completed projects, and special studies of particular countries or issues. In gaining access to such materials, I agreed to certain ground rules. I agreed to paraphrase instead of quoting directly (to the extent that this was feasible, sometimes direct quotes were necessary to convey the full meaning of a particular point). I also agreed to make only general reference to the source, not to cite title, date, and so forth. Thus all references to internal Bank documents are not cited in the notes to this book.

Many observations come out of my detailed interviews with Bank staff and officials which numbered approximately 300 during the course of the research conducted for this study. The quotations from these interviews are liberally sprinkled throughout the study, and they stem from my extensive notes compiled immediately after the interviews took place. It would be highly inappropriate to name the people at the Bank who were so generous with their time and observations. In any event in some places the reader who knows the Bank will undoubtedly be able to identify the source.

The fact that neither internal Bank materials nor interviews with Bank staff and officials are cited in the notes means that the notes are generally confined to published sources. In a strictly academic sense, then, the study is not fully annotated. This is the inevitable consequence of my agreements with Bank officialdom about my use of their sources. Failing such agreements, I would never have been able to obtain the requisite access to an institution which even by Washington standards has a reputation for being rather reticent about revealing what it is doing.

1

Historical Evolution and Changes under McNamara

The departure of Robert S. McNamara as president of the World Bank on June 30, 1981, marked the end of thirteen years of his presidency and of an era for the world's preeminent international development organization. It was an era characterized by two major changes: a vast expansion in the flow of financial resources from the Bank to the countries of the developing world and a significant reorientation in the kinds of projects those resources financed. Particularly after 1973 the Bank diversified the sectoral allocation of its funds away from an almost exclusive concern with funding projects of basic economic infrastructure toward projects explicitly devoted to the alleviation of poverty in less-developed countries. At the same time it was vastly expanding the amounts of its development lending, the Bank was also becoming the world's largest antipoverty agency. It was in the forefront as the international development assistance community entered an era of poverty-oriented development projects.

The Bank before McNamara

A product (along with the International Monetary Fund) of the Bretton Woods conference of July 1944, the International Bank for Reconstruction and Development, now known almost exclusively as the "World Bank," began formal operations at its headquarters in Washington, D.C., on June 25, 1946. Its twin functions were explicit in its name. It was to assist in the reconstruction of the war-ravaged economies of Europe and Japan and in the "development"—the term was open to numerous interpretations—of the "less developed" world. The Bank's first four loans, approved in mid-1947, were for reconstruction of Denmark, France, Luxembourg, and the Netherlands. Its first development loan was made to Chile for two small projects in March 1948.

From its inception the Bank was both determinative and reflective of current thinking about development. In the two decades between its first development loan and the presidency of McNamara, the Bank had a strong tendency to equate development with economic growth. The principal developmental goal was the expansion of the aggregate growth rate, and the projects the Bank undertook to finance in the developing world tended to be judged by their prospective contributions to this objective. Edward S. Mason and Robert E. Asher, in their monumental history of the first quarter century of the Bank, summarized this view as follows:

The Bank recognized that investments of many kinds were needed for development but frequently implied that one kind was more essential than any other. The relative ease with which it could finance electric power, transportation, and economic infrastructure projects . . . made it an exponent of the thesis that public utility projects, accompanied by financial stability and the encouragement of private investment, could do more than almost anything else to trigger development. Projects to develop electric power and transport facilities were accordingly considered especially appropriate for Bank financing. At the same time the Bank was led to eschew certain fields traditionally open to public investment, even in the highly developed free-enterprise economies: namely, sanitation, education, and health facilities. Investments in these so-called "social overhead" fields were widely considered to be as fundamental to development as are investments in hydroelectric sites, railroads, highways, and "economic overhead" programs. The contribution of social overhead projects to increased production, however, is less measureable and direct than that of power plants, and they can be completed without large outlays of scarce foreign exchange. Financing them, moreover, might open the door to vastly increased demands for loans and raise hackles anew in Wall Street about the "soundness" of the Bank's management. It therefore seemed prudent to the management during the first postwar decade to consider as unsuitable in normal circumstances World Bank financing of projects for eliminating malaria, reducing illiteracy, building vocational schools, or establishing clinics. The Bank became the leading proponent of the view that investment in transportation and communication facilities, port developments, power projects, and other public utilities was a precondition for the development of the rest of the economy.[1]

This view in fact persisted well beyond the first postwar decade; it was still operative when McNamara assumed the presidency of the Bank in 1968. It was clearly reflected in the Bank's sectoral lending allocations. Between fiscal years 1961 and 1965, 76.8 percent of all Bank lending was for electric power or transportation. Only 6 percent was for agricultural development, and a paltry 1 percent for social service investment.[2] In the case of the International Development Association (IDA, the Bank's "soft-loan" affiliate created in 1960), about half of the lending between 1961 and 1965 was for electric power and transportation, only 18 percent for agriculture, and only 3 percent for social services.[3]

The total lending of the Bank and IDA for all purposes from their respective beginnings until McNamara's presidency was not great. This totaled approximately $13 billion through June 30, 1968. Much of this represented commitments to developed rather than poor countries. By 1968 the Bank had loaned about $857 million to Japan, $398 million to Italy, $290 million to France, and $236 million to the Netherlands. Reconstruction lending per se ended in 1955, but there continued substantial lending to developed countries until about 1967.[4] Development loans had a slow beginning but soon attained an annual level of $300 to $400 million, persisting at this level until fiscal 1958. Between then and the beginning of McNamara's presidency in 1968, loans for development purposes tended to vary between about $700 and $800 million a year.[5]

In retrospect the World Bank before McNamara was, relatively speaking, a remarkably conservative institution. It was basically a project lender. The projects it financed were quite traditional, as it shunned riskier sectors in the borrowing nations. The Bank was particularly conservative in the ways it judged the performance and creditworthiness of its borrowers. For some years the principal index of creditworthiness was a country's debt service ratio—the ratio of a country's interest and amortization payments on its public and publicly guaranteed debt to the country's earnings from exports of goods and services. The Bank put considerable emphasis on domestic savings rates, public sector fiscal and monetary probity, the growth of output and investment in different sectors, and efficiency in the use of domestic resources. As Mason and Asher note, "the early literature of the Bank is full of references to 'sound' economic policies, 'sound' fiscal and monetary policies, and 'sound' policies of various other kinds, with the clear implication that the distinction between sound and unsound policies is as obvious as the distinction between day and night."[6]

It was a comfortable if not complacent time. The objective was growth, and growth could be technocratically orchestrated regardless of the political systems in the countries that were the recipients of Bank loans. Much of this was also related to the Bank's desire to establish and verify its own creditworthiness. The Bank was in part a cautious lender because of its own need to borrow to finance its lending program, and "it was clear from the start that whatever lending policy the Bank might want to pursue would be strictly conditioned by the necessity of finding U.S. investors who were willing to buy its securities or accept its guarantee."[7] This was less strictly conditioned as the years went by but, nevertheless, kept the Bank from venturing into sectors and countries where lending could be thought to jeopardize the quality of its loan portfolio. The Bank in the pre-McNamara years avoided a role as a *development agency* in favor of the more traditional role of *bank*.

The McNamara Years

A vigorous debate continues on whether the World Bank under McNamara changed for better or worse, but there is no denying that the institution experienced some remarkable changes during his tenure.

Funding clearly increased, from 62 new projects approved by the Bank and IDA in fiscal year 1968 to 266 in fiscal 1981. In fiscal 1968 these new commitments totaled $953.5 *million*; in fiscal 1981, $12.4 *billion*.[8] By the end of fiscal 1981 the total cumulative lending commitments of the Bank and IDA were $92.2 billion.[9] Of this amount all but $13 billion were committed during the McNamara years. This means that almost 86 percent of all Bank/IDA lending occurred during those years. Even after correcting for the notorious inflation of that interval, Bank/IDA lending under McNamara grew approximately fivefold in real terms. This substantial growth in lending was accompanied by a growth in the staffing needs of the Bank. In fiscal 1968 the total staff numbered 1,574. By fiscal 1981 it had grown to 5,201. The professional staff numbered 767 in fiscal 1968; in fiscal 1981 it was 2,552.[10] The World Bank, while becoming by far the world's largest official lender for the development of low-income countries, also became a bureaucracy.

But there were also important changes in the *composition* of Bank and IDA lending, and these serve as the basis for the inquiry that follows. The Bank in the McNamara years, and particularly since 1973, became increasingly devoted to the alleviation of poverty in its developing member countries. (The membership of the Bank, which totaled 36 nations in 1946, now numbers 141.) The benchmark event or turning point was McNamara's Nairobi speech, his address to the Board of Governors of the Bank delivered on September 24, 1973. McNamara focused on the dimensions of world poverty, particularly on the very little done in the previous two decades to increase the productivity of subsistence agriculture in poor countries.[11]

But McNamara's Nairobi speech was only the beginning. A series of sector policy papers outlined Bank thinking about sectoral poverty concerns, notably rural development, basic education, basic health, and low-cost housing, and suggested roles for the Bank in attacking poverty problems directly. The Bank's Development Research Center turned much of its attention to questions of poverty and income distribution. A volume produced in 1974, *Redistribution with Growth*, became somewhat of a landmark citation.[12] Much of the Bank's own research work was increasingly given over to questions about poverty alleviation. More recently, the Bank was in the vanguard of theoretical work on a "basic human needs" approach to development.

The McNamara reorientation of the Bank away from its almost exclusive concern with basic economic infrastructure toward antipoverty work was most dramatically reflected in changes in the Bank's lending activities for development. In fiscal 1968 Bank lending for agriculture and rural development amounted to only $172.5 million, 18.1 percent of its total lending. By fiscal 1981 it had risen to $3.8 billion, 31 percent of total lending.[13] Bank lending for agriculture and rural development in the single year of fiscal 1981 was almost four times such lending during the Bank's entire existence from 1946 to 1968.[14]

There were also pronounced changes in lending within the agricultural sector. Lending for irrigation and other projects of agricultural infrastructure declined in relative importance, while lending for poverty-oriented rural development increased. Between fiscal years 1974 and 1978, approximately 75 percent of the 363 agriculture and rural development projects approved by the Bank contained what is called a "small-farmer element or component."[15] Over 50 percent of the Bank's lending for agriculture and rural development in 1974 to 1978 was accounted for by 210 rural development projects defined by the Bank as "those projects in which more than half of the direct benefits are expected to accrue to the rural poor."[16]

Other lending changes were also apparent. Increasing concern with problems of urban poverty led to lending for low-cost housing and slum rehabilitation projects. From 1972, when the Bank made its first housing loan (for a project in Dakar, Senegal) through the end of fiscal 1981, the Bank undertook 52 basic urbanization projects representing total loan commitments of $1.6 billion.[17] Lending for industrial development increased, with greater attention to the potentialities of small-scale industry.

In the education sector the pre-McNamara years were characterized by no lending at all for primary education and very little for nonformal education. The Bank estimated, however, that 21.2 percent of its educational lending would be for primary education and 24.6 percent for nonformal education over the fiscal years 1979 to 1983.[18]

Health components came to comprise an increasingly important proportion of the Bank's rural development and other projects. Approximately $202 million were committed for health components of projects over the fiscal years from 1976 to 1981.[19] The Bank funded large countrywide nutrition projects in Brazil and Colombia. In addition the Bank had approved 23 population projects by the end of fiscal 1980, involving Bank lending of $421.9 million.[20] While small in aggregate amounts, Bank lending for health and population activities represented other new directions under McNamara.

In general, lending for the traditional activities of power, transportation, and telecommunications increased in absolute amounts but declined as a percentage of the Bank's lending operations. In fiscal 1968 lending for these activities constituted 57 percent of total Bank lending.[21] By fiscal 1980 this figure was only 39.[22]

Such changes in the Bank's lending program, while of central importance to the themes of this study, were not the only significant changes under the McNamara presidency. There were changes in the composition of the staff. The percentage of the professional staff coming from the United States, the United Kingdom, and other economically developed countries declined whereas the percentage from developing countries increased. There was also a perceptible increase in the percentage of women although the total number of women on the Bank's professional staff remains small. As of fiscal 1980 women constituted 12 percent of the professional staff, an increase from 6.3 percent in fiscal 1968.[23]

There were many internal organizational developments. Entirely new units were created, reflecting both the increase in Bank work and its reorientation toward questions of poverty alleviation and income distribution. These included the Agriculture and Rural Development Department created in 1973, the Urban Projects Department created in 1975, and the Population, Health, and Nutrition Department created in 1979. The Bank's Development Policy Staff increased greatly in size and importance to the point where the organization's research expertise on some questions of economic development became unrivaled. A policy-planning department was established in 1972. The Operations Evaluation Department created in 1975 represented an effort at self-criticism and evaluation. Its principal task was to audit and draw lessons from the implementation of the Bank's manifold development projects.

All of these changes had profound implications for the work of the Bank. The social dynamics of the organization were fundamentally altered. Before McNamara the Bank was in a sense a club characterized by much cultural homogeneity; now it is a bureaucracy with a good deal of heterogeneity. Before, management was benevolently paternalistic; under McNamara it was greatly centralized, much more hierarchical.

The pace of work also speeded up. The number of projects approved per staff member increased. Loan commitments per staff member increased from $1.59 million in fiscal 1968 to $1.95 million in fiscal 1978.[24] This resulted in what some members of the Bank's own Staff Association referred to as an assembly-line approach to project preparation. Pressure increased to grind out projects to meet the year's quantitative goals.

If the Bank changed internally, it also changed in the character of its external relations. The substantial increase in the commitment of Bank resources and the associated qualitative changes in lending had pronounced effects upon the Bank's role in the international development assistance community. At a time when the low profile was much in vogue elsewhere, the Bank became an increasingly visible institution. Its general development policy orientations, the kinds of specific projects it financed, and its conflicts with recipient countries became the subject of increasing journalistic, political, and public comment and debate—in marked contrast to the lack of attention given the Bank when it was in many ways almost an appendage of the U.S. Treasury Department. The Bank's active involvement—indeed its central role—in the substantive debate about the goals of development in the 1970s, particularly the goal of poverty alleviation, brought it into increasing conflict with regimes in the developing world not noted for their urgent concern for these matters.

Such involvement also brought the Bank into conflict with important figures in the U.S. government. There was increasing disquiet, especially within the Congress, with the growth and poverty-oriented redirections of the Bank. This disquiet sharply increased with the advent of the Reagan administration in 1981. Few in the administration seemed to share McNamara's concerns with subsistence farmers and shantytown dwellers.

Poverty Alleviation and Its Implications

What motivated the new poverty-oriented concerns in development assistance? What motivated McNamara's World Bank? There were undoubtedly numerous, complex conditions, many of which may be summarized in the following observation: The process of economic growth as it occurred in many developing countries in the last several decades appeared to bypass the poorest people and in some cases even worsened their circumstances, despite some impressive achievements in aggregate terms.

The problem was the apparent failure of the trickle-down strategy of development.[25] The impressive growth rates and sectoral achievements in many developing countries were apparently not translated into an improvement in real living conditions for the "absolute" poor who constitute, according to a conservative estimate, at least 40 percent of the population of such countries.[26] Even within countries such as Brazil and Mexico, where growth is thought to have been exceptional, there are very large areas of desperate poverty (in this case rural Mexico or northeast Brazil). For many countries income distribution, as measured by indicators of relative inequality or by measures of absolute impoverishment, appeared to worsen noticeably as economic growth proceeded.[27] The problems of unemployment and under-employment came to the fore as urban industry was unable to absorb the increments to the urban labor force.[28] Neglect of agricultural development contributed to a crisis of production and productivity. According to one account, "a large majority (nearly four-fifths) of the population of underdeveloped territories are supported on a level of productivity that still implies a risk of famine."[29] In the light of these and other seemingly intractable problems, it is conceivable that the development assistance effort had to change to deal with poverty directly; the traditional practice of waiting for the slow diffusion of the benefits of growth simply did not work.

The Bank of course is not the first institution to treat the socio-economic conditions of the poor. If one wishes to search for the roots of concern for the poor, one may retreat through the millennia to the study of the world's great religions and philosophical systems. A more contemporaneous and mundane example is to be found in various Indian national plans, which have stressed the importance of anti-poverty objectives.[30] The work of the International Labor Organization (ILO) after 1969 on the employment needs of developing countries was of undeniable importance. During the 1970s a number of international forums focused directly or indirectly on poverty-oriented issues. These included a conference in Cocoyoc, Mexico, held by the United Nations in 1974, where the objective was to "redefine the whole purpose of development . . . to ensure the quality of life for all . . . "; the Third World Forum, organized in 1975 to "facilitate the creation of a more just world order"; the 1975 report of the Dag Hammarskjold Foundation, which argued that the satisfaction of peoples' basic needs should be at the core of the development process; the 1976 World Employment Conference of the ILO, where the central theme was the importance of making basic needs satisfaction the prime focus of national and international development efforts; and the Tinbergen report on *Reshaping the International Order* which called for the elaboration of new development strategies emphasizing basic needs satisfaction, poverty eradication, self-reliant and participatory development, and development attentive to ecological considerations.[31]

Two major policy initiatives of the American government—one antedating by many years the World Bank's newer concerns, the other coterminous with them—were particularly illustrative of poverty-oriented emphases. One was the Alliance for Progress, an initiative begun in 1961 which marked "a dramatic and fundamental reorientation of Washington's policy toward Latin America."[32] While the primary objective of the Alliance was an increase in rates of economic growth, its second objective was a more equitable distribution of national income.[33] The Alliance aimed at reforms in the region's economic and social systems and proposed specific policy reorientations in agriculture, health, housing, education, and other sectors that in many significant ways preceded World Bank initiatives a decade later.

A second major effort was embodied in the U.S. Foreign Assistance Act of 1973, popularly known as the New Directions legislation. The act mandated a change in "our whole approach to development by concentrating on the needs of the poor."[34] Henceforth the American bilateral assistance program was to focus on the fundamental problems of the "poor majority"—food and nutrition needs, population, health, education, and human resource development.[35] The overriding objective was to "help improve the lives of masses of people who live under conditions of extreme poverty, malnutrition, and disease."[36] According to one observer, "this was a marked departure from previous U.S. aid schemes which had concentrated on high-technology, capital-intensive, industry-based growth for almost two decades."[37]

The Bank then was not a deus ex machina. Poverty alleviation was not invented with McNamara's Nairobi speech of 1973. But the Bank rapidly moved to the vanguard of international efforts on the anti-poverty front. Partly this was because it skillfully distilled the work of others—in academe, in international forums and organizations, and in some developing countries themselves. Partly it was because of its own intellectual leadership role in this area, especially after the creation of its Development Policy Staff in 1971. But mainly it was because the Bank possessed the *resources* to make the new poverty-oriented emphases operational. While others còuld write reports, elaborate theories, make proclamations, and perhaps carry out some limited endeavors in the field, the Bank could back up its new antipoverty concerns with the transfer of substantial sums of money.

The transfer of money by the Bank for poverty-oriented work had a number of significant implications for its operations. One of these was the tension created between McNamara's goals of substantially increasing resources transferred to developing countries by the Bank and of reorienting the Bank to play a predominant role in the international antipoverty effort. The goal of transferring resources, or "moving money," as it is sometimes called, was more readily attained via big, traditional infrastructure projects—through loans for steel mills, for example. Poverty-oriented projects appeared to be typically smaller in their commitment of resources, more time-consuming, more staff-intensive, more difficult to implement, more requiring of skills in which the Bank was still relatively deficient. How to move a lot more money while doing a lot more on behalf of poverty alleviation thus became a central tension of the Bank's work under McNamara.

A second major implication concerned the Bank's role as a bank in contrast to its role as a development agency. The officials interviewed at the Bank for this study were very quick to point out that the institution is first and foremost a bank. It makes loans. It has to be concerned about creditworthiness of borrowers, interest rates, amortization schedules, and the like. Like any other bank it does not give things away. It does not subsidize undertakings. As the treasurer of the Bank has pointed out, it has to provide "unmatched protection and strength for creditors and shareholders."[38]

In fact, however, the World Bank has always been something more and something less than a "real" bank. In its functions of technical assistance, research, in much of its country economic work, in its more innovative development projects, in its involvement in desperately poor countries, in its role in the international marketplace of ideas through its publications and the speeches of its president, the World Bank has always differed substantially from a standard bank. Obviously, if the Bank were to become increasingly involved in antipoverty activities in developing countries, it had to become less of a bank and more of a development agency.

A third implication of the Bank's poverty-oriented concerns under McNamara relates to the Bank's larger role in the international system. The Bank in the McNamara years became a more overtly reformist institution. But this reformist role, in which social and distributional concerns were added to primarily economic and growth-oriented objectives, did not fundamentally alter what may be considered the Bank's primary objective. This has been variously phrased, but in essence it amounts to the goal of modernizing the international economy in its capitalist variant for the sake of its long-term preservation. In the 1950s and 1960s an overriding concern was with growth, and development projects to facilitate growth were viewed as principal contributors to this primordial goal. In the 1970s certain socioeconomic reforms came to be seen—by the Bank and by others—as essential in this effort. McNamara at the Bank confronted a situation not unlike that before Franklin Roosevelt during the Great Depression. For both the task was to preserve the prevailing system through reforms whose necessity was not previously understood or well tolerated. Means were significantly altered in the pursuit of long-standing ends.

Evaluating the Bank

These considerations suggest that the political economy of poverty-oriented development strategies is a complex and controversial topic. So is the role of the World Bank in the design and implementation of such strategies. In addressing these subjects, there is an array of conflicting analytical and normative orientations. It is accordingly difficult to formulate criteria for evaluating the Bank's work, particularly its work under McNamara on behalf of poverty alleviation in its developing member countries.

There are strikingly divergent (indeed almost diametrically opposed) viewpoints on this question. On the one hand, a leftist or "radical" interpretation is that the kinds of antipoverty efforts in developing countries discussed in subsequent chapters of this study amount to a mere utopian pipedream. From this perspective, such efforts in developing countries (with a few exceptions, such as Cuba) are viewed as not politically feasible because such countries are "dependent capitalist" states. They lack a growth-promoting "national bourgeoisie" because the most powerful political actors are closely tied to foreign capital. They are thus "structurally inhibited" from pursuing poverty-oriented strategies because these would transform the status quo from which the elites derive benefit. In such political systems policies designed to combat poverty would be mere palliatives or tokenism at best and probably counterproductive. The only "real" solution lies in the revolutionary uprooting of the dependent capitalist system and its wholesale replacement by some variant of socialism.

Opposed to this line of reasoning is a "conservative" critique of the Bank which in its most extreme guise argues precisely the reverse, that the Bank's operations are *promoting* socialism in developing countries. According to this line of argument, the Bank's efforts are *undermining* capitalist development. In the United States this line of argument spread from academic into policy circles with the arrival of the Reagan administration. Early in the administration, for example, its budget director protested that the Bank "has supported state planning efforts in some countries" and "has not been vigorous in using the leverage inherent in its large lending program to press recipients to redirect their economies toward a market orientation."[39]

This was only one of the conservative complaints about the Bank. Whereas leftists were concerned that Bank funds might not reach the poor at all, conservatives seemed to be concerned that they might in fact reach them, contribute to their empowerment, and possibly even result in changes of regimes away from capitalism. One prominent conservative critic argued in this fashion when he severely criticized loans for "collective farming" in Tanzania.[40] Whereas leftists argue that much World Bank lending simply winds up back in the pockets of developed-country exporters and multinational corporations (through contracts awarded in connection with Bank projects), conservatives tend to argue that *not enough* is winding up back in their pockets. While leftists see the terms of Bank lending as too onerous to be supported by the public treasuries of developing countries, and therefore as contributory to a vicious circle of external indebtedness (requiring still more loans), conservatives tend to see the terms as too liberal. In their view much Bank lending (and all IDA lending) represents a "giveaway."

On a range of criteria for judging the Bank, therefore, both leftists and conservatives give it bad marks—but for completely different reasons. Public debate about the role of the Bank has alternated between one or another of these bifurcated positions. Under the Reagan administration the terms of the debate in the United States have generally been established by the conservatives, and their arguments are dealt with extensively in the concluding chapter of this study (on policy issues and options currently confronting the Bank). In some other countries, for example, Canada and the Scandinavian countries, the terms of the debate about the Bank more often have been established by the left.

Each of these lines of argument has important implications for the study of the World Bank and its efforts under McNamara to give a poverty-oriented slant to development. According to each argument, the Bank is not part of the *solution* at all; it is part of the *problem* (though for entirely different reasons).

Teresa Hayter succinctly states the leftist view of the Bank as problem, arguing that "The existence of aid can be explained only in terms of an attempt to preserve the capitalist system in the Third World. . . . [T]he exploiting classes relinquish the minimum necessary in order to retain their essential interests."[41] As another book on the Bank put it: "If one is convinced that in most low-income countries immediate, wholesale shake-ups of society—in other words, revolutions—are necessary before real progress can occur, he will probably consider the Bank counter-revolutionary, meaning that, in his view, the institution is worse than useless."[42]

The conservatives see the Bank as part of the problem because, as an editorial in the *Wall Street Journal* argued, it is promoting "harebrained schemes" in developing countries at the expense of sound development polices.[43] Such policies would entail greater attention to the private sector, free enterprise, and, in general, "supply-side" economics applied to the Third World. Instead, the conservatives argue, the Bank emphasizes national planning and bloated public-sector bureaucracies requiring high taxes to support them and thwarting the development of the private sector which should be the real engine of growth. In this sense, then, the Bank and its programs constitute impediments to development.

This study sides with neither the leftist nor the conservative critique of the Bank. It adopts a centrist view, emphasizing the Bank's essentially *reformist* role as a development institution. It adopts the normative position of Albert O. Hirschman, the chief academic representative of the reformist persuasion. According to Hirschman, reformers need to explore "how social change short of cataclysmic revolution actually happens."[44] This in turn requires attention to the *politics* of such non-cataclysmic social change. An important element of such politics is the existence (or, more commonly, the forging) of a pro-change coalition. Such a coalition does not only involve domestic actors within developing countries; it may also, and frequently does, involve the World Bank.

In this study reform is viewed as preferable to either revolution or reaction and the World Bank is viewed as an agent of reform. Given this orientation to the Bank's involvement in socioeconomic development in poor countries, the discussion in this study largely concerns various ways of promoting reform rather than ways of promoting revolutionary activity or (at the other extreme) arresting progress. The study readily accepts the implication of this, that the possible contributions of the Bank on behalf of socioeconomic change may very well be somewhat prosaic. The Bank is limited in what it can do for a great variety of reasons. But this limitation does not call for systematic derogation of its work. Rather, it encourages a sober assessment of its role and highlights the fact that the major commitments on behalf of change must in the final analysis be made by the developing countries themselves. Most of these countries, if they opt for change at all, are far more likely to opt for either liberal reformism or authoritarian social change (the "revolution from above") than for the genuine revolution suggested by radical models.

The radical model, which for long dominated the academic debate about the Bank, suffers from a number of problems that make it singularly inappropriate to employ as a basis for judging its poverty-oriented work. Its most serious flaw is that it vastly oversimplifies existing political reality in contemporary developing countries. It "overdetermines" that reality. As an analytical tool the model has proved notoriously long on abstractions and notoriously short on the generation of systematic empirical research. Moreover the radical model often seems wrong. It tends to conclude that "ultimately, revolutionary socialist movements are likely to succeed because of the failure of capitalism to eradicate underdevelopment and the limited capacity of the world capitalist system to defend itself against mounting revolutionary activity in the underdeveloped areas."[45] It therefore ignores the limited amount of truly revolutionary activity in most underdeveloped areas, political trends in developing countries that seem profoundly antirevolutionary, and, especially, the range of alternative political forms (not just socialist ones) that are likely to supplant dependent capitalism. It neglects the fact that revolutions are not always necessary for meaningful social change to occur. Nor are they always capable of achieving what they claim to achieve (such as income or wage equality). The frequent ossification of putatively revolutionary regimes in the postrevolutionary period raises the question of which kind of regime—the revolutionary, the reformist, or other (unlabeled) variants—produces more continuous and enduring changes.

The conservative model, which currently dominates the *political* debate about the Bank, is also inappropriate as a criterion for evaluating the Bank's antipoverty activities. Many of the reasons for this are adumbrated in the concluding chapter, but the essential reason is that it is fixated on private-market solutions to the problems of development and gives little if any importance to the provision of "public goods." It substitutes the profit motive for the achievement of development. While the World Bank does make a relatively modest annual profit, and while earning a profit may sometimes be compatible with helping the poor, the Bank is not a private firm and cannot be evaluated as if it were.

On balance therefore, the present study sides with those of reformist tendencies. Its criteria for evaluating the World Bank's poverty-oriented initiatives are not those of either its leftist or conservative critics. They are essentially those of its reformist defenders. Such a reformist defense of the Bank speaks to both the leftist and conservative critiques. The ensuing discussion demonstrates that the Bank's poverty-oriented projects are consistent with the institution's long-standing emphasis on economic growth, that the Bank places great stress on cost recovery and on such associated notions as the affordability of the benefits provided by its projects, and that the Bank also stresses the importance of the policy environment within recipient countries as crucial to project effectiveness. These are things of which conservatives can generally be expected to approve. The left is fond of contending that Bank funds do not reach the truly poor. While there may have been more than a modicum of truth to this assertion a decade or two ago, the Bank's sharply increased antipoverty lending which is the focus of this study belies the argument now. Both right and left are concerned that Bank projects do not pay enough attention to "institution-building" issues or to project "software." As a result they are alleged to make insufficient contributions to long-term development. But this too is increasingly belied by the historical record. That record demonstrates the Bank's concern with ensuring that the development projects it finances make many contributions beyond simply the capital installations themselves.

Perhaps it is inevitable that the Bank should be subjected to severe criticism from the ideologues of both left and right. Those on the left at bottom desire that the Bank contribute to *revolutionary* change, something it is most clearly not in the business of doing. Those on the right appear to desire that the Bank become a mere underwriter of the plans of private investors for the developing world. But this too would be alien from the Bank's developmental role. The profit motive alone will not solve the problems of underdevelopment.

The Bank is thus vulnerable to crosscurrents of criticism in the same way as any organization that eschews ideological extremes. Judgments about the utility of the Bank must therefore be made in the light of what it is that its programs are trying to attain and not in the light of externally prescribed criteria, which are frequently irrelevant to its developmental objectives. Under McNamara those objectives were basically summarized in the phrase "growth with equity," to be attained in an incremental, reformist fashion. While some social costs are inevitable in any pursuit of these objectives, the Bank's approach sought to minimize disruptive consequences of a social or political nature. The approach is justified by its contribution to qualitatively better societies in developing countries. While far from being the perfectly egalitarian societies of the radical visions or the free-market paradises of the right, these societies would be improvements over what they were when the Bank commenced its operations.

2

The Bank and Its Activities

The poverty-oriented work of the Bank begun under McNamara had numerous implications for virtually every aspect of the institution. But these implications cannot be adequately discussed without some prior knowledge about the Bank's constituent members and principal tasks. The World Bank is one of three component members of the so-called "Bank Group": the World Bank, the International Finance Corporation, (IFC), and the International Development Association (IDA). The International Finance Corporation (IFC) was established as an affiliate of the Bank in 1956. Unlike the other components of the Bank Group the IFC is oriented primarily toward the private sector. It raises loan and equity capital designed to encourage the growth of private enterprises in developing countries, in situations where investment would apparently not be undertaken without IFC participation. The corporation also assists investors with technical expertise. Occasionally, the IFC lends to public enterprises when it is clear that their assistance will ultimately be channeled to the private sector.

The IFC is unique among the international lending institutions in at least two respects: it makes equity as well as loan investments; it is permitted to make commitments without government guarantees. Its loans are generally structured on commercial terms with maturities from seven to twelve years. It frequently supplements its own resources through syndications, especially through the sale of participations in its own loans. It facilitates equity investment either by underwriting or through private placements with foreign and domestic investors.

The IFC is comprised of 113 member countries, 92 of which are developing countries. It has its own staff and is legally and financially separate from the Bank. Its fiscal 1980 operations consisted of 55 projects in 30 countries, representing total commitments of $681 million (including syndications). This represented about 6 percent of total Bank

Group lending in that fiscal year. Cumulative gross commitments as of June 30, 1980, totaled approximately $3.2 billion. The corporation has its own capital base derived from member country subscriptions, and as a result of a capital increase in 1977 it has significantly expanded its operations in recent years. (Over 21 percent of its total cumulative commitments were made in fiscal 1980 alone.)[1]

The other component of the Bank Group is the International Development Association (IDA). Frequently referred to as the "soft-loan affiliate" of the Bank, it forms an important part of this study. Whereas the World Bank began operations in 1946 and makes long-term loans on near-commercial terms to developing countries for economic development projects, IDA was created in 1960 for the purpose of supplying interest-free credits to the poorest of these countries. IDA, however, does not have its own staff, officers, or buildings. The staff and officials of the Bank are the staff and officials of IDA. IDA is simply a "window" of the Bank.

But there are some important differences between the Bank window and the IDA window. The Bank and IDA transfer resources to different countries (with a few exceptions called "blend" countries because the transfer of resources to such countries is marked by a blend of Bank loans and IDA credits). Bank loans go to the better-off among the developing countries; IDA credits go to the poorest. The cut-off point for IDA lending as of fiscal 1981 was a country per capita income of $730; countries with per capita incomes above $730 were generally considered ineligible for IDA credits. The Bank and IDA transfer resources on vastly different terms. The interest rate on Bank loans is currently 11.6 percent; the only charge on IDA credits is an annual service charge of 0.75 percent.[2] The maturity on a typical Bank loan is 15 to 20 years; on IDA credits it is 50 years.

The Bank and IDA obtain the resources they transfer from vastly different sources. The Bank possesses a capital base supplied from subscriptions from its member countries and uses this base as collateral to enter national and international bond markets with the sale of its securities. The principal source of IDA funds is periodic replenishments, grants to IDA from the wealthier of its member countries. There is also a marked difference between the Bank and IDA in the size of total commitments; new Bank loans in fiscal 1981 totaled $8.8 billion compared to IDA credits of $3.4 billion.[3]

The two institutions support projects in the same sectors, yet the sectoral composition of Bank loans and IDA credits shows noteworthy differences. In fiscal 1978, for example, 58 percent of IDA credits were for agriculture and rural development; only 5 percent were for industrial development. By contrast, the Bank loaned 32 percent of its total lending for agriculture and rural development, 20 percent for industry.[4] To some extent this is a result of the correlation between agricultural needs and the needs of the low-income countries to which IDA grants credits. There may, however, be Bank lending for poverty-oriented projects in middle-income developing countries, and there may be IDA lending for traditional projects of economic infrastructure in low-income developing countries. The poverty-oriented nature of a project is not the principal criterion for determining whether the project receives a Bank loan or an IDA credit; that criterion is, rather, the level of development and creditworthiness of the country in which the project is located. Despite these differences between the Bank and IDA, there is an important similarity. All projects, whether Bank or IDA funded, must meet the same standards for technical feasibility, economic and financial rates of return, capacity for implementation, and so forth.[5]

Reference is consistently made here to "World Bank" or "Bank" for purposes of stylistic convenience. When "World Bank" or "Bank" is used as a noun, it means the Bank plus its administrative fiction, IDA.[6] When "Bank" is used as an adjective (as in "Bank lending," "Bank commitments," "Bank staff and officials," and so forth), it means the same thing. In instances where there are important differences between the Bank and IDA, such as in the discussion of country allocation criteria for lending, a distinction is clearly made and IDA is referred to separately.

Levels of Bank Activity

What does the World Bank do? This most basic of questions about the Bank does not permit a simple answer. The most obvious answer is that the World Bank makes long-term loans to developing or less-developed countries for economic development projects. IDA, as has been pointed out, makes interest-free credits for the same purpose. The cumulative loan commitments of $92.2 billion the Bank and IDA had made through June 30, 1981, were extended in 3,094 operations.[7]

While loans for such development projects appear to constitute the essence of the Bank's work, they are by no means the whole story. It is more accurate to view the totality of the Bank's work as taking place at quite distinct levels of activity.

The Bank in the International Marketplace of Ideas

At the international level the Bank's role is as a consciousness raiser about development. It heightens sensitivities to the major tasks of development and contributes new ideas about how to accomplish these tasks. The Bank performs this role in several ways.

One is through the annual addresses of its president, presented each year to the annual meeting of the Board of Governors of the Bank. Under McNamara these addresses came to take on the aura of state-of-the-world speeches. The Nairobi speech of 1973 concentrating on rural development, the Washington speech of 1975 with its emphasis on urban development, and the valedictory address of 1980 have become historic documents on the subject of international development.

A second way in which the Bank performs its role of international consciousness raising about development is through the publication of its sector policy papers on development issues. These began in 1972 and have resulted in the publication of twelve such papers. Each paper summarizes the problem area (such as health needs of developing countries), recounts the state of existing knowledge in the area, and proposes policy redirections designed to address development needs better, particularly of the poorest people in developing countries.

A third key aspect of the Bank's consciousness-raising role is of more recent vintage. In his 1977 address to the Board of Governors McNamara proposed that the Bank begin work on an annual volume to be called the *World Development Report*. The report was to be "a comprehensive analysis of development problems, and of the policies of developed and developing countries that affect them."[8] Four such reports have been issued to date, generally coinciding with the staging of the annual meeting.

A fourth aspect of the Bank's work in the international marketplace of ideas is its own research activities. Many of the categories of the research program are directly relevant to the Bank's newfound concerns with the alleviation of world poverty. Much recent research work, for example, has been in the area of rural development. The largest category of current research is on the subject of population and human resource issues, including the central question of employment.

These and related activities constitute the most general level of World Bank tasks. They tend to be the tasks that make the headlines. McNamara's annual addresses received extensive press treatment every year, the sector policy papers were seen as the Bank's latest thinking about development priorities, the *World Development Reports* in the short span of their existence acquired the status of somewhat of a bible in the international development community, and the Bank's research work was often seen as representing the "cutting edge" or "frontier" of contemporary development issues. Many would argue that these activities are the most important activities of the World Bank. They tend to judge the worth of the Bank by the extent to which it performs well its role in the international marketplace of ideas.

The Bank in Country Dialogues

A second level of generality to the Bank's work concerns its interactions with developing member countries. This level of Bank activity is frequently summarized in the phrase "country dialogue." It refers to the Bank's country economic work, the most tangible product of which is the Bank's well-known country economic reports on individual borrowing countries. The country dialogue marks the translation of the Bank's general precepts in the international marketplace of ideas into country-specific contexts. If, for example, trade liberalization and enhanced export performance are important ingredients of the Bank's general prescriptions at the international level, what might these imply for the concrete case of Brazil? If greater attention to small-holder agriculture is deemed by the Bank to be the hallmark of a strategy designed to alleviate rural poverty and, at the same time, assist in increasing food production in developing countries, what might this imply for the specific case of agricultural policy in Nigeria? The country dialogue therefore concretizes the Bank's more general concerns at the country level. The Bank and the country debate, discuss, and dispute the basic contours of country policy in the aggregate and in key sectors.

The Bank's Work on Development Projects

Descending the ladder of generality, one arrives at the Bank's project work. The implementation of a specific development project may be very far removed from the international marketplace of ideas and even from the country dialogue in the recipient country. The project represents another level of specificity. There is a progression from general nostrums about small-holder agricultural development to more specific recommendations for agricultural policy changes in a Bank member country to a specific small-holder-oriented rural development project in the country.

This descending order of generality in the Bank's work represents a fundamental distinction in the Bank's tasks that goes to the heart of the evaluation of its activities. There is increasing leakage as one goes from the general to the more specific. Each descending level of Bank activity is a less perfect representation of the level that preceded it. The country dialogue inevitably results in major modifications of the line taken by the Bank at the level of the international marketplace of ideas. The specific development project inevitably results in similar modifications of the line taken at the level of the country dialogue. This sequence has extremely important implications for evaluating the Bank's effectiveness. If, for example, the Bank's project work is a highly imperfect implementation of its prescriptions in the international marketplace of ideas, is it appropriate to evaluate the Bank on the basis of the success or failure of that work? Is the Bank's project work really the bottom line of the institution's activities? Or should it be judged by its success in its international consciousness raising about development or in persuading developing member countries to adopt more rational development policies?

The present study gives relatively more attention to the Bank's project work than to the other two levels of its activities, partly out of simple necessity because it is not possible to discuss the entire sweep of the Bank's antipoverty initiatives in the McNamara years. But a more important reason for the relative amount of attention given to project work relates to some philosophical presuppositions. The inclination here is toward the view that "by their deeds ye shall know them." The assumption is that it is appropriate to focus primarily on where the Bank actually spends the bulk of its money. Accordingly, this study adopts the view of project work as the bottom line of the things that the Bank does.

Raising Consciousness about Development

McNamara's Annual Addresses

McNamara made eight addresses during the period covered by this study (1973 to 1980). Extracting the major themes from them on the subject of world poverty, they may be identified as follows:

- The attack on world poverty can only succeed in the context of economic growth. The emphasis on poverty alleviation does not in any way signify a sacrifice of the Bank's growth objectives for developing countries.

- There needs to be far greater concern than previously with the problems of absolute poverty, greatly increased assistance designed to increase the productivity of the 40 percent of the population of the developing countries that have not been able to contribute significantly to national economic growth nor to share equitably in economic progress.

- The major ingredient of a strategy to combat absolute poverty is a far-reaching program of rural development in less developed countries. Such a program must focus on the problems of small-holder agriculture.

• Another major component of a strategy to combat absolute poverty is a comprehensive program of urban poverty alleviation. In this regard McNamara proposed a multipronged attack on the problems of urban poverty designed to make the cities of the developing world absorptive mechanisms capable of providing productive employment for all those who need and seek it.

From 1973 onward McNamara gave increasing attention to the international context of development. Several of his addresses also painted a dismal picture about the trade deterioration of developing countries, the consequences of worldwide inflation, the staggering increase in the price of oil, and the slowdown in the growth rates of advanced industrial countries. It cannot be said that McNamara spelled out a thorough strategy for the adjustment process, but he gave particular emphasis to the following:

• There must be significant restructuring in the patterns of use and production of energy, on the part of developed and developing countries.

• There must be a vast expansion in the production of basic food grains in the developing countries so as to reduce their current heavy reliance on food grain imports.

• There must be a substantial, rising flow of capital resources to the developing countries. For the Bank this entailed an increase in its capital and thus in the amount it could lend; for IDA, larger replenishments. For the developed countries, it meant the recognition that the effects of inflation alone would require major increases in official development assistance.

• The middle-income developing countries need to monitor closely and limit their contraction of additional external debt. Relief from the debt problem was seen to lie in lengthening the average maturities of obligations, broadening the number of commercial banks engaged in financing the developing world, and expanding the number of countries serviced by the private markets.

• Industrialized countries must reduce tariff and nontariff barriers to trade. This was regarded as perhaps the single most important step that the developed countries could take to assist the developing countries.

• A global compact is needed between the North and South to address the "nature and magnitude of the problem, the action required to solve it, the relative responsibilities of the parties for taking such action, and the costs and benefits to each of doing so."[9]

• The objectives for developing countries must be realistic. Closing the gap in per capita income between the developed and the developing countries was simply not a feasible goal. It should not be the primary development objective of the developing countries. What was more important, according to McNamara, was to seek to narrow the gaps between themselves and the developed countries in terms of the quality of life: in nutrition, literacy, life expectancy, and the physical and social environment. The critical development problems in the 1980s and beyond will concern population increase ("the greatest single obstacle to economic and social advancement of most of the societies in most of the developing world"), employment, food security, and the alleviation of absolute poverty.[10]

The most important requirement for dealing with the staggering national and international problems was political will and political commitment. While the importance of this was consistently recognized by McNamara in his addresses, little or nothing was said about how the formidable political obstacles to most of his proposals were to be overcome. The general point remained: the developing countries must recognize that the bedrock responsibility for dealing with poverty resided within their own domestic economic, political, and social systems, and the developed countries must facilitate efforts to alleviate poverty by entering into accommodative arrangements with developing countries. The chief justification for such arrangements was that the developed and developing countries shared a mutual interest in the restoration of world economic growth (without which there could be no poverty alleviation).

Who can say with certitude what the impact of McNamara's annual addresses was? At a minimum they kept before the international development community a clear sense of the awesome tasks before it. While the addresses did not comprise a full-scale strategy for completing these tasks, they did put forth pieces of necessary, if not sufficient, requirements for achieving the twin goals of economic growth and poverty alleviation.

Sector Policy Papers
The Bank's sector policy papers on key development issues translated many of McNamara's general ideas in his annual addresses into proposals for action. The Bank produced such papers in a great number of areas, including housing (May 1975), urban transport (May 1975), rural electrification (October 1975), village water supply (March 1976), development finance companies (April 1976), rural enterprise and non-farm employment (January 1978), agricultural land settlement (January

1978), and employment and the development of small enterprises (February 1978). When all the papers were added together, they amounted to a formidable collection of analyses of underlying problems, recommendations for action, and implications for the Bank's work. They heralded the Bank's orientation on sectoral questions to the entire international development community, but, more important, they provided clues as to the kinds of projects the Bank was likely to finance. Two examples of such papers, those on health and education, illustrate the Bank's consciousness-raising technique.[11]

The central problem identified by the health paper was that, despite large expenditures, efforts to improve medical care for the majority of the population in developing countries had only a modest impact. The most important reason for this, according to the Bank, was the typical overemphasis on sophisticated, hospital-based services to the neglect of preventative public health programs and simple primary care provided at readily accessible facilities.

The analysis had implications for the Bank's lending program. Future health projects would include elements designed to deal with this problem: there would be emphasis on the development of basic health infrastructure, the training of paraprofessional staff and community health workers, the promotion of proper nutrition, the provision of maternal and child health care, family planning, and endemic and epidemic disease prevention and control.

The education paper identified a number of problems. An important one was the continuing failure of most countries to provide a basic education to the widest possible segment of society. The Bank argued that too much emphasis continued to be placed on secondary and university education for a minority, not enough on basic primary education for the majority. A corollary of this involved the disequilibriums in the relationships between education and employment opportunities in developing countries. Educational efforts in such countries were not sufficiently geared toward skill training consonant with realistic employment opportunities. To some extent these shortcomings were shared by the Bank's own educational lending, which before McNamara was concentrated on "hardware" projects in restricted subsectors and on formal, secondary, and postsecondary education.

As in the case of health, the analysis of educational problems led to policy redirections of the Bank's work. The primary emphasis in the future was to be on the provision of "low-cost, minimum, mass education in poor countries with low primary school enrollment ratios."[12] A second priority was to design educational projects in such a way that education would be more adequately related to the workplace in developing countries.

Overall, the sector policy papers represented a substantial challenge to conventional wisdom. They pointed out the legacy of problems left by applications of more traditional theory and in virtually every case suggested policy redirections that were significantly at variance with received ideas about the sector. This policy iconoclasm embroiled the Bank in controversy with the professional establishment in these sectors (the established doctors vs. paramedical workers, the traditional educational establishment vs. basic education) as well as with the policy-making establishment in both developed and developing countries.

As with McNamara's addresses, it is difficult to ascertain the full impact of these papers. The publication of the papers placed the Bank in the forefront of thinking about development issues. They provoked international policy debates, shook up the establishments, produced far-reaching reassessments of policy, and stimulated additional research designed to expand the analyses and recommendations. In this sense they were very important contributions to the Bank's role in the international marketplace of ideas.

World Development Reports

The Bank's *World Development Reports* constituted voluminous information on the state of world development and the problems and potentialities of future development. The first two reports (1978 and 1979) were principally extended discussions of the major themes raised in McNamara's annual addresses. Thus the twin development goals of rapid economic growth and the reduction of absolute poverty were consistently restated in these reports. The 1978 report, however, contained a finding that generated a great deal of interest—the projection that there would still be 600 million people in absolute poverty in the world in the year 2000, assuming that the growth rates projected for the period 1975 to 1985 were maintained to the end of the century and a certain postulated relation between income distribution and aggregate growth rates.[13] It seems more probable there would be over one billion people in this condition.

The 1980 report was more thematic, focusing on human resource development and the contribution provided by education, training, health, and nutrition programs. The report was noteworthy for stressing not only the direct benefits that programs in these areas confer but also the indirect role of human development as investment for growth. The 1980 report was distinctive in a number of other ways. It offered an innovative examination of the complex and reciprocal interrelationships between health, nutrition, education, and fertility. It engaged in the rare exercise of actually examining the lessons learned about the comparative efficacy of different country programs and policies for stimulating human development. The report examined some political and administrative constraints to the effective implementation of programs and projects in this area, as well as ways based on experience for dealing with them.

The 1981 report adopted as its theme the subject of national and international adjustment to the post-1973 shocks in the world economy. The report contained a comprehensive overview of international economic developments in the 1970s with special attention to developments in the areas of trade, energy, and external finance. But the most distinctive feature of the report was a lengthy analysis of the diversity of country experiences in adjusting to these developments. The report offered highly instructive country profiles of adjustment processes in both the oil-importing and oil-exporting countries. From these it built a number of generalizations for national and international policy.

While these *World Development Reports* lacked the rhetorical flourishes that gave vitality to McNamara's annual addresses, and while they were not as detailed in their policy recommendations as the Bank's sector policy papers, they became increasingly important contributors to the international development debate. Their continuing search for the most cogent themes of contemporary international political economy could only increase their contribution.

The Bank's Research Program

No discussion of the World Bank's main tasks in the international marketplace of ideas would be complete without reference to its research activities. The McNamara years witnessed a major expansion of the Bank's research program. The Bank did not have a separate budget for research until fiscal year 1972. By fiscal 1980, however, expenditures on formal research by the Bank had grown to $11.4 million.[14] As defined by the Bank, formal research consists of "relatively large studies that are reviewed by the Bank-wide Research Committee . . . and smaller studies, often of an exploratory or state-of-the-art kind, undertaken wholly at the discretion of individual departments with their own resources."[15]

As of October 1980 the Bank's formal research program involved 83 ongoing projects. The bulk of these were carried out by its Development Research Center and its Development Economics Department (both under Hollis B. Chenery, the Vice-President for

Development Policy); the rest, in collaboration with various external research centers. Expenditures by subject category reflected many of the newer poverty-oriented concerns of the Bank under McNamara. Research on agriculture and rural development, for example, claimed $1.9 million of the $11.4 million research budget in fiscal 1980. This was followed by research on industrial topics ($1.5 million), population, health, and nutrition ($1.3 million), education ($1.3 million), and employment studies ($1.2 million).[16]

The themes of the Bank's poverty-oriented research are indicated by some of the studies currently underway. Among the substantial amount of research projects conducted in agriculture and rural development is a study of a multifaceted program in the central region of Malawi. The study examines the effect of the program on crop yields, productivity, and the extension of agricultural credit. Other studies are being conducted on agricultural investment in the Indus Basin of Pakistan, the management and organization of irrigation projects (with attention to such social considerations as the effects of the projects on the traditional African extended family system), food distribution projects, constraints on the adoption of farm technology in northern Nigeria, and the impact of agricultural development on employment and poverty in India. The Bank is also attempting to consolidate existent knowledge on rural development in China in the hope of integrating China's development experience with that of other major developing countries.

The largest research category in terms of number of studies is that of population and human resources, with twenty-four ongoing studies. One major area of emphasis in this category is employment, with studies examining such issues as the linkages and contrasts between formal and informal labor force participation in Malaysia and India, the extent to which agricultural projects undertaken by the Bank benefit landless or near-landless rural households dependent on wage employment, and the ways in which economic growth affects certain socioeconomic indicators (through an examination of distribution and growth in Brazil). There is a study of the socioeconomic consequences of migration patterns in the Middle East and North and West Africa. Population studies have been initiated examining the determinants of recent fertility rate declines in Sri Lanka and South India, and the association between population growth and rural poverty in India, Kenya, Nigeria, and Sri Lanka.

The Bank likes to think of this research as being on the cutting edge of development studies, but this has been disputed by some researchers in the academic community who maintain that the Bank by and large follows the path breaking that allegedly occurs in academe. The matter may be clarified by distinguishing between two distinct roles of the Bank. In one role, the Bank conducts original research, much of it quite innovative. In another the Bank translates the research results of others external to it, bringing such results to the attention of a wider audience in the international development community.

The Bank, sensitive to some of the criticisms of the academic community, undertook between 1977 and 1979 to set up Specialized Research Advisory Panels of outside experts to evaluate its research in six fields. The conclusions of these panels clarify the debate about the importance of bank research. The panel that investigated the Bank's research on agriculture and rural development found "a large output of high quality" that had "quite likely contributed to the shift in lending policy toward the small farmer and the rural poor."[17] A similar panel exploring the Bank's research on income distribution and employment noted "the high quality and varied character of Bank income distribution research." The Bank had developed a "leadership role" in this field. Similarly, regarding employment research, "an evident feature is the generally high quality of the output. . . . Many of the authors have been acknowledged as experts in the field."[18] In the area of industrial development and trade, a review panel was "impressed by the overall high quality of Bank research."[19] A transportation research review panel found that "the overall accomplishment has indeed been impressive, clearly placing the Bank and its collaborators in a preeminent position among the world's leading research centers on problems of transportation in developing countries."[20]

In some areas, however, the Bank's marks were not as high. In population research, for example, the effort was deemed "small and fragmented"; the Bank's research in this area needs to be "more substantial and more focused."[21] Yet on balance it appears that the external experts did not necessarily share the view that the Bank's research work was lagging and not leading the development research efforts of others.

There was another criticism of the Bank's research work under McNamara that appeared to be more serious. While the bulk of the institution's research seemed to be of undeniable importance in an intrinsic sense, there was considerable question about the status, importance, and operational relevance of this work within the institution itself. The consistent impression obtained in several years of research conducted at the Bank for this study is that the people carrying out research within the institution were largely divorced from the operational staff. There was a tendency for the latter to view the former as misplaced academics who never built a dam or laid a road; there was a tendency for the former to view the latter as dam and road builders incapable of scaling the higher reaches of abstraction. There was thus some tendency for each to view the other as irrelevant. The Bank's research work was probably taken more seriously by the academic community outside the Bank than by many staff within the institution itself.

This matter was also examined by the various external review panels, and their findings regarding it were not as favorable as their judgments about the intrinsic quality of the Bank's research. The panel on research in agriculture and rural development found that "the direct impact of research on agriculture lending has been marginal."[22] A panel examining the Bank's research on commodities found that it had "not yet made any significant contribution to the operational and the policy roles of the Bank, and the direction of the work still underway is hardly more promising in this respect."[23] The panel studying employment research argued that "the relationship between the subject matter of research and the operational needs of the Bank has not always been evident."[24] Even the otherwise laudatory panel on research in industrial development and trade felt that considerably more attention needed to be given to research application and dissemination.[25]

A recent Bank review of the research program was very sensitive to these lines of argument. It concluded that it was not possible to ascertain "whether the entire research program has been significantly responsive to Bank operational needs."[26] While pointing out that "about two-thirds of the research is directed toward directly supporting operations and only a third is allocated to serving broader objectives," it acknowledged that there were "insufficient links between operational staff and researchers, especially at the conception and design stages of research."[27] It also acknowledged that from fiscal 1972 through fiscal 1980 only about 10 to 15 percent of the Bank's research resources were devoted to application and dissemination.[28]

These kinds of observations have led the Bank to explore new ways of organizing its research efforts. Particular attention is being given to integrating formal research with the Bank's country economic and sector work. Greater emphasis is being placed on policy-relevant research, somewhat less on arid abstractions of the past. But the disquiet with some aspects of the Bank's research program and the recent changes this has provoked should not obscure the central point, that the program has, with all its faults, marked one more important contribution by the Bank to the international marketplace of ideas.

Country Economic and Sector Work

A second important component of World Bank activity is its country economic work. Such work is the principal responsibility of the country economists in the Bank's various regional divisions. The basic task of such personnel is the continuous monitoring of a country's economic performance—both macro- and microeconomic. Bank staff responsible for economic work engage in frequent interactions with officials from developing countries concerning the ways in which performance might be improved (from the vantage point of the Bank of course)—interactions that, as might be expected, are not always uniformly amicable.

Country Economic Reports
The most tangible product emanating from this work is the country economic report. Such a report has generally been produced annually or biennially for countries in which Bank operations are extensive. Major economic reports on smaller borrowers are produced less frequently. A more recent tendency is to produce a comprehensive economic report and to follow it up with a number of economic memorandums, or updating reports, instead of producing a comprehensive volume every year.

These country economic reports are for the most part comprehensive assessments of macroeconomic performance. They give great attention to recent trends in aggregate economic growth and growth prospects, to balance-of-payments data and especially export performance, and to the principal features of fiscal and monetary policy. The reports also frequently deal in considerable detail with performance and prospects in specific sectors, such as the agricultural sector. The reports therefore are veritable gold mines of economic information. They are also supposed to provide an essential frame of reference for subsequent Bank operations in the country, particularly at the project level. The reports represent the World Bank's judgments about countries. This is why not only the decision makers in the Bank or in the country concerned but numerous outside observers—large commercial banks, other bilateral and multilateral institutions, investigative reporters and academic scholars—are keenly interested in the assessments of developing countries contained in these reports.

From the standpoint of function within the overall scheme of the Bank's work, however, what is frequently more important than the reports' substance is the process of their elaboration. The preparation of these reports provides an opportunity for a continuing dialogue between Bank officials and officials in recipient countries. The preparation process facilitates and concretizes the dialogue. Frequently, to hear the Bank's country economists tell it, the report has served its function before it has ever been written. Indeed sometimes reports never reach final, official form. They go through successive draft presentations as the dialogue between Bank officials and officials in the Bank's developing member countries evolves.

Assessment of Economic and Sector Work

The general orientation of the economic and sector work is one that, albeit for a stated change on the part of the Bank toward a concern with poverty alleviation, is still heavily weighted with traditional concerns. It was evident that the economists who contributed to this work and who were interviewed for this study were very cognizant of the dichotomy between the Bank's stated policy orientations and the dictates of economic necessity—on the one hand, the Bank's professed concern under McNamara about social and distributional issues in development, and, on the other hand, a necessity, by virtue of economic developments in individual countries, to address more traditional questions of financial management and policy reform emphasizing the promotion of growth. Typical issues therefore have included various features of trade policy, debt management, exchange rate policy, domestic interest rates, industrial policy, agricultural issues, and user charges for public services.

The Bank has made remarkably little effort to assess the impact of its work on these issues in the various countries where the country dialogue is of long standing. As a result no systematic comparative assessment is available of the impact of this economic and sector work or, to put it more directly, of its leverage on recipient countries. Recourse must thus be had to more or less anecdotal evidence which is an insufficient basis for comprehensive conclusions. Several years ago, however, management of the Bank asked the chief economists in the various regional departments to make an assessment of some of the achievements and shortcomings of the economic and sector work in the countries within their respective spheres of concern. The reports produced by these assessments were obtained in the research conducted for this study. While stopping considerably short of the kind of in-depth analysis that the Bank still requires, they do provide some of the country economists' own critique of economic and sector work.

In one of the areas of its more traditional concerns, the Bank evidently considered itself relatively successful in influencing various aspects of trade policy among some of the countries its economists assessed. The two major themes of Bank advice in this area have been export promotion and trade liberalization. The Bank was judged to have had particular success in Mexico and India (the two largest cumulative Bank/IDA borrowers) with its recommendations for export promotion policies. It also claimed to have had considerable influence in the modification or elimination of import restrictions and other policies aimed at greater trade liberalization in these two countries. In Algeria and Mexico it was found that the Bank had had a clear impact upon external debt management.

On other items of traditional macroeconomic significance, however, the Bank's own economists found that its impact on domestic policy formulation and implementation had been more ambiguous. This was particularly true regarding exchange rate adjustments. In this area the Bank has been a fairly consistent exponent of devaluation, arguing that distortions between domestic and foreign prices inevitably spill over into negative balance-of-payments repercussions. While many of its member countries have historically balked at devaluation for political reasons, the Bank has sometimes been a key influence in the decision to devalue. Ghana is an illustration of this. Until 1978 the government of Ghana consistently held out against the Bank's recommendations. By August 1978, however, with inflation running at 116 percent, export growth stagnant, and import demand overwhelming, the government devalued the currency by 58 percent.

The Bank's analysis of the impact of its economic and sector work revealed some success in affecting interest rate policy in Ghana, Nigeria, and Senegal. This was generally in the direction of increasing such rates to reflect the real opportunity costs of capital. However, its impact upon such politically sensitive issues as public savings and the expansion of the tax base has been relatively minimal. Bangladesh and Mexico are cases in which the Bank's recommendations in this regard have invariably confronted the political volatility of these kinds of issues.

Regarding industrial policy, the Bank's assessments concluded that it apparently had had only a very marginal impact in many of the countries studied. For example, the Bank was relatively unsuccessful in the Philippines in convincing the government to implement policy changes that would have improved industrial efficiency. In Tanzania the timing of the Bank's criticism of the government's Basic Industry Strategy, as well as its concern with the poor performance of public sector enterprises, was interpreted by the country as an implied criticism of its basic social goals and alienated the Bank-country relationship.

The internal assessments indicate that the Bank has had considerably more impact upon the implementation of policy in the agricultural sector, especially in increasing efficiency, production and output levels, and service extension. In Mexico the Bank influenced the country's use of limited domestic water resources, through its encouragement of the redirection of agricultural investment toward the humid tropics, and also the allocation of Mexican government resources to small-scale irrigation and other rural works programs. In India the Bank successfully persuaded the government to raise the efficiency of fertilizer production and distribution. In the Philippines it was associated with policies aimed at the better definition of agricultural programs, especially regarding rice production, while in Senegal the Bank, in part due to its recommendations for a major overhaul of the domestic pricing system, helped to persuade the government to stop subsidies on agricultural inputs.

Influence on Structural Reform
Any generalizations concerning the impact of Bank policies and advice on the agricultural sector must be qualified when it comes to the question of structural change, however. The implication from Bank reports seems to be that such topical areas within the sector work as tenancy, prevalent forms of farm organization, and local rural labor markets were often insufficiently treated. The Bank's influence on land reform was very often marginal. This was particularly evident with the uncertainties related to the application of land reform measures arising in Mexico and the Philippines. The issue points to a broader, often cited criticism of the Bank's inability to have much impact upon structural reform and institutional modernization.

The Bank's recommendations on user charges appear to have had only limited success in influencing national policy. A dichotomy of interests usually existed between the Bank, which generally pushed for higher user charges in the interest of cost recovery, and the governments, which were reticent to undertake initiatives of such political sensitivity. In Mexico, for example, the Bank historically had no success in persuading the government to raise irrigation charges. The Bank's Bangladesh mission had similar problems with water charges there. The Bank, however, was successful in persuading the government of Ghana to raise tariffs for telephone, water, and electrical services.

As part of the review of the impact of its economic and sector work, the Bank commissioned more intensive studies of that work in three of its most important borrowers—Mexico, India, and Tanzania. The reports emanating from these country studies provide a more systematic analysis of the issues and effects of this aspect of the Bank's work.

The economic and sector work on Mexico is of long duration and rates as one of the most thorough country economic works the Bank has undertaken. In the 1950s and 1960s, Bank economists judged the performance of the Mexican economy largely in terms of the standards of economic growth and external financial stability, and by those standards it was generally considered by the Bank to be performing well. Then, in economic missions to Mexico in 1969 and 1970, the Bank was the first to highlight the problems of poverty, population growth, and unemployment. By the Bank's own admission, the populist policies followed by the administration of Luís Echeverría (to the presumed neglect of financial stability) imposed something of a strain on Mexico's relations with the Bank, and the macroeconomic policy advice offered by the Bank over the years 1974 to 1976 appears to have had little impact. With the advent of the administration of Jóse López Portillo, the Bank dispatched an economic mission to Mexico in 1977 which was reported to have had a significant influence on the administration.

The Bank's conclusion was that its advice had generally helped to strengthen the hands of the technocrats in the Mexican bureaucracy but had considerably less impact when it ran counter to deep-rooted political constraints or was otherwise at variance with the general thrust of Mexican government policy.

Within this general assessment the Bank concluded that in some areas its influence appeared to have been substantial—on the state petroleum monopoly, in different ways at different times (in pressing for a more active exploration policy and improved financial returns in the 1960s, in restraining the pace of development now); on reducing import restrictions and encouraging a somewhat more outward-looking orientation of Mexican industry; on the operational efficiency of some Mexican ports; and on external debt management, if only by continually reiterating the Bank's concern at the growth of Mexico's external indebtedness.

But the Bank's advice evidently had less impact when it ran counter to what are sometimes euphemistically described as "political realities." Thus "constantly repeated exhortations" (the quote is from the Bank's own assessment) on taxation and public savings, the pricing policies of public enterprises, irrigation charges, railway passenger service, and industrial efficiency met with a rather limited response. The poor financial performance of various Mexican public enterprises offers testimony on this point. For years the Bank urged that irrigation charges should be raised and that uncertainties over the application of land reform policy should be cleared up, but little action was taken. Vested interests in Mexico successfully resisted attempts to bring about the introduction of more progressive taxation of incomes. Political considerations consistently outweighed the Bank's recommendations for reducing railway passenger service and improving the efficiency of road transport.

Even in those areas where the Bank demonstrably had some impact, the actions taken by the Mexican government fell far short of what the Bank recommended. In general, while the Bank's economic and sector work appeared to have made a real contribution to policy making, it did not appear to have had any comparable influence on what might be called institutional modernization and reform. Nor did the Bank really carry out much in the way of in-depth analysis of long-term development issues.

The Bank's own assessment of its economic and sector work in India concluded that there was a discrepancy between the way some high-level Indian officials saw the Bank's work and the way in which the Bank saw itself. Most Indian officials did not see the Bank as having more than a marginal impact on official thinking or government policy. Some staff within the Bank itself, moreover, were of the opinion that the Bank's economic work on India was too superficial to carry weight with the Indian authorities. Their feeling was that too much effort was put into the annual economic reports and not enough resources were devoted to in-depth study of long-term structural problems.

But Bank analysts preparing a report on the Bank's impact in India were of the belief that the work was more influential than either Indian officials or staff within the Bank itself were prepared to admit. The Bank consistently pressed India for the simplification of controls over industry and foreign trade and for more vigorous export promotion. Family planning, food security, and the need to expand irrigation were other constantly recurring themes. The analysts concluded that export promotion, trade liberalization, petroleum development, and fertilizer production were areas where the Bank's work had some effect. They also felt that the Indian Ministry of Agriculture valued highly the contributions that the Bank made to raising the efficiency of the extension service, introducing improved methods of water management, promoting the expansion of grain storage, and so forth. Still, it was discovered that the Bank's reports are seen by "no more than a handful of senior officials of the Government of India," and with a few exceptions, "Indian industrial policy does not seem to have been particularly responsive to Bank advice."

The Bank's relations with Tanzania on matters of economic and sector policy are interesting because of the socialist government and its pursuit of collectivist and other policies thought antithetical to customary Bank emphases. The relationship between the Tanzanian government and the Bank has never been an easy one, and the relationship has tended to be strained whenever a basic tenet of policy was thought to be questioned. An agriculture sector study of 1974 led to something of a confrontation with the government because of the Bank's criticisms of the village-development (*ujaama*ization) policy and the Bank's espousal of a "production first" strategy, with the Bank seemingly giving low weight to income distribution or regional equity goals. The latter were, at least rhetorically, major governmental emphases. Similarly, a Bank economic mission of July–August 1976 produced a draft that again aroused governmental sensitivities. Some officials in the Tanzanian government saw the report as having the hidden objective of seriously criticizing basic Tanzanian social goals. The Bank's concern about the good performance of public sector enterprises was so interpreted. Another example was the report's discussion of Tanzanian income distribution which was "thought to be critical to no useful end."

The Bank's agricultural sector work, however, led to a periodic dialogue with the Tanzanian Ministry of Agriculture which is recalled by the pragmatists within the ministry as having helped them pursue output and efficiency goals at a time when they were simultaneously being asked to achieve a range of social and political objectives. A recent Tanzanian assessment of the Bank concluded that there has been a significant improvement in the Bank's perception of *ujaama*. As a result of the most recent basic economic report on Tanzania the Bank and the government agreed to move ahead with the exploration of trade policy, including import tariff levels and structures; agricultural producer prices, input pricing, and agricultural marketing; the transportation system; management systems for parastatal enterprises; and more general work on the instruments, especially prices, and institutions necessary to make market socialism work.

Poverty Concerns in the Bank's Country Economic Work
Coverage of economic and sector work in most countries is still heavily oriented toward macroeconomic issues, but there was increasing attention to questions of income distribution, poverty alleviation, and basic human needs. The Bank's regional divisions produced assessments of the economic and sector work conducted under their auspices. The general conclusion was that such work, despite some significant reorientations, had only been able to "scratch the surface" of the poverty-oriented issues.

There seem to be a number of reasons for this. One involves the difficulties that arise from doing field work on these issues. The political volatility and constraints surrounding poverty concerns are another explanatory factor. Lack of manpower within the Bank is another; it simply was not possible to give sufficient attention to poverty issues while continuing the large amount of more traditional macroeconomic work. But a very important reason for the relatively limited amount of poverty-oriented economic and sector work had to do with the views of some Bank staff members themselves. Many traditional country economists at the Bank did not think it bad that the institution's country economic and sector work had changed surprisingly little since the poverty-oriented emphases began. They were not terribly concerned that the work generally did not deal explicitly with income distribution issues. In their view a well-done macroeconomic report would cogently speak, albeit indirectly, to almost all poverty-related concerns. They were openly skeptical of efforts to address income distribution or employment generation in a manner which they viewed as divorced from the overall evolution of the economy of the country in question. They were scornful, for example, of the monitoring work of the unit created within the Urban Projects Department to oversee the employment impact of the Bank's urban work. In the process there were serious conflicts between some of the chief economists in the Bank's regional departments and the urban poverty staff. On rural poverty, there was the belief among some staff members responsible for economic work that the alleviation of extreme rural poverty was an automatic consequence of any development activity in rural areas, not a separate decision variable that should enter into the analysis of policy trade-offs. Another part of the problem was the constancy of man-years allocated to country economic work in staffing decisions at the Bank in the recent past. This created problems because, while in theory the country economists were given new poverty-related tasks, "we were not told to stop doing anything we had been doing."

Another reason is the rather remarkable continuity in country discussions with borrowers over the years despite the high turnovers of country economists whose terms are usually not much more than about two years. To some extent, because many country economists dealing with the Bank's major borrowers—Brazil is a good example— were among the younger, newer breed of more socially conscious economists recruited during the McNamara years, the high turnover seemed to provide opportunities for smuggling in socially oriented concerns into the economic and sector work program. But to a greater extent the presence of representatives from a newer generation had no effect at all.

There seemed to be two explanations for this. One concerned directives from higher officials who had been schooled in the Bank's previous emphasis on growth and relatively unschooled on distribution and related matters. The economic and sector reports were produced in accordance with the guidelines contained in operational policy memorandums. These provided detailed terms of reference for the country economists in the preparation of their reports—a sort of annotated outline. Even after the inception of the Bank's poverty-oriented directions, such memorandums gave much greater emphasis to traditional macroeconomic themes than to the newer social and distributional concerns.

The other explanation for continuity in traditional reporting was to be found in the powerful socialization process to which World Bankers were subjected as they began to accumulate some years within the institution. Even the socially conscious might in large measure succumb, however indirectly, to the norms and ambience of neoclassical emphases. Too great a concern with poverty in the economic and sector work program would, to some extent at least, have been perceived by many important individuals within the Bank as deviant behavior.

It was perhaps not surprising therefore that the Bank's regional divisions reported that for a large number of countries the knowledge and understanding of the poverty problem had not yet reached the point where they could adequately incorporate it into the development policy debate. A 1978 report from the Policy Planning and Program Review Department of the Bank stated that the long-term reorientation of work in the lending program could only be achieved if the information base about poverty conditions were expanded. Describing its work in eastern Africa, the Bank's regional report pointed out that "it was seldom possible to probe very deeply into any problem area. Most of the limited resources were tied up in trying to obtain descriptions of economies of member countries and in keeping track of changes in production, public finances, external debt, monetary position, balance of payments, policies, and institutions." As a result the bulk of work done in country economic memorandums on the poverty problem was usually of an initial, exploratory nature. The West African regional report concluded that income distribution issues could not be the focus of further study as long as better statistics were unavailable. It also claimed that the Bank's knowledge was still deficient in the areas of small-scale industries and employment creation, while on population issues, apart from elementary analysis, the Bank was deemed largely guilty of neglect.

This did not mean that nothing was accomplished, however. In the area of basic needs analysis, for example, the Bank completed studies of Pakistan and Turkey in fiscal 1978, and basic needs missions were sent to The Gambia, Mali, Somalia, and Sri Lanka in fiscal 1979. Basic economic reports on Afghanistan and Indonesia emphasized the primacy of meeting basic needs in their focus of analysis, while recent studies of Brazil, Costa Rica, El Salvador, Guatemala, Haiti, Kenya, Venezuela, and Zambia all gave some attention to employment questions or to other themes related to the social or distributional dimensions of development. Coverage of the basic needs front was expanded to include nine additional countries in fiscal 1980.

Reports dealing with the employment situation were produced for a number of countries, including Brazil, Indonesia, Mexico, Portugal, Sri Lanka, Thailand, Venezuela, and the Caribbean region. They undoubtedly shed considerable light on the complexity of the relationship between basic needs, income distribution, and employment, but the Bank's actual influence on government policies was more difficult to ascertain. It was generally accepted within the Bank that many of these issues remained inadequately investigated. The Bank admitted that "for most countries, the dynamics of rural nonfarm employment and of nonformal urban employment are poorly understood."

Income distribution was a focus of investigation for a number of studies, notably on Brazil, Kenya, Mexico, Sri Lanka, and Tanzania. Evidence related to the Bank's influence on this topic was scanty. The analyses and recommendations that arose from the basic report on the nature and causes of regional income inequalities in Thailand provided a basis for reorientation of the Bank's lending strategy there, but the example seemed to be more the exception than the rule.

Few countries were the subjects of in-depth population studies (namely, Brazil, Kenya, Korea, and Pakistan). Neither was education treated extensively. Exceptions were special reports on Brazil, Mexico, and Sri Lanka which proved to be exemplary. But on the whole coverage of nonformal education and of education's linkages with agriculture, health, and other social services remained weak.

All of this meant that the Bank's poverty-oriented redirections in its project work under McNamara were not sufficiently backstopped by the analytical work being conducted in the economic and sector work program. There was in fact insufficient interface between what was transpiring in project work in a given country and what was transpiring at the same time in economic and sector work on that country. "Motivation" was frequently outrunning "understanding," to employ Hirschman's terminology.[29] Poverty-oriented projects were often undertaken in the absence of a thorough understanding of the nature and causes of poverty within individual countries.

Overall, then, the issue seemed to rest upon the dichotomy between Bank pronouncements and actions. This was emphasized in a Bank report that identified poverty studies in country economic and sector work as "marginal tasks" only to be undertaken "if sufficient additional resources were made available in the budget." Moreover, even if such work was somewhat more oriented toward poverty concerns in the latter McNamara years, the question still arose as to the impact of this work on such crucial Bank issues as country allocation criteria and loan decisions.

The Bank's Project Activities

The third component of the World Bank's work is related to the development projects it funds. For at least the first two decades of the Bank's existence, the definition of a project was relatively simple. A road, a port, a dam, a steel mill, an irrigation network: these were readily identifiable projects. The McNamara years, however, witnessed a considerable expansion in the concept of a development project. A rural development project, for example, may include agricultural credit for small-scale farmers, small-scale irrigation works, agricultural extension and research, basic rural education, and other social services.

According to two officials at the Bank, a project may be defined as "an optimum set of investment-oriented actions, based on comprehensive and coherent sector planning, by means of which a defined combination of human and material resources is expected to cause a determined amount of economic and social development. . . . [E]ach Bank project constitutes a discrete unit of operation, with its own appraisal, negotiation of terms and conditions, legal documents, board presentation, disbursement procedures, and supervision. Depending on the objectives and circumstances, the Bank loan may finance a minor or a major part of the items packaged in a project, and the project itself may be limited to a small fraction of the development program for the sector or embrace the whole program."[30]

The Bank is undoubtedly hindered by the dictates of its project-oriented approach. While it has with increasing frequency stretched the definition of a project, it still engages in very little program lending, if such lending is defined as "the financing of imports that are not specifically directed to particular capital installations."[31] As Mason and

Asher define it, a program loan is designed to finance a particular kind of foreign exchange deficit—"a deficit arising from planned foreign exchange expenditures in excess of the foreign exchange prospectively available for a national development program."[32]

In fiscal 1980, following McNamara's suggestions in his 1979 annual address, the Bank began a program of structural adjustment lending. As defined by the Bank, "this type of nonproject lending has the specific objective of helping countries reduce their current account deficit to more manageable proportions over the medium term by supporting programs of adjustment that encompass specific policy, industrial and other changes designed to strengthen their balance of payments."[33] Among these specific changes to be suggested by the Bank were programs for promoting investment in nontraditional exports, for adjusting domestic production to higher energy prices, for reappraising price and fiscal incentives so as to ensure the more efficient mobilization of domestic resources, and for making institutional changes to improve production and marketing systems.

Immediately the question arises as to the distinction between this type of Bank lending and the traditional balance-of-payments support funded by the International Monetary Fund, or the previously limited amount of program lending funded by the Bank itself. The Bank went to some length to try to effect such a distinction but it was not always easy to make. The basic distinction seems to be that between programs "designed to meet the immediate consequences of crises" and programs "finding solutions to a country's underlying, long-term structural problems."[34] The Bank's structural adjustment lending envisaged "the probability of multiyear programs being worked out and supported by a succession of loans."[35] Nevertheless, the Bank's annual report for fiscal 1981 explicitly noted that "structural adjustment lending by the Bank is complementary to support for adjustment programs provided by the International Monetary Fund. . . . This has required the development of procedures for ensuring closer collaboration between the staffs of the two institutions."[36] There has been some criticism of the Bank's structural adjustment lending on the grounds that it encroached on the preserve of the Fund.

Although structural adjustment loans appear to be much needed by many developing countries, particularly in the current international economic and financial circumstances, the World Bank continues to hew quite closely to its lending for specific development projects. In fiscal 1980 only eight nonproject loans were approved. These totaled only $522.5 million and accounted for only 4.6 percent of the Bank's total lending.[37] In fiscal 1981 seven structural adjustment loans were approved. These totaled $717 million, or about 7 percent of lending.[38] The Bank recently estimated that its total lending for structural adjustment or related programs would approximate only 10 percent of its overall lending in the immediate future.

Not only does this severe limitation on program lending appear incommensurate with some of the financial needs of developing countries; it also raises some serious questions about the overall impact of the Bank's operations. Frequently, sectoral policies in the recipient country are not at all conducive to effective project implementation. If in the case of rural development, a project that appears technically sound confronts governmental pricing, interest rate, marketing, and other policies that run counter to its objectives, the net effect of the project may be questioned.

Various metaphors may be used to describe this situation: the project may be an "island of sanity" in a sea of irrational policies; it may "swim against the tide" of such policies; it may amount to what has aptly been called "pushing on a string." Inevitably, many Bank projects travel this isolated route, especially in rural development where sectoral policy in many developing countries is still oriented toward large-scale, commercial, quasi-corporate, or export-oriented agriculture. This raises crucial questions concerning the link between projects and programs, how to design projects so that they have maximum or optimal effect upon the adoption of sectoral policies the Bank is attempting to encourage. How can a project have major catalytic effects? How can it be an opening wedge for further policy changes? How can its demonstration effects be maximized?

One formal way the Bank attempts to address this problem is by attaching project conditions the recipient country must meet before the loan becomes effective, or, following effectiveness, must meet to secure successive disbursements of funds from the Bank. Less formally, the Bank seeks assurances from the recipient country concerning matters of sectoral policy likely to affect the implementation of the project. These assurances and conditions vary widely from project to project. In a nationwide rural development project in Mexico, for example, the Bank obtained thirteen assurances from the Mexican government, including ceilings on the incomes of those eligible to benefit from irrigation works, certain regulations on interest rates, limits on the installation costs for rural electrification, a target date for the implementation of the extension component of the project, and so forth. In the Bank's first rural development project in northeastern Brazil nine assurances were obtained from the Brazilian government, including an agreement that the government would conduct annual reviews of the progress made in expanding lending to small farmers in the project area, present a report for further action by the Bank, and carry out the actions jointly agreed with the Bank. Perusal of project documents reveals a plethora of such conditions and assurances for each approved project.

There are several big hitches, however. Analysis of project conditions generally reveals that they do not really touch upon the most important issues within the sector but tend to confine themselves to relatively minor matters (such as the reorganization of a project unit, or the use of consultants, or the restructuring of project financial accounts) presumably deemed amenable to the recipient government. The second consideration is an obvious but important one: the Bank can obtain all of the assurances it wants, but it is up to the recipient country to make good on them, and the Bank does not always possess the leverage or supervisory capability for seeing to this. Prompt disbursement on Bank loans is highly valued in the institution, but it is difficult to determine how often the Bank refuses to make a loan effective or to disburse on an effective loan because a recipient country fails to meet the assurances or conditions.

Despite the fact that there is an apparent need for more program lending, and that the Bank engages in many other activities besides its development projects, it must be emphasized (because it is often overlooked) that the real heart of Bank activity is its work on these projects. Economic development projects require identification, preparation, appraisal, negotiation, and supervision. These elements of the project cycle for each individual project, multiplied, for example, by the 247 Bank/IDA projects approved in fiscal 1980, mean that the bulk of staff time at the Bank is devoted to work on projects.

Project work entails two major activities: field missions and the preparation of reports. Identification missions, frequently including the staff of other international development institutions, seek to locate promising projects or stimulate their development. Preparation of a project, in the words of a key official at the Bank, "covers all the steps necessary to bring a project to the point where its technical, economic, and financial feasibilities have been established and it is ready for appraisal."[39] The formal appraisal of a project is undertaken by an appraisal mission to the field. Once a project has been negotiated and approved, its implementation is overseen by supervision missions, detailed at least every nine months or more frequently in the case of active projects.

Just as the country economic report is the most important report to emerge from the country dialogue and performs a function going well beyond the written document itself, the project appraisal report plays a key role in the Bank's project work. The appraisal report, produced for every project ultimately approved by the Bank (with the exception of structural adjustment projects), describes the proposed project in infinite (and often inordinate) detail: the nature of the works to be carried out, the nature of the intended beneficiaries, the economic and financial justifications for the project, project assurances and conditions, and so forth.

All future work on the project—from project supervision to project evaluation at the time of completion of the project—is carried out in terms of the guidelines contained in the appraisal report. The report in fact establishes the parameters within which all subsequent project work proceeds. Many of the problems identified by the Bank during the supervision phase are judged problems because some project developments are at variance with what the project appraisal report said should happen. There may, for example, be cost overruns on the project, or there may be delays in disbursements on the loan, costs and delays not envisioned in the project appraisal report. When the Bank's Operations Evaluation Department, the unit charged with auditing completed projects, analyzes what has occurred during project implementation, it has a strong tendency to evaluate the project in terms of the conditions laid out at the time of appraisal. Indeed, although projects inevitably undergo some modification during implementation, the phrase "at the time of appraisal" has a certain sacred quality to it. Project sloppiness may be grudgingly tolerated, but it is not looked upon with great favor. What is considerably more favored is the project that did what the original appraisal report said it would do.

In this regard the report of the External Advisory Panel on Population (August 1976), a panel set up to evaluate the Bank's experience in population projects, commented upon the appraisal reports of such projects. The comments of the panel are applicable to appraisal reports in other areas as well. In the opinion of the panel, "The very thoroughness of the Bank's approach often tends to lend a spurious solidity to the project as defined: from the language and content of appraisal reports the projects appear overly definitive in areas of uncertainty, overly specific and detailed, . . . overly assured in their assertion (seemingly normal to the Bank) that something will happen as projected if the document says so; overly confident that . . . the outsiders know better than the insiders what to do."

The reporting function of the Operations Evaluation Department is of increasing importance. This unit is supposed to reach an overall conclusion about the successes, failures, and attendant lessons of projects. It is also supposed to call attention to the implications of projects for the Bank's overall policies, practices, and procedures. Its principal product is the project performance audit report (PPAR), frequently produced in conjunction with outside consultants.

While the PPARs also hew quite closely to the guidelines laid out in the appraisal reports, they contain occasional social and political analyses highly rare in Bank reports. As a result the reports tend to be critical of certain project features. Livestock projects in Ecuador were deemed to have ignored the importance of the land reform issue. A cooperative farms project in Tunisia failed to take into account the power of the individual farmer's attachment to the soil. A project in Malawi was a "heavy political liability," and another in that country "preempted the activities of local people who had organized themselves to provide their own conservation works." A series of land settlement projects in Malaysia "raise a big issue for the Bank regarding the high costs of a settlement strategy with high-income targets." Similar observations were contained in all of the project performance audit reports examined for this study.

The PPARs were also quite candid on the more conventional questions relating to the correspondence between the projects' attainments and what the appraisal report said they would attain. The reports indicated that the economic and financial rates of return estimated in the appraisal reports were often considerably in excess of the rates actually obtained by the projects. In a number of the reports examined for this study, the rates of return were less than half those estimated at the time of appraisal. These and other findings of the PPARs again illustrated the suspect nature of the technical niceties of the project appraisal report. The *Annual Review of Project Performance Audit Reports*, made public by the Bank for the first time in February 1978, in no sense conveyed the richness of detail and the analytical insights contained in the original PPARs (of which the *Annual Review* was a sanitized summary).

"Institution Building" and Technical Assistance

An important but little understood achievement of Bank projects is "institution building." This goes well beyond the more immediate objectives of projects. The Bank's investments and financial resources are a necessary but not a sufficient condition for achieving development. Institutional development—increasing the ability of institutions and agencies within recipient countries to formulate development objectives and to work toward meeting them—is another essential requirement. The Bank has engaged in a fourfold institution-building effort. It has contributed to the creation of entirely new institutions (such as the Colombian National Railways and National Planning Office), established new project units in existing ministries (such as in virtually all of its education projects), reorganized existing institutions (such as those managing large agricultural estates producing rubber, coconut, and palm oil in Indonesia), or strengthened existing institutions with emphasis on general organization and management, financial management, and training (such as in highway projects in Indonesia).

One way in which such institutional development takes place is through the Bank's provision of project "software" and technical assistance—training, advice-giving, and the provision of expertise. These are crucial ingredients for the long-term sustenance of projects in all sectors. Indeed in some ways the Bank may be understood as a large technical assistance agency. It provides advice, furnishes consultants, and assists recipient countries in myriad ways related to general economic and specific project management.

The Bank has come to an increasing awareness of the importance of this aspect of its work. In many of its earlier projects, there was a decided tendency to employ expatriates instead of nationals to implement projects. In part this was a realistic assessment of the small pool of qualified manpower in countries that were the recipients of Bank resources, but in part it was also an institutional bias on behalf of efficiency and neatness in the implementation of projects—itself a reflection of western ways of doing things. Another prominent tendency in Bank projects was the use of autonomous project implementing units instead of the regular line agencies of government. The assumption was that in this way the projects would escape the inefficient bureaucracies thought to characterize most developing countries.

Gradually, however, there emerged realization of the need to work through nationals within recipient countries and, wherever possible, through the regular line agencies of government. The realization was the product of a number of factors. Limited evidence seemed to suggest that project performance might not be as dramatically affected by the use of expatriates and special units as was once thought. Moreover it was realized that, while special units might be preferable for building the infrastructural components of many projects, long-term maintenance and responsibility for project works would almost certainly have to rest with regular bureaucratic agencies. Thirty-two of 49 Bank agriculture and rural development projects audited by the Operations Evaluation Department in 1980 lodged implementation with these regular agencies. In 32 such projects audited in 1981, *all* were so implemented.

A Bank review conducted in the late 1970s revealed a pattern of institutional results by *activity* and *subsector* (but not by *country*). While very few countries seemed to have had institutional failures in *all* subsectors, some subsectors and activities consistently have had better or worse results over long periods in most countries. The Bank's most successful institution-building efforts tended to be found in industrial projects, telecommunications, development finance companies, and some utility projects (mainly power). In agriculture the projects most successful at institution building appeared to be those involving relatively autonomous operations with modern or standardized technologies: plantations, tea, and coffee growing. (By contrast, low-technology agriculture has proved probably the most difficult activity to organize and manage.) Among activities, technical and financial aspects of projects generally attained good progress with a less satisfactory performance in training, maintenance, interagency coordination, and the promotion of sectorwide reforms.

In some instances it has been possible for the Bank to attain perhaps its ultimate institution-building goal, the creation of strong organizational intermediaries in developing countries that can, in effect, function like "mini-Banks." If such intermediaries can be created and/or strengthened with Bank assistance, they can "retail" the funds the Bank supplies. The Bank can then become a "wholesaler" of development assistance funds, perhaps extending such funds for entire sectoral programs instead of lending for a multiplicity of small projects. The recipient institutions—as a result of Bank-financed staffing and training programs, organizational and managerial planning, assistance with financial systems (accounting, auditing, financial planning)—develop their own project identification, preparation, and appraisal capabilities.

A good example of this evolution is the Bank's support for agencies supplying agricultural credit in developing countries. In the Indian agricultural sector, for example, it worked to develop a nationwide institution to act as a channel for funds. It began its agricultural credit work in India by supporting state-level projects throughout the country. But it recognized that the creation of a central institution would be a more efficient way to proceed. Accordingly, its support was crucial for the institutional development of the Indian Agricultural Refinance and Development Corporation (ARDC). Two large projects enabled ARDC to become the central financial intermediary for the disbursement of agricultural credit in India. The Bank worked with ARDC to develop its project appraisal, supervision, and control capabilities, and as a result ARDC disbursements are running at more than $100 million per year.

In another preferred model of Bank institution building, a first project in a given sector assists in the creation or strengthening of an agency in the recipient country. Thus created or strengthened, the agency then serves as the chief implementing organization for a whole series of subsequent projects. Examples of such experiences are numerous in the history of the Bank. One comes from efforts over the years at irrigation rehabilitation in Indonesia, where eight projects were implemented by an agency of the government created as a result of the first project. With Bank assistance the agency attracted and maintained a corps of experienced full-time engineers, spent considerable time on the development of improved water management at the farm level, conducted numerous training sessions for farmers and extension personnel, and coordinated the provision of water with that of other agricultural inputs. A similar example comes from work with the Jordan Electricity Authority (JEA). At the time of the first thermal power project in Jordan (mid-1973), the JEA was still in its formative stage with a very small staff. With institution-building assistance (the JEA was organized on the basis of recommendations of management consultants funded by the project) it developed from a small entity with virtually no project implementation capacity into a major public utility which is well-managed and semiautonomous. Its staff now plays a large part in the planning and supervision of new power projects, and JEA has gone on to additional project execution of other Bank-funded projects.

The provision of technical assistance and project software is difficult to quantify and is not as precisely measurable as the attainments of the physical objectives of the projects the Bank undertakes. Nevertheless, the Bank has learned that it is one thing to build schools; it is quite another to develop new curricula, train teachers, and, in sum, to educate. It is one thing to build factories, quite another to train the workers to operate them and the managers to manage them. Building new roads is a notable achievement; maintaining them once they are built is frequently a difficult proposition. Irrigation installations count for little without proper water management. Family planning and other health clinics will go unused without adequate training of health, population, or nutrition workers. While there is no denying the great need for basic capital facilities in the countries to which the Bank lends, since they are important contributors to the growth of national income, they are not enough to sustain development. As a result the

Bank has given increasing emphasis to requirements for the long-term sustenance of its projects in all sectors, and this has been reflected in the provision of teaching materials, curricular innovations, and the training of teachers for the ongoing success of its education projects; agricultural extension efforts for the success of its rural development projects; "industrial extension" on behalf of small- and medium-scale industries; maintenance components for the long-term success of highway projects; good water management in irrigation projects; and the training of paramedical workers in health projects. Such emphases illustrate anew the great breadth and diversity of the Bank's work on development projects.

3

Constraints on the Bank

The post-1973 crisis associated with petroleum price increases and recession in the industrialized countries had a devastating effect on many developing countries. This was exacerbated by the second round of petroleum price increases in 1979.

In 1973, the year in which McNamara announced his intention to move the Bank in a more poverty-oriented direction, the cost of petroleum imports for the oil-importing developing countries stood at $7 billion (in current dollars). By 1980 the bill was projected to reach $67 billion.[1] The aggregate current account deficit of the low-income, oil-importing developing countries in 1973 was $4.9 billion, or 2.4 percent of gross national product. By 1980 it had risen to $9.1 billion, or 4.5 percent of gross national product.[2] More adverse were the trends among the middle-income, oil-importing developing countries. In 1973 the aggregate current account deficit for this group of countries was $6.7 billion, constituting only 1 percent of gross national product. By 1980 the figure had risen to $48.9 billion, or 6 percent of gross national product.[3]

One consequence of these sharply rising costs was increased recourse by the oil-importing developing countries to private commercial banks to finance their deficits. The borrowings of the middle-income developing countries from the world's private banking system increased from $53 billion in 1973 to approximately $251 billion in 1979.[4] It has been estimated moreover that as much as $300 to $500 billion may have to be added to developing countries' debts from now until 1985 if their financial needs are to be met.[5] About 60 percent of commercial bank credit was concentrated in only eight middle-income developing countries. Perhaps the most extreme case of this increment in external debt among the middle-income countries was Brazil. The Brazilian external debt was projected to reach approximately $60 billion by the end of 1981.[6]

According to the Bank's *World Development Report* for 1981, the outstanding medium- and long-term debt of developing countries reached $438.7 billion by the end of 1980, compared with only $67.7 billion in 1970. While the Bank found that the growth of debt was not excessive in relation to gross national product or exports, it also found that significant changes in the composition of the debt had increased the burden of servicing it. The share of official creditors in the debt of the middle-income, oil-importing countries fell from 43 percent in 1970 to 27 percent in 1980, so that private creditors now account for almost three-fourths of the total.[7] Average maturities fell from 20 years in 1970 to 12.7 years in 1980.[8] Interest rates rose dramatically. The combination of these factors meant that only 22 percent of borrowed funds were available in 1980 for buying imports and adding to reserves (after amortization and interest payments). In 1970 the figure was 43 percent.[9]

The external capital requirements of the developing countries show little signs of moderating. They are enormous merely to support fairly modest rates of per capita economic growth. For the least developed countries the aggregate external capital needs were estimated at $11 billion annually during the 1980s and $21 billion annually during the 1990s to support a 3.5 percent growth in per capita gross national product. External capital needs of the middle-income countries may be as high as $155 billion annually by 1985 and $250 billion by 1990.[10]

What do these developments have to do with the antipoverty work of the World Bank? They heighten the tension between the Bank's role as a mover of money and its role as an alleviator of poverty. The overwhelming financial needs of the developing countries since 1973 arguably oblige much greater attention to money moving just to keep these countries afloat; never mind the poverty conditions within them. According to this line of argument, the Bank should be much more concerned with the aggregate transfer of financial resources than with its antipoverty work. Unless some innovative ways can be found for combining the Bank's roles as transferrer of resources and alleviator of poverty, there may be a retreat from antipoverty concerns in the years immediately ahead. This is because the 1980s are not seen as a time for bold new initiatives on the world antipoverty front, any more than on the American domestic front.

The adverse international financial developments of the post-1973 period also raise the question of the relationship of the World Bank to its sister Bretton Woods institution, the International Monetary Fund (IMF). Stripped to its essentials, the Bank's principal role is to supply long-term capital for economic development projects. The Fund's role was conceived as markedly distinct: it was to supply short- and medium-term balance-of-payments financing for nations experiencing temporary or cyclical (not structural) disequilibriums in their external accounts. As the current account deficits of numerous developing countries ballooned in the post-1973 years, country after country was obliged to have recourse to the Fund. Such countries read like a who's who of World Bank borrowers, ranging from some of the largest (Mexico with an IMF loan in 1976, India in 1982) to some much smaller but politically significant (Jamaica in 1977). But access to successively larger tranches of IMF resources is conditional upon the borrowing countries' adopting the economic and financial austerity measures required by the Fund. Since these usually involve a contraction of public credit as well as other measures (holding the line on wage increases, reducing food and other subsidies) felt by many to have an adverse impact upon the poor in the affected countries, the issue is posed of a possible conflict of objectives between the Bank and the Fund. What happens when the supply of recipient-country counterpart funding required for disbursement on a Bank loan is sacrificed on the altar of fiscal austerity to meet the demands of an IMF stabilization program? The issue is particularly relevant to the kinds of Bank poverty-oriented projects discussed here. Since these may be seen as less directly productive undertakings than more traditional projects, they may be especially susceptible to the demands for austerity. The possible conflict between the IMF's short- and medium-term recipes and the World Bank's long-term objectives is bound to be a central issue of international political economy in the years immediately ahead.[11]

Another point about the economic-financial context of the Bank's work also bears emphasis. The multilateral development banks, of which the World Bank is by far the largest, have in recent years supplied no more than about 6 to 7 percent of the total net external receipts of the developing countries.[12] Indeed, despite the growth of the Bank under McNamara, one estimate held that it still provided only about 1 percent of the total (internal and external) capital needs of these countries.[13] Even in important sectors in which its lending has tended increasingly to be concentrated, the developing countries' capital requirements dwarf the amounts supplied by the Bank. Until recently the Bank's share in total agricultural investment in less-developed countries was on the order of only between 1 and 2 percent.[14] To provide but one-half the required capital spending and 20 percent of the required spending for recurrent costs to rectify food deficits in low-income countries would require foreign assistance of $12 billion annually in the 1980s (in 1975 dollars), approximately $8.5 billion more than that currently provided.[15] Even in the transportation sector, in which the Bank was extensively involved in the past, the Bank's contribution to total investment requirements at its height still represented less than 4 percent of total public and private transport investment in less-developed countries.[16] Such data underlie McNamara's observation in his 1974 annual address to the effect that "[a]s large as the Bank program is, . . . it is totally inadequate to meet minimum development objectives."[17] The Bank under McNamara was increasingly in the position of having to run faster just to stand in the same place.

This also has its implications for the institution's antipoverty work. It underlines the importance of the Bank's activities not necessarily related to its aggregate transfer of resources. The Bank's technical assistance and institution-building roles take on added importance. It becomes incumbent upon the Bank to attempt to increase the catalytic, demonstration effects of its poverty-oriented lending. The Bank is obligated to seek out those areas where even a relatively small amount of assistance may provide the opportunity for exercising leverage on behalf of antipoverty concerns. Its research work on poverty alleviation assumes more significance. The figures on the percentage of developing countries' investment needs supplied by the World Bank reiterate the contention that the vast bulk of development tasks must be undertaken by the developing countries themselves. Many of the investment priorities such countries establish, including whatever investments for antipoverty purposes they may choose to undertake, are beyond the control of the World Bank.

So also are virtually all of the political developments within the Bank's developing member countries. A central question concerns the nature of the regimes in the developing countries with which the Bank deals. From the standpoint of a concern for poverty alleviation, the majority of such regimes suffer numerous deficiencies. If the assumption is made that there is some correlation between democratic regimes and public policy output on behalf of the poor, then the number of democracies among the developing countries is a source for concern. As Robert A. Packenham has pointed out, the proportion of democracies among the developing countries has never been greater than 25 percent since World War II; usually, the figure has ranged between 10 and 20 percent. As he notes, "the modal types of political system in the Third World are neither communist nor democratic but rather undemocratic and unstable types of regimes . . . military, single-party, multiparty, monarchical, etc."[18]

Such considerations about politics in developing countries raise questions about the work of the World Bank. While that work principally concerns economic development and not political democracy, the apparent failure of the two to coincide in many countries calls into question one of the main historical arguments for development assistance programs. Should the Bank loan money to undemocratic regimes? Should it try to encourage democratic ones? If a regime lapses into authoritarianism (or worse), should the Bank attempt to exercise leverage on behalf of political reform by withholding loans? What about the systematic violation of elementary human rights? Should the Bank take a stand?

In recent years these and related kinds of concerns became the subject of congressional actions in the United States. In 1977 Section 701 of the International Financial Institutions Act required that the American representative (the executive director) to the World Bank "oppose any loan, any extension of financial assistance, or any technical assistance" to countries that engage in a "consistent pattern of gross violations of internationally recognized human rights unless such assistance is directed specifically to programs which serve the basic human needs of the citizens of such countries."[19]

Officials of the World Bank have generally looked with some disquiet upon these sorts of restrictions. In practice, they argue, the Bank has to deal with the world as it is and not as the Bank might like it to be. The Bank continues to loan to numerous undemocratic regimes; indeed there are conspicuous examples—Indonesia, Korea, the Philippines—of such regimes among the largest borrowers from the Bank. But the Bank makes loans to all kinds of political regimes, even some ostensibly socialist ones—Tanzania, for example. The Bank might prefer to find reasonably democratic regimes and contribute to their development with loans. (A good contemporary example might be Costa Rica.) If economic development can really contribute to democracy, this is an ideal situation and should be encouraged. If, however, democracies are few or dwindling, or if economic development and various kinds of authoritarian regimes seem to go hand in hand, this does not mean that lending should stop.

Why should lending continue in the face of an unfavorable political situation in recipient countries? One explanation relates to the money-moving function of the Bank. Making loans on political grounds (such as considerations about democracy or human rights) would greatly reduce the aggregate amount of resources transferred by the Bank. It might mean not making any loans at all to a majority of developing countries. (Some of the implications of doing this are discussed elsewhere in the study.)

A second explanation is more prevalent at the Bank. According to this line of argument, the mere existence of an antidemocratic or authoritarian regime is no reason to stop lending when there are large numbers of desperately poor people in such countries. Even if more democratic or politically humanitarian regimes do not result from the Bank's involvement, the satisfaction of basic human needs or the conquering of absolute poverty—or some modicum of increase in human welfare—may be among the outcomes. By this logic the Bank's presence in thoroughly undemocratic countries may be even more crucial than its presence in countries that really care about human rights or feeding their poor. Who else will make loans to small farmers in Pinochet's Chile?

But this does not negate the central point, that the World Bank under McNamara operated in a political context that was not noticeably hospitable toward democratic political development or even the kinds of economic development the institution was increasingly attempting to promote. The political leverage of the Bank was thereby reduced in several ways. It was diminished by the nature of many of the regimes with which it had to deal and by the Bank's own very reduced conception of what is meant by "politics." At the World Bank, politics is the establishment of a new administrative agency within a recipient country. Politics is the replacement of a nondynamic agency head by a more dynamic one. Politics is bureaucratic squabbling or interagency competition for the scarce resources that the Bank provides. The political context within which the Bank operates reduces the Bank's political impact, if by such impact is meant wholesale changes in the nature of political regimes. It should not therefore be the expectation that the Bank's poverty-oriented projects are by themselves going to pull down retrograde regimes or perhaps even significantly alter their defining characteristics. Political problems can apparently be overcome only in a much narrower sense.

The discussion is once again relevant to the Bank's reorientations toward poverty concerns since 1973, because the poverty-oriented activities of the Bank were much more politically controversial within recipient countries than were its more traditional undertakings. This was foreshadowed eight years ago by Escott Reid, a former official of the Bank, when he wrote that poverty-oriented work involved the Bank "in efforts to influence the general development policies of the countries which borrow from it on issues much more politically delicate, much more traditionally domestic, than issues related to growth in the gross national product on which the Bank Group has in the past attempted to exert leverage or influence."[20] What Reid could have added is that the political elite in most recipient countries does not care about the poor majority. Where there is the absence of political will and commitment, it is difficult for the Bank to be effective. It is especially difficult to be effective on a large scale, since governments may tolerate piddling efforts to help the poor but they will not tolerate efforts that cross a certain threshold and really amount to something. This was a mammoth contextual constraint on the Bank's poverty-oriented operations in the McNamara years.

Besides political constraints within recipient countries, there is a range of constraints on Bank operations stemming from the influence of principal donor countries, particularly the United States. The ensuing discussion of the financial bases of Bank operations points out how voting power at the Bank derives from member countries' capital subscriptions. The familiar Bank response to arguments about the concentration of voting power in the hands of a few developed countries is to contend that decisions on individual loans or on more general questions of Bank policy are based on consensus and not on the crude tabulation of votes. There is no doubt, however, that the U.S. government retains an extremely important, decidedly preeminent role in the operations of the Bank. The Bank's operations in Peru were minimal following the nationalization of the International Petroleum Company by the government of Juan Velasco in 1969. The Bank made no new loans to Chile under Salvador Allende from 1970 to 1973. Nor did it loan to Peronist Argentina from 1973 to 1976. McNamara agreed that there would be no additional lending to unified Vietnam following the domestic political controversy in the United States attendant upon an IDA credit to that country in fiscal 1979. In seeking to understand the Bank's actions in these and related instances, the attitude of the U.S. government emerges as a prime explanatory variable.

This does not mean that the United States (or other major donor countries) runs the World Bank. An accurate assessment of the real weight of U.S. influence on the Bank must await a more complete description of historical relations between the Bank and the United States than is currently available. Nevertheless, there can be little doubt that the shift from the Ford to the Carter administration had largely favorable consequences for the Bank. Similarly, the recent change from the Carter to the Reagan administration portends a whole new context for the Bank's operations. The commitment to multilateral development assistance on the part of the new administration is dubious at best. Early in the administration, Budget Director David Stockman proposed revoking the U.S. pledge to the sixth replenishment of IDA and reducing the U.S. contribution by half. This underscored anew the impact donor countries can have on the Bank's work.

Because the Bank, like any large bureaucratic organization, operates within a certain economic and political framework, some elements of this framework—such as many developing countries' needs for huge amounts of external resources to which certain conditions can be attached—provide opportunities for expanding its development role. Other elements, however, constitute very serious impediments to the Bank's work. These are frequently overlooked by critics of diverse ideological persuasions. Those who see aid as imperialism apparently assume that aid agencies can obligate recipient countries to do or not to do just about anything. Those who fault the Bank for not doing enough—in the amount of its lending, the kinds of projects it funds, or the limited amount of influence it sometimes seems to have in orienting the development policies of many countries—seem to assume exactly the same thing.

The Financing of the Bank and IDA

Capital subscriptions from member governments comprise one aspect of Bank resources. The Bank makes a distinction between "paid-in" and "callable" capital. Each country joining the Bank is assigned a capital subscription following consultation between the Bank and the applicant and approval by the Bank's Board of Governors. Upon joining, the country pays in 10 percent of its subscription—1 percent in gold or U.S. dollars and 9 percent in the country's own currency. The remaining 90 percent of its subscription is callable, not paid in but subject to call by the Bank if it is required to meet Bank obligations for borrowings or guaranteeing loans.[21] There have been periodic increases in capital subscriptions, the latest authorized in January 1980.

The primary way, however, in which the Bank finances its lending operations is by selling obligations to private investors and to the instrumentalities of governments. The Bank borrows as well as lends. Bank borrowing on capital markets has grown in proportion with the tremendous increases in Bank lending. Aggregate borrowings for fiscal years 1975 to 1980 were $30 billion, whereas such borrowings in the preceding six fiscal years were only $8.6 billion.[22] The Bank's outstanding debt as of June 30, 1980, stood at $29.7 billion.[23] As of June 30, 1970, its total outstanding debt was only $4.6 billion.[24]

The voting power of individual members of the Bank is determined by the size of the members' capital subscriptions. A member receives 250 votes plus one additional vote for each share of stock it holds. A share of Bank stock is worth $100,000 (in 1944 dollars). The employment of such a formula means that the United States obtained 21.11 percent of the total number of votes in 1980; the United Kingdom, 7.82; West Germany, 5.32; and so forth. By contrast, Ecuador possessed 0.18 percent of the votes; Peru, 0.29; and Uruguay, 0.20. Even such a large and important developing country as Brazil possessed only 1.19 percent of the total voting power.[25]

The financing of IDA is a substantially different story from that of the Bank. IDA obtains the overwhelming bulk of its resources through periodic replenishments from its wealthier member countries. (Its other source of funds, amounting to only $100 million in fiscal 1980, stems from profits on Bank loans which are transferred to IDA.)[26] Replenishments are appropriations to IDA. In the case of the United States they must be appropriated by the Congress. Unlike the Bank, which has its capital to loan against and can enter international capital markets with the sale of its securities, IDA has fundamentally only these replenishment funds plus the small amount of Bank profits; if they are not delivered, there is no IDA. Delays in appropriating the funds, particularly on the part of the United States, have periodically affected the level of IDA activity.

These facts about the method of financing of the Bank and IDA give rise to several problems. The Bank's Articles of Agreement lay upon it an extremely conservative proviso, that its outstanding and disbursed loans cannot exceed 100 percent of its subscribed capital plus reserves. While that percentage was approximately 60 as of fiscal 1980, it was projected to approach 100 very rapidly as future disbursements were made on previous commitments.[27] There was thus a necessity for a capital increase. Without it there would have been a leveling off of new Bank lending (and thus a decrease in real terms).

In January 1980 the Bank's Board of Governors authorized a $40 billion increase of the Bank's capital stock. This occurred when countries casting three-fourths of the total votes of the membership approved the proposal. The paid-in capital subscription of the United States under this proposal was $658.3 million. After much congressional debate it was agreed that the American paid-in contribution to the capital increase would be stretched out over a six-year period. (In this newly negotiated general capital increase, only 7.5 percent of the subscription was to be paid-in; 92.5 percent would be callable.) The increase was designed to finance a 5 percent yearly growth in real

Bank lending, assuming, roughly, an inflation rate of 7 percent (thus a nominal increase in Bank lending of 12 percent). With greater inflation there could still be a real growth in lending, but the Bank would need another capital increase since the lending is tied to the level of the Bank's capital plus reserves.

The negotiated American contribution to the sixth replenishment of IDA engendered an extensive debate within the Congress. IDA is seen by many of its critics as a giveaway. The most recent replenishment was negotiated by donor countries in 1980. Totaling approximately $12 billion for the three-year period commencing July 1, 1980, the replenishment entailed pledges from 33 countries. The American share in the sixth replenishment was $3.24 billion, or 27 percent of the total. (This was a reduction from the 31.2 percent American share of the fifth replenishment.) A distinctive feature of the sixth replenishment was the participation of several middle-income developing countries, including Argentina, Brazil, and Mexico.

Originally, the United States was to contribute its sum in three equal installments of $1,080 million each. But the Reagan administration proposed that the three-year contributions be graduated, rising from $540 million in fiscal 1981 to $850 million in fiscal 1982 to $1,850 million in fiscal 1983. For a time no American money was forthcoming, and IDA was obliged to survive with funding from its other major donors in a procedure known as "bridge financing." Eventually, such donors refused to continue their contributions while the United States was in arrears, and at one point approximately $1.5 billion of IDA projects had been approved for which funds to disburse were unavailable. Following protracted congressional squabbling, the United States contributed about $700 million to IDA in fiscal 1982 (in comparison with the $1,080 million originally pledged). Other donors, operating under an escape clause in the replenishment agreement, also scaled down the level of their contributions. As a result IDA entered dire financial straits. Its new commitments for fiscal 1982, originally programmed at $4.1 billion, had to be cut back to $2.6 billion, forcing some severe country allocation decisions.

There appeared to be several kinds of concerns about the financing of the Bank and IDA in the McNamara years. One was that the Bank may have grown too big and too fast during those years and in some sense had become overindebted to creditors. This did not appear to be a valid fear, however—chiefly because of the extraordinarily low debt-to-equity ratio of the Bank.[28] Moreover the Bank's callable capital is solely for the protection of its bondholders; it cannot be used in the Bank's operations, for disbursements, or for administrative expenses.

Since the Bank's total outstanding debt was only about 68 percent of its total capital and reserves as of June 30, 1980, it seemed impossible to argue that the Bank was overextended and in danger of going under.[29] Opposition to a larger role for the Bank (through a capital increase and collateral for entering securities markets) did not appear to be made on the grounds of requisite financial probity but politically. Much of the opposition to the further growth of the World Bank came from those who wished to reverse the growth of multilateralism.

A second concern related to where the Bank borrowed. After the first round of petroleum price increases, the Bank borrowed substantial amounts from petroleum-exporting countries. Borrowings from such countries rose to 57 percent of total marketings in fiscal 1975. Included in these amounts was the largest single borrowing ever made by the Bank — $750 million of ten-year U.S. dollar bonds sold to the Saudi Arabian Monetary Agency in December 1974.[30]

Such borrowings gave rise to fears in some circles of excessive Bank dependence on Arab countries and to an Arab takeover of the World Bank. One controversial article written at the time was entitled "Whose World Bank?" and the implication was clear: the Bank was in the hands of the Arabs.[31]

The facts are quite otherwise. As of June 30, 1980, the Bank's total outstanding debt was $29.7 billion. Of this amount $5.4 billion (18 percent) was held by public and private investors in the United States, $8.2 billion (27.7 percent) by investors in West Germany, $4.2 billion (14.1 percent) by investors in Japan, and $4.7 billion (15.9 percent) by investors in Switzerland (which is not, however, a member of the Bank). Only $4.2 billion of the Bank's total debt (or 14.2 percent) was held by members of OPEC, and, of this amount, only $2.8 billion (or 9.4 percent of the Bank's total indebtedness) was held by investors in countries customarily called "Arab."[32]

It may be argued that Arab and OPEC countries, given their vast financial holdings accumulated in recent years, should be holding more, not less, of the Bank's debt (and should also have a greater share of its subscribed capital and voting power). It is debatable whether the fact that Arab countries hold such a distinct minority of the Bank's debt is a good thing. If the United States or other major donor countries are reluctant to increase their contributions to the Bank's capital or to IDA's replenishments, one solution is to seek greater amounts of funding from alternative sources — chiefly Arab and OPEC nations. Also overlooked by those making arguments about Arab control of the Bank is that the way to gain control of an institution is to hold its stock, not debt. Saudi Arabia, for example, holds 5.6 percent of the Bank's debt but only 1.6 percent of its stock.[33]

Some other concerns about Bank financing under McNamara were more directly related to the qualitative reorientations of Bank lending. One such concern was that the emphasis on Bank lending for poverty-oriented development projects under McNamara damaged the quality of the institution's loan portfolio. Such projects were often perceived as riskier undertakings than more traditional infrastructure projects, and their increasing importance in Bank lending was thought by some to have compromised the Bank's long-standing reputation for the utmost in financial and technical probity.

Financial officers at the Bank firmly disputed the contention that increased involvement in poverty-oriented projects had reduced the creditworthiness of the institution. The Bank's treasurer remarked that in eleven years he had never heard anyone in the private financial community voice a concern about poverty orientations per se. Rather, in his view, the concern was more with Bank lending to specific countries that private financial powers might not like—Afghanistan, Ethiopia, Vietnam, and so forth—and not so much with specific Bank projects they might not like (such as poverty-oriented ones). As he put it, "the emphasis must be on country creditworthiness—if all our money were going to Bangladesh, Tanzania, and the like, then we'd have a problem. But not because it's going for poverty projects." He saw the Bank as much more prudent on some of these matters than private commercial lenders. As he phrased it, "They don't even have projects, much less rates of return for such projects!"

Does the rate of return on antipoverty projects differ substantially from the rate on more traditional projects? The answer to this question requires distinguishing between various kinds of rates of return. In the Bank's lexicon there are financial, economic, and social rates of return. The Bank's financial analysis identifies the money profit accruing to the entity undertaking the project and is concerned with the entity's ability to meet its financial obligations and finance future investments. Economic profit, in contrast, measures the effect of the project on the fundamental objectives of the whole economy. Economic costs and benefits may be larger or smaller than financial costs and benefits, and, in order to reflect true resource constraints, they are derived using "shadow" or "efficiency" prices rather than market prices.

As the Bank became increasingly concerned with poverty alleviation, it began to experiment with an expanded system of analysis that can accommodate additional policy objectives, including effects on the distribution of income. In social rate-of-return analysis, for example, a social wage rate might reflect both the benefit of increased income in terms of impact on the poor and the cost in terms of reduced savings and reinvestment. The determination of social prices is very difficult, however, since it requires judgments about the relative value of consumption by different income groups.

Future costs and benefits of a project can be discounted to present values using an agreed-upon discount rate. Projects with positive net present values would be viable undertakings. An alternative approach, which is more common in the Bank, is to calculate an internal rate of return. This rate of return is essentially the discount rate that results in project benefits and costs being equal. The larger the benefits, the higher the discount rate must be to bring benefits down to the level of project costs, and hence the higher will be the internal rate of return.

Most rates of return calculated by the Bank are economic or financial rates of return; social rates of return are rarely used, even for poverty-oriented projects. Where project benefits cannot be quantified at all, it is not possible to calculate any rate of return. In poverty-oriented projects such as the Bank's rural development projects, it is difficult to conceptualize a financial rate of return. The focus tends toward the projects' effects on the growth of output. Rate-of-return analysis is thus an extremely complicated undertaking which even some staff interviewed within the Bank professed not to understand fully.

This caveat having been registered, however, it does not appear that the Bank's antipoverty projects have suffered from bad rates of return (whether economic, financial, or some hybrid of the two). While evidence so far available is extremely limited because not enough poverty-oriented projects have been completed to facilitate a definitive assessment, audits of completed rural development projects indicate generally acceptable (and, in some cases, clearly better than acceptable) rates of return. This result seems mainly attributable to sharp increases in the incremental output and thus incomes of small-scale farmers.

A corollary consideration goes well beyond the results of the project itself. If overall country creditworthiness is satisfactory, it may not be crucial for individual projects to manifest a satisfactory rate of return. This subject is, however, considerably more complex than appears at first glance. For, in the words of a regional chief economist at the Bank, "the fact that the projects financed offer good economic rates of return does not mean that it is easy for the government concerned to capture enough of the benefits to cover debt service. This is particularly the case when the project concerned is for economic or social infrastructure not offering a direct financial return (such as roads or schools). In such cases debt service must be paid from general government revenues."[34]

To the extent, then, that antipoverty projects generate less revenue for covering debt service than more traditional projects (mainly because of less export revenue), there is a problem. But the problem is in a sense solved if the condition of general government revenues is such as to permit efficient debt service. In this respect loans for poverty-oriented projects are no riskier than loans for traditional projects, provided that by "risk" is meant that the loan will not be repaid. The loan is repaid by the government no matter what the economic or financial rate of return on the individual project itself. The fact is that there have not been any of these kinds of losses on World Bank loans. There has never been a default on a loan. There has never been a write-off of a loan. There is no debt rescheduling. It is unlikely that this situation will change with loans for poverty-oriented projects.

It is highly doubtful that an excessive preoccupation with poverty-oriented projects has damaged the financial reputation of the World Bank. In the final analysis the question may not turn on either country or project creditworthiness but on whether the international financial markets accept the creditworthiness of the Bank. The research conducted for this study revealed no hard evidence of the Bank's having difficulty in raising funds because of its poverty-oriented lending policies. A more likely concern is quite the reverse, that an excessive concern on the Bank's part for financial probity might damage the poverty-oriented projects. This concern could lead the Bank to cut back on its most innovative projects. It could lead to some very narrow criteria for identifying the success of projects—to strictly financial and economic rather than social, political, or institution-building criteria. It could curtail lending to countries seriously committed to antipoverty efforts but whose overall financial situation is marginal. Societies in transition would suffer. It could lead the Bank to neglect innovative sources for channeling its funds; for example, nongovernmental intermediaries might find it difficult to secure governmental guarantees. These appear to be more probable dangers than increasing poverty-oriented work and its innovativeness.

The Bank's Organization

A number of features of the Bank's organization under McNamara appeared to produce difficulties for the conduct of its poverty-oriented activities. (An organization chart showing the formal organization of the Bank is included in appendix A.) Foremost was the centralization of the Bank in Washington. Of the Bank's professional staff approximately 94 percent are located in its headquarters in Washington. Although the Bank has 26 resident missions in individual member countries and three regional missions (in East Africa, West Africa, and Thailand), these are staffed by only about 150 professional personnel out of a total professional staff of 2,552.[35] The vast bulk of the Bank's most important decisions are taken at its headquarters in Washington. Major inputs into these decisions come from the missions that periodically go out to visit the developing member countries.

This organizational approach had a direct bearing on the Bank's efforts to combat poverty in the McNamara years. It was difficult for this mission-oriented approach to provide the sustained picture of rural and urban development processes that appeared a requisite for the Bank's decision making in these areas. The choice was between top-down and bottom-up approaches to development and poverty alleviation, and the Bank's approach was basically top-down. Rural poverty alleviation, however, required local-level knowledge and expertise that the Bank arguably did not possess in sufficient abundance. A corollary of such centralization difficulties was insufficient participation of the poor recipients in the design and implementation of most poverty-oriented projects. These aspects of the Bank's organization had an impact on implementation. In rural development projects some of the Bank's project designs were seriously flawed. In urban poverty projects insufficient participation of the intended beneficiaries also adversely affected project implementation. Maintenance of project works was a particularly frequent problem.

The World Bank under McNamara was centralized in another way—internally. Within its headquarters in Washington decision making tended to be highly centralized. This was an issue of singular concern to the Bank's Staff Association. As a report of the association put it, "information about operational and administrative policies is disseminated in a selective one-way communication process from the top down." It was claimed by the association that "middle managers play little more than a foreman's role."[36] This approach was considered to have had an adverse impact on the Bank's poverty-oriented work. A considerable number of Bank staff and officials interviewed for this study felt that McNamara's penchant for centralized decision making, taken together with his allegedly excessive preoccupation with quantification, led to an emphasis on quantity over quality in the decision-making process about poverty-oriented projects. The priority placed upon the prompt meeting of targets and directives from higher management was sometimes seen to be at the expense of the nuances, subtleties, and ultimately the quality of the Bank's address of poverty alleviation.

The Bank under McNamara also seemed to suffer from some lack of imagination in its management of poverty-oriented work. While poverty-oriented projects by their very nature cut across disciplinary boundaries, the organizational structure of the Bank was very traditional. Many of the poverty problems of developing countries seemed to require a regional development approach that would integrate rural and urban projects and give more systematic attention to the employment requirements of such countries. Yet the relationship between the problems of rural and urban poverty was not adequately addressed by the Bank with its somewhat arbitrary subdivisions of "rural projects," "urban projects," "educational projects," "industrial projects," and so forth. If the Bank was calling for a more integrated approach to the problems of poverty, then it also seemed to require its own more imaginatively integrated organizational structure.

A somewhat peculiar organizational feature of the Bank concerns the role of its executive directors. There are five appointed and fifteen elected directors. Those appointed are from France, Japan, the United Kingdom, the United States, and West Germany. The others are elected through a complex system of country groupings; one director represents the group of countries that elected him. Elections occur at the meeting of the Board of Governors and are for two-year terms.

The executive directors, however, seemed to have relatively little power in McNamara's Bank. The Bank was very much a management-run institution. This was despite the fact that the directors were required to approve every commitment of funds for development projects as well as major changes in Bank policy (such as the interest rate on Bank loans). But the directors' approval of these things was more or less a formality. In practice projects were approved by the operational management of the Bank and ratified by the directors. During the course of the research for this study no single instance was discovered of a project's being turned down by the directors.[37] Management also had great flexibility in determining what matters of general policy it would submit to the directors for review. Bank mythology had it that the comments voiced by the directors in their weekly meetings were fed back into the design of future projects and the formulation of future policies, but there was very little evidence that this was in fact the case. This seemed to reflect management's fears that control and guidance of the Bank by the executive directors would adversely politicize the institution. This was the alleged reason why the Bank's country-programming papers, which spell out its lending program for individual countries for the succeeding five years and are reflective of the Bank's criteria for the country allocation of its funds, were not seen by the directors. The notion was that this would lead to higgling and haggling, pork barrels, horsetrading, and the like.

The Bank might have suffered in some ways from the weakness of its executive directors. An example concerns the issue of Bank accountability. During the McNamara years the notion grew—particularly within the U.S. government—that the Bank was insufficiently accountable to its member countries, especially its principal donor countries. One solution might have been to attempt to make the Board of Executive Directors a more effective instrument for communicating information about the Bank's decisions to member governments. The executive directors also might have had a more active role to play in the poverty-oriented work of the Bank. As the Bank's chief political officers they might have been more skillfully employed in negotiating poverty-oriented programs with potential recipients of the Bank's resources.

Country Allocation and Performance

Much of the remainder of the present study is devoted to a detailed discussion of the Bank's work on specific development projects initiated in the latter years of McNamara's presidency. But these projects did not simply emerge willy-nilly. Behind them were determinations about the countries within which the projects were to be located.

This is another area where the distinction between the Bank and IDA is crucial. Two factors—a country's per capita income and its creditworthiness—appeared to determine whether a country was an "IDA country" or a "Bank country." In theory, the lower a country's per capita income, the more it should qualify for IDA lending. Also in theory, the less creditworthy a country, the more it should qualify for IDA lending. ("Creditworthy" in this sense refers principally to the country's access to private capital markets. If a country clearly had such access, it was not supposed to be eligible for IDA money.) If a country passed a certain per capita income threshold (currently $730), or if it became creditworthy in the narrow sense of obtaining access to private capital markets, the country was supposed to "graduate" (or "maturate") from IDA to Bank lending. Along the way some countries pass through an intermediate zone as "blend" countries. (The question of how to determine when a country should graduate from Bank lending altogether is discussed later.)

"Creditworthiness" has traditionally been a crucial concept in the lexicon of the Bank. Theoretically, the more creditworthy a country, the more it is a candidate for Bank loans. Some shorthand quantitative indicators have been utilized for assessing creditworthiness. These include a country's debt service ratio, the public sector deficit as a percentage of gross domestic product, and a country's total savings and total investment, as well as its savings and investment rates. In theory, the higher the debt service ratio, the lower the creditworthiness; the higher the public sector deficit as a percentage of gross domestic product, the lower the creditworthiness; the higher the savings and investment rates, the higher the creditworthiness; and so forth. On the basis of such indicators a number of countries seemed to be experiencing creditworthiness difficulties as of mid-1980 (when the research on this topic was conducted). Rather obvious examples included Ghana and Zaire. Some other countries appeared to be only marginally creditworthy, including Egypt, Jamaica, Nicaragua, and Turkey.

Once it was determined whether a country was an IDA country, a Bank country, or a blend country, allocational factors came into play. One of these was population size. Lending revealed a "small-country bias." According to statistical analyses conducted at the Bank, a country with a population five times larger than another country would only get one-half again as much money. A number of factors explain this bias. One is the "lumpiness" of development projects. There is a minimum project size below which a project would lose viability, and, when this minimum size (quite large in an absolute sense) is divided by a small country's population, it introduces a small-country bias. Another factor is the Bank's policy on portfolio diversification. As a general rule no country is supposed to receive more than 10 percent of the Bank's outstanding loans. With such a ceiling on lending to countries that "should" receive more money on strict per capita lending grounds, the small-country bias is reinforced. In addition a great number of small countries have lately joined the Bank. The necessity of making some loans to all countries reinforces the small-country bias. In making its decisions on country lending, the Bank introduced a statistical corrective to reduce the small-country bias, but some element of bias remained nevertheless.

Also important in the determination of country allocations in the Bank under McNamara were a range of country performance considerations that went beyond creditworthiness narrowly defined but were very closely related to it. The Bank distinguished between economic management and equity performance. The former included both quantitative and qualitative assessments of a country's management of its economic growth, foreign trade, and fiscal and monetary policy. Assessments were also made of the performance of the country's public-sector institutions, such as state enterprises. The relationship to creditworthiness was obvious; the better the economic management, the better should be the creditworthiness.

It was difficult to measure economic management, but it was doubly difficult to assess a country's equity performance. There was very little evidence on longitudinal changes in country income distributions. The Bank referred to such social indicators as life expectancy, literacy, and infant mortality. Primary school enrollment ratios received attention. There was some qualitative evidence on government policies and programs. The adoption of rural development policies by recipient countries was given considerable weight. But Bank staff emphasized that there were no one or two best quantitative indicators that the Bank employed crossnationally to measure equity performance.

Having determined as best it could a country's level of performance on economic management and equity grounds, the Bank then attempted to assess the extent of its own recent and historical impact on these levels. "Bank impact" thus defined was, again, largely a subjective judgment.

There were at least two other factors that appeared to enter into the Bank's judgments on country allocations in the McNamara years. One was the level of interest the country itself manifested in borrowing from the Bank or IDA. The most common reason for a country's (rather infrequent) lack of interest in borrowing was the conditionality attached to Bank loans or IDA credits. Obviously, if a country was not interested in borrowing money from the Bank or IDA, there would be no allocation of funds to that country.

An additional factor in country allocation was that of "absorptive capacity." This refers to a country's ability to use the loan or credit effectively. It was most obviously a factor in the poorest IDA countries but concerned some Bank countries as well. It was, however, a difficult factor to quantify. One indicator the Bank used was disbursement shortfalls on its own projects under implementation. If these were chronic, they tended to indicate an absorptive capacity problem.

As a practical matter, it was virtually impossible for the Bank to quantify these various country allocation criteria or even to systematize them in a precise, rigorous fashion. In the latter years of McNamara's presidency, however, a limited, experimental effort was made to quantify the process of country allocation. By assigning scores to a number of performance indicators, and by combining such scores in an unweighted manner with other factors such as a country's population size or absorptive capacity, a unit within the Bank's central economic staff attempted to arrive at very rough approximations of projected country allocations for the next five-year lending period.

A number of factors about this effort, which may be deemed roughly akin to the "country risk" analysis of some private commercial banks, should be stressed.

First, a high degree of subjectivity entered into the assessment of countries. Qualitative judgments regarding governmental policies were obviously unavoidable, and, where qualitative judgments were employed, substantial room for debate was opened.

Second, while staff within the Bank were understandably reluctant to reveal the Bank's "ratings" of countries, it is noteworthy how few surprises were to be found among the Bank's assessments. Students of development will not be surprised to learn that the Bank has generally considered economic management good in countries like Korea, Brazil, Colombia, Kenya, Malawi, or Cameroon. Similarly, it is understandable that the Bank has generally looked with favor on equity performance in countries like Costa Rica, Yugoslavia, Sri Lanka, or Tanzania. Conversely, that the Bank in recent years found Zaire noticeably unimpressive on economic management grounds or Nicaragua (under Somoza) unimpressive on equity grounds will certainly not startle students of such countries. While the Bank is extremely reluctant to state precisely for public consumption how it views a member country's performance, it may be reported that the vast majority of Bank assessments do not differ greatly from what might be considered as educated common sense about development performance.

Third, the procedures by which an effort was made to systematize the assessments of countries, and thereby the process of country allocations, took place at the staff, or technical, level of the Bank. Being highly experimental and subjective, and thereby open to various methodological objections from other staff within the institution (particularly in the regional divisions and departments), the procedures were never officially sanctioned by the Bank's higher management nor by the executive directors. The proposed country allocations and the proposed country lending programs that emerged from rudimentary efforts at quantification served as the basis for an exchange of opinions ("negotiations" is perhaps too strong a word) with the staff of the Bank having regional responsibilities.

These efforts to systematize country assessments were closely coordinated with the essentially qualitative exercise that marked the preparation of country programming papers. These are the most confidential reports produced within the Bank. They spell out Bank or

IDA lending targets for the next five years. They contain candid assessments of recent developments in the borrowing country, including some discussion of recent social and political developments (highly rare by the Bank). They discuss, sector by sector, the proposed lending strategy for the upcoming period. They also discuss the kinds of projects to be processed during the period and how such projects fit into the overall lending targets.[38] The end result of these complex, interactive procedures is a set of country allocations. Each Bank or IDA borrower is programmed to receive a certain amount of Bank or IDA resources over the subsequent five-year lending period, and recommendations on these amounts are accompanied by frank, terse assessments of the countries concerned.

A topic that has generated a considerable amount of interest concerns the role of "politics" in these country allocation decisions. A principal element of the mythology of Bank lending has always been the contention that loans are made on the basis of economic criteria alone. Political considerations are alleged to have no part in loan decisions. This position has often been reiterated by official spokesmen for the Bank. Approval of loans to the Pinochet government in Chile is a case in point. According to one press report on the favorable vote of the U.S. government, the executive director for the United States "stood by the long-standing Treasury position that World Bank loans should be judged on economic merits alone and not on 'political' grounds."[39]

This formulation of the matter appears, however, far from accurate. Political criteria have certainly entered in. Bank lending to Chile is clearly a case in point. In the initial years of the Pinochet regime, Chile was an horrendous performer on economic and financial grounds. On December 24, 1975, for example, the Bank produced a report that painted an exceedingly grim picture of the situation in that country: "The Chilean economy in 1975 is suffering its worst depression since the 1930s. Industrial production for the year will be some 22–25 percent below the level of 1974, construction is down 30 percent, mining output has fallen 10 percent, and services will be down around 15 percent. Real GDP will decline by 12–15 percent. The effect of deteriorating terms of trade reduces the economy's real income by an additional 4 percent relative to 1974." Yet two weeks later, on January 7, 1976, a copper sector project appraisal report recommended a Bank loan to Chile of $33 million. Two additional loans to the country followed. It was difficult to explain these actions with reference to arguments about creditworthiness. Much more plausible were arguments on political grounds, particularly the importance which a Republican administration in the United States attributed to a show of support for the Pinochet government.

There seem to have been other instances in which political considerations were paramount. In some cases there was pressure to increase proposed allocations for reasons of political importance. Egypt was a good example of this. Tanzania probably was also, with lending designed to show that the Bank could be forthcoming toward socialist regimes. Similarly, countries such as Jamaica or Turkey were sometimes supported for essentially political reasons and not in conformity to the strict Bank canons of performance and creditworthiness. There were also a number of countries that, strictly speaking, appeared to be candidates for "graduation" from all Bank lending entirely. Romania and Yugoslavia would appear to be two such countries, and Korea could likely also be included. But there was some feeling that Bank lending to post-Tito Yugoslavia should continue as a show of support to the international community, and it was considered unlikely that the Reagan administration would look with favor upon the cessation of all Bank lending to Korea, whether or not such an action would appear to be justified on strictly economic grounds.

The Bank's poverty-oriented thrust under McNamara raised some particularly difficult questions of country allocation. There were some sharp internal debates on lending to countries whose development policies (or lack thereof) were the object of intense international controversy. Should there, for example, have been Bank lending to Nicaragua under Somoza, where a less poverty-oriented regime could hardly have been imagined? The debate over lending to Pinochet's Chile was perhaps the most publicized example. Another debate occurred concerning loans to Ethiopia following the overthrow of the emperor; such lending is now sharply reduced from previous levels. Country allocation decisions were of course present before the poverty-oriented redirections of the Bank. But they seemed to become more political as the commitment of countries to the Bank's antipoverty objectives began to be taken into account in the struggles over allocative priorities. These struggles were not always resolved in favor of the countries with a serious commitment to alleviating poverty, as is obvious from the record of Bank lending in recent years.

It must be reiterated that such political considerations were extremely difficult to quantify and, as such, it was difficult to assign weights to their importance when measured against all of the other variables the Bank considered in reaching its broad decisions on its lending program. Political factors seemed to enter in to a greater extent for countries that were highly salient to the interests of the foreign policy of the most important donor countries (most notably the United States) or countries whose development policies, for whatever reasons, were highly conflictual and thus the subject of relatively intense international attention and controversy. The point, however, is that this still left a whole range of countries—the clear majority of the Bank's recipient countries—that were not so salient or so conflictual. In these countries the weight of political variables was likely to be considerably less and the correspondence of country allocation decisions to the norms discussed here accordingly greater.

What, finally, of graduation? It has proved relatively easy to ascertain when an IDA country should graduate into the Bank. Since IDA was founded in 1960, twenty-nine countries have been phased out of IDA borrowing as a result of improvements in their economic situation.[40] IDA is currently considering steps to graduate all recipients with a per capita income above $500.

Graduation from the Bank is supposed to be principally dependent on a country's level of per capita income and what the Bank calls "reasonable access to private capital." Countries reaching a certain threshold income and having such access are supposed to graduate from Bank lending. In January 1982 the Bank's executive directors approved a new graduation policy that stipulated a country per capita income of $2,650 (in 1980 dollars) as the cutoff point for triggering Bank analysis of the need for continued Bank assistance. (Graduation therefore is *not* automatic at this figure.) According to a recent U.S. Treasury Department report, however, "there are no precise guidelines nor an explanation of what this more rigorous analysis should entail. Moreover there is no per capita income ceiling on eligibility for IBRD loans, and in the past key questions concerning timing, scale, and content of the phaseout lending program have been decided on an ad hoc basis."[41]

Graduation first became an issue at the Bank around 1972, when it was widely noted that the Bank was still lending to the likes of Finland, Greece, Iceland, and Yugoslavia (to which it still lends). Since the Bank first formulated its graduation policy in 1973, eight countries— Iceland, Finland, Israel, Ireland, Spain, Singapore, Greece, and Venezuela—have graduated. Nearly all had a per capita income level well above the supposed threshold level established in 1973 at the time they stopped borrowing from the Bank. A number of other major borrowers crossed the threshold between 1973 and 1979. According to the Treasury Department report, another group of major borrowers—including Algeria, Brazil, Chile, Korea, Malaysia, and Mexico—appear likely to cross the threshold in the 1980s.[42]

From time to time there has been a controversy within the Bank about whether graduation should be based on an *absolute* or a *relative* measure of per capita national income. If based on the former, graduation would mean that sooner or later the Bank would work itself out of a job since presumably at some point *all* countries would reach the absolute threshold figure. If based on the latter, countries would graduate when their per capita income reached a certain proportion of some developed countries' incomes (and the graduating countries had "reasonable access to private capital"). One "graduation paper" sent to the Board of Executive Directors proposed such a relative measure but met with considerable opposition. Thus the sequential progression remains: IDA country to blend country to Bank country to graduated country, with the stages in the progression being defined principally by absolute measures of per capita income and by judgments of country creditworthiness and access to private capital markets.

A Bank Ideology?

Do the Bank's performance criteria and the way in which these are employed to make country allocation decisions suggest anything about a Bank ideology? The dominant ideology, widely shared throughout the Bank, may be identified as that of neoliberalism (using the term "liberal" in the classical sense). The principal objective of such neo-liberalism is economic growth. The principal routes to growth are seen to lie, domestically, through capital accumulation (savings and investment) and, externally, through export expansion and diversification. Ingredients of neoliberalism derivative from these basic goals — ingredients highly prevalent in Bank documents, publications, and interviews with Bank staff and officials — include fiscal and monetary probity; "getting prices right," or removing obstacles to the free-market determination of prices, wages, interest rates, user charges for public services, and so forth; a sound currency; external economic equilibrium; export dynamism; economic stability; and, through all of these things, a favorable investment climate. Deviations from any of these elements constitute deviations from prevalent Bank norms and are likely to be the subject of the country dialogue between the Bank and the deviating country.

It was found, however, that the vast majority of World Bankers reject the notion that these emphases indicate an ideology at all. In their view, as expressed in repeated interviews, all of this is neutral. It is simply sound economic and financial management, technocratically orchestrated and applicable to any kind of economic system—be it capitalist, socialist, the "third way," or whatever. This technocratic neoliberalism is tenacious and was certainly far from totally discarded as a result of the reorientations, real and proposed, of Bank activities since 1973.

Nevertheless, the antipoverty emphases of McNamara since 1973 posed some serious challenges to the prevalent Bank ideology. The result was a somewhat ambiguous pastiche of concepts and approaches. Thus, while there was heightened emphasis on questions of poverty and income distribution, this did not mean that the prevalent growth concerns could be forgotten. While there was a heightened concern for the social aspects of rural development, this did not mean any less attention to the requirements for increasing agricultural production. While there was a heightened concern for the consumption needs of the poorest, this did not mean that national savings and investment rates should fall. While a heightened concern for poverty and income distribution presumably entailed more concern for the political and social aspects of economic development, Bank loan decisions were still held to be governed by purely economic considerations. While poverty-oriented development projects were by their very nature riskier and more innovative than traditional projects, they still had to meet traditional canons of economic and financial analysis.

The result after 1973, then, was a rather tenuous gluing together of some markedly divergent approaches. Poverty-oriented emphases sometimes seemed to have been pasted on to the prevalent ideology without, however, altering its fundamental slant. This was in a certain sense very convenient. It enabled the Bank to do anything it wanted to do, to some an enviable position. It seemed to justify almost any project, study, new direction, or strategic retreat. It came close, however, to making the Bank all things to all people and thus not enough of anything to any of them. It raised in stark form the question of the comparative advantage of the Bank, and it opened up the Bank to criticism of diverse sorts. On the right, critics claimed that the new Bank emphases represented giveaways, welfare programs, money wasted on projects of marginal rates of return. On the left, the Bank's poverty-oriented emphases were alleged to be creating a new stratum of rural and urban elites in developing countries. That the attack on the Bank could come from such widely divergent quarters was perhaps in part a reflection of some of the divergent emphases in its post-1973 ideology.

The Bank's Theory of Poverty Alleviation

Attempting to alleviate poverty without having a theory about how to do it is simply throwing money at problems. What was the Bank's theory? Did it have one? By "theoretical rationale" is meant the general intellectual underpinnings for its country-specific and project-specific work of a poverty-oriented nature.

Redistribution with Growth

In 1974, shortly after McNamara's Nairobi address, the Bank's Development Research Center (jointly with the Institute of Development Studies in Sussex, England) produced a volume that has come to possess a semiofficial status. Entitled *Redistribution with Growth* (*RWG*), the volume marked the Bank's effort to spell out its general approach to poverty alleviation in developing countries. The overwhelming majority of interviews conducted with Bank staff and officials indicated basic agreement with the major arguments of the book. Despite much theoretical ferment within the institution in recent years, the outlines of a strategy for alleviating poverty presented in *RWG* retain their semiofficial status eight years after their initial publication. That is why it is important to ascertain the essential arguments of *RWG* and indicate why they survived efforts at alternative theoretical formulations, such as those identified with a basic human needs approach to development.

Absolute and Relative Poverty

The volume makes the fundamental distinction, also made in McNamara's speeches and in other Bank publications, between absolute and relative poverty. Absolute poverty, which McNamara has defined as "a condition of life so degraded by disease, illiteracy, malnutrition, and squalor as to deny its victims basic human necessities," is in *RWG* defined by a per capita income benchmark. The absolute poor is that population in developing countries living below two poverty lines of annual per capita incomes of $50 and $75 (in 1971 prices). This formulation was rather crude in its measurement of the concept; subsequent work became more sophisticated, referring, for example, to the income needed in different societies to purchase a minimum nutritional bundle in those societies. This crudeness aside, *RWG* attempted to specify the percentages and numbers of absolute poor in various developing countries. In India it was estimated that 44.5 percent of the population, numbering 239 million individuals, were below the $50 poverty line in 1969. The next greatest number of the absolute poor in that year were in Pakistan (East and West), where 32.5 percent of the population, or 36.3 million people, were estimated below this line.[1]

In *RWG* relative poverty refers to the extent to which the income share of groups of individuals or households differs from their population share. Even if the basic human necessities of the lowest 10 or 20 percent of the population are satisfied, they may be considered among the relative poor if their absolute incomes are less than, for example, one-third of the national average per capita income. *RWG* and McNamara consistently gave greater emphasis to absolute poverty than to relative poverty (or more simply, inequality). According to *RWG*, "the limitations of a purely relative approach are self-evident; changes in relative equality tell us little about changes in income levels of the poor unless we also know what has happened to total income."[2] For McNamara, relative poverty "means simply . . . that some citizens of a given country have less personal abundance than their neighbors. That has always been the case, and granted the realities of differences between . . . individuals, will continue to be the case for decades to come."[3]

When reference is made therefore to the World Bank's new antipoverty focus, it is principally in terms of absolute poverty. Rather little is said about relative poverty or inequality. *RWG* argues that "a concern with income distribution is not simply a concern with income shares but rather with the level and growth of income in lower-income groups."[4] For *RWG* and the Bank there was relatively little concern in subsequent years with income shares; the heightened concern for distributionally oriented development projects essentially meant a concern with the "level and growth of income in lower-income groups."

Poverty Alleviation and Economic Growth

A key question of *RWG* is whether the pursuit of poverty alleviation might be at the expense of growth. This was a particularly important question for the World Bank because of the Bank's long-standing preeminent concern with growth. Too great a concern with "premature" income distribution might be thought to have seriously adverse effects on growth, chiefly because of the disruption of the presumed relationships between income concentration, savings rates, and growth. Some country evidence is alleged to illustrate this. Perón's Argentina, Castro's Cuba, Allende's Chile, Sri Lankan experience in the mid-1970s, and current-day Tanzania are frequently cited examples of how excessive preoccupation with distribution might be at the expense of growth.

This question has attracted considerable attention in the economic literature in recent years. A widely quoted assertion is that of Irma Adelman and Cynthia Taft Morris, who concluded from their statistics that economic growth "is accompanied by an absolute as well as a relative decline in the average income of the very poor."[5] In a more recent study David Morawetz concludes that there is no clear relationship between growth and cross-sectional inequality or between growth and longitudinal inequality.[6] Morawetz points to some highly differential country experience in this regard. In the case of relative poverty it appears that the share of the poorest people in gross national product seems to have increased or remained constant in a large number of countries. These include China, Colombia, Costa Rica, El Salvador, Iran, Israel, Korea, Puerto Rico, Singapore, Sri Lanka, and Taiwan. In another group of large countries, however (including Argentina, Brazil, India, Malaysia, Mexico, and the Philippines), it appears that the share of the poorest people declined.

In the case of absolute poverty Morawetz argues that only in China and Mexico is it agreed that large-scale impoverishment of the poor has not occurred. Such impoverishment may well have occurred in Bangladesh, Brazil, India, Indonesia, and Pakistan. But Morawetz is cautious, noting that the countries in which impoverishment is alleged to have occurred include at least as many slow growers as fast ones.[7] Another approach to analyzing this question, involving complex simulations of the growth effects of hypothetical income redistributions and employing numerous assumptions about savings functions, demand profiles, and the like, tends to argue for the neutrality of income redistribution effects. Redistribution is not likely to have particularly perverse effects on growth nor to be particularly growth stimulating.[8]

RWG reached its own conclusion. It argued that "the cross-section evidence does not support the view that a high rate of economic growth has an adverse effect upon relative equality. . . . [T]he objectives of growth and equity may not be in conflict."[9] It further suggested that "the trade-off between distribution and growth—if it exists in a given country—may well be an intermediate phenomenon limited to the period that is required to make the investment in the poor productive."[10] *RWG*, in short, was relatively sanguine about the supposed trade-offs between distribution and growth. Poverty-oriented projects could therefore address themselves to both concerns. While optimistic, this orientation implied the formidable task of designing policy instruments and development projects to reconcile the twin goals in specific countries and specific historical contexts.

RWG discussed four approaches to the problem of raising the welfare of the low-income groups: (1) maximizing the growth of gross national product, (2) redirecting investment to poverty groups, (3) redistributing income or consumption to poverty groups, and (4) transferring of existing assets to poverty groups.[11] The favored strategy was the second. The first had the problem of "relatively weak linkage between the poverty groups and the rest of the economy."[12] The third had "too high a cost in terms of foregone investment to be viable on a large scale over an extended period."[13] The fourth was considered unfeasible because "political resistance to policies of asset redistribution makes this approach unlikely to succeed on any large scale in most countries."[14] In this respect the essence of the *RWG* approach was on increasing the productivity, incomes, and output (and through these, the welfare) of the absolute poor. This also coincided with McNamara's annual addresses since 1973.

Shortcomings of the Bank's Approach

There appeared to be at least two deficiencies in this conceptualization of the problem. One was insufficient attention to the factors that generate poverty. The World Bank's causal chain was very short. Why were people poor? Because they lacked jobs. Because they were unproductive. Because they produced insufficient output. This explanation bordered on the tautological. Why did they lack jobs? Why was their productivity low? Why didn't they produce enough? A paper on poverty in Latin America argues that "it is only valid to study poverty within the framework of some theory of income distribution and social inequalities in general . . . the causes of poverty are rooted in the same mechanisms that determine general inequalities prevailing in each society. To concentrate our attention on poverty should not become a substitute for the concern about inequalities in the distribution of welfare."[15] The World Bank's approach to poverty alleviation under McNamara could, however, be considered such a substitute. It lacked an adequate theory of income distribution and social inequalities in general. This lack gave rise to considerable contradictions and ambiguities in Bank work at the project level.

The second deficiency was the lack of a sophisticated political theory for implementing the proposed distributional redirections. *RWG* discusses what it calls the "political framework," but it has relatively little to say on the subject. The essential political judgment, "thematic to the volume as a whole," is that "intervention which alters the distribution of the increment to the overall capital stock and income will arouse less hostility from the rich than transfers which bite into their existing assets and incomes."[16] It is questionable therefore whether this can really be called a "redistributive strategy," as *RWG* calls it, when it argues that "the key factor is the emergence of a coalition of interests able to grasp power that sees some advantage in implementing a redistributive strategy."[17]

The essence of *RWG*'s political framework is the emergence of a reformist coalition. The central problem is that the elite must make some concessions to the poor. *RWG* considers only two options whereby the elite would make such concessions. One is out of enlightened self-interest, but this is not considered very likely at all. The other involves intraelite competition in which one segment of the elite reaches out to the poor for support. But this necessitates analyzing the contradictions within the elite (such as rural vs. urban interests, national bourgeoisie vs. dependent bourgeoisie, subcategories of the rural and urban elites, and so forth) from country to country, issue to issue, epoch to epoch. *RWG* engages in virtually none of this. Its reformist coalition concerned with the distribution of the growth increments appears to emerge as a deus ex machina. In the absence of a theory of the politics of redistribution with growth, there were only hortatory utterances like "political will" or, in McNamara's 1978 annual address, "sustained political courage."[18] This excessively voluntarist approach was grossly inattentive to questions of socioeconomic and sociopolitical context and structure. It was, however, to be expected from the Bank. "Owned" by its member countries, the Bank had obvious difficulties in making explicit distinctions among them in terms of their commitment to redistribution with growth.

International Dimension

RWG deals principally with the question of income distribution within countries. It has relatively little to say about distribution between countries. The Bank's position on the latter issued mainly through McNamara's annual addresses.

A distinction is customarily made between the middle-income developing countries (such as Argentina, Brazil, Korea, Mexico, and Taiwan) and the countries of the Fourth World, the IDA countries with per capita incomes below $730. The needs of the two groups of countries are seen as different by the Bank. For the middle-income countries the principal concessions required of the rich countries are in the areas of trade and investment. The essence of the argument is that there should be fewer barriers to trade erected by the developed countries, and there should be greater investment flows with a more equitable division of the profits between the developed-country investors and the developing recipient countries. For the poorest countries the principal requirement is sharply increased amounts of official development assistance. These twin themes were perhaps most forcibly stated in McNamara's 1978 address to the Board of Governors.[19]

Another line of argument is remarkably similar to the arguments put forth by *RWG* concerning absolute poverty and relative poverty within countries. What is more important to the World Bank is the absolute poverty of developing countries, not the gaps between them and rich countries. The relative gap, the per capita income of the developing countries as a proportion of the per capita income of the developed countries, remained constant at around 7 to 8 percent over the period 1950 to 1975. But the absolute gap widened greatly. From $2,191 greater in 1950, the average gross national product per capita of the countries in the Organization for Economic Cooperation and Development grew to $4,839 greater than that of the developing countries by 1975.[20] Projecting historical growth rates into the future provides rough estimates of the years required to close the absolute gap. It would take Brazil 362 years; Turkey, 675; Panama, 1,866; China, 2,900; and Mauritania, 3,224. Morawetz argues that narrowing the absolute gap appears to make more sense as a development objective than narrowing the relative gap. But even narrowing the absolute gap would require centuries, and it is unclear that it could really ever be narrowed.[21]

In his 1977 annual address McNamara was very forceful on this point: "[C]losing the gap was never a realistic objective in the first place. Given the immense differences in the capital and technological base of the industrialized nations as compared with that of the developing countries, it was simply not a feasible goal. Nor is it one today."[22]

When the World Bank refers therefore to a "new international economic order," it is not referring to international income redistribution. Rather, what is being proposed are certain reforms of the existing international system which would improve the terms on which the poor countries relate to it. What is definitely not being proposed is a total transformation of that system.

But the Bank has not really been in the forefront of those championing a new order. This is understandable given the constraints on its operations discussed in the previous chapter. Many of the proposals for such a new order emanating from the developing countries have proven unacceptable to the developed countries which are the principal donors of Bank and IDA resources. It is not considered wholly appropriate for the Bank to take the lead in endorsing southern proposals for a new order of North–South relations. As embodied in resolutions of the Sixth Special Session of the United Nations General Assembly (May 1, 1974) and subsequent documents and proclamations, such proposals include a range of initiatives regarding commodities, international trade, reform of the international monetary system, development assistance, international industrialization, the transfer of technology, regulation and control over the activities of transnational corporations, and so forth. The developing countries have called for international commodity agreements to regulate and stabilize world markets for raw materials and primary commodities, for enlarged tariff preference arrangements for exports of manufactured and semi-manufactured products, for additional participation in IMF decision making, for an increase in their share of international industrial production through the financing of industrial projects and industrial relocation, for more developed-country support for the development of indigenous technology within developing countries, for the adoption of an international code of conduct for multinational corporations, and numerous other measures. With the notable exception of its emphasis on the negative aspects of industrial-country protectionism and its understandable emphasis on the need for increased flows of development assistance, the Bank has given relatively greater attention to necessary policy reforms within developing countries.

By the same token the latter have focused on the perceived inequities of the international system. While intellectuals from developing countries were in the forefront of those formulating poverty-oriented development strategies, such strategies took a back seat in numerous international forums where the southern viewpoint was expressed. According to one analysis, "the position voiced by the South is that basic needs objectives are to be achieved through economic growth, which in turn is to take place through implementation of the new international economic order."[23] The same analysis goes on to observe, "the South is absolutely unwilling to endorse the basic needs approach as its main priority."[24]

One of the difficult issues currently confronting the international development community therefore involves ways in which to link the concerns of intra- and international equity. The developed countries have seen the principal obstacles to poverty alleviation as residing within the developing countries themselves. They view the developing countries' concerns with various aspects of a new international economic order as a smokescreen devised by the poor countries to hide their own lack of attention to the poor within their borders. For their part the developing countries have tended to view the great attention to their poverty problems as another kind of smokescreen constructed by the developed countries to avoid their having to make any concessions to the poor countries at the international level. The task confronting the World Bank and other institutions concerned with international development seems increasingly to be that of designing an effective linkage between commitments on the part of developed countries to improve international equity with commitments on the part of developing countries to ameliorate their intranational inequities. Stating the task in this way, however, simply serves to underscore the immense difficulties confronting any attempt to conquer poverty in the developing world.

Basic Human Needs Alternative

Since the publication of *RWG* and the translation of its theoretical approach into specific poverty-oriented development projects, there emerged within the international development community and the World Bank one potentially competing approach called the "basic human needs" (BHN) development strategy. More recently, a number of papers were produced within the Bank that took issue with some of the postulates of *RWG* and formulated an alternative strategy for poverty alleviation. Indeed, although some critics of the World Bank saw the BHN approach as central to the Bank's poverty-oriented efforts, BHN was not able to supplant the approach outlined in *RWG*. Why it was unable to do so says much about the nature of the institution.

The basic needs approach includes several elements, all aimed at overcoming absolute poverty in a way deemed by its proponents as more direct and efficient than the *RWG* strategy. The first entails the specification of the basic needs themselves. Principal emphasis is placed on the satisfaction of material needs, and a Bank paper specified minimum acceptable levels for food, nutrition, drinking water, basic health, shelter, and basic education. Differences among observers as to what constitute basic needs have prevented agreement on a core bundle of such needs. There are also differences about priorities among basic needs. There seems to be general agreement that material needs take priority over nonmaterial needs, but, apart from this, efforts at defining a hierarchy of basic needs have been unsuccessful.

A second aspect of the BHN approach involves the specification of indicators for measuring basic needs. The Overseas Development Council uses a composite index of the physical quality of life (PQLI), comprised of indicators of literacy, infant mortality, and life expectancy.[25] A Bank paper suggested that attention be focused on the core indicators for each basic need identified which, with appropriate weighting, might be combined into a composite basic needs index. As a proxy for such an index, the paper suggested life expectancy at birth or literacy.

It is generally agreed that what constitutes a minimum acceptable level of basic needs is culture-specific and varies from country to country. In practice, however, this admonishment about cultural specificity is frequently ignored when it comes to establishing indicators for BHN. Another Bank paper defined the needs by way of indicators apparently designed for general employment. The food requirement, for example, was deemed at about 2,350 calories per day per adult male. Safe drinking water should be within reasonable access, defined by the Bank as within 200 meters in urban areas.

A third issue concerns the measurement of progress in meeting basic needs. It is argued that increases in per capita income do not necessarily translate into increases in basic needs attainment and that some other yardstick is required. A debate has ensued on what this yardstick should be. The Overseas Development Council employs a disparities reduction rate, which measures the annual rates at which the disparities between individual developing countries and the developed country with the best performance on indicators of life expectancy, infant mortality, and literacy are being reduced. Success at disparity reduction in this sense might or might not be correlated with annual increases in per capita income.[26]

BHN Attainment Strategy

In its simplest variant the BHN approach involves establishing an inventory of core basic needs, formulating targets, calculating what it would cost to eliminate the shortfalls by a specified date (usually taken, without the greatest of logic, to be the year 2000), and assigning a figure to the amount of external development assistance that would be required to do the job.

So conceptualized, the BHN approach appeared difficult to contest. There were formidable technical problems, such as the difficulties of establishing quantitative targets, and there were some heroic assumptions, such as those that had to be made to arrive at a dollar figure for meeting basic needs. But the approach seemed to make sense with regard to absolute poverty, appeared at least feasible in a financial sense, and, above all, contained indisputable moral and ethical appeal.

In practice, however, there were many objections to the BHN approach. One of the key questions to arise was whether basic human needs, so defined, could be met by the income-productivity-output approach identified with *RWG*. Advocates of a BHN persuasion argued that the income-productivity-output approach was a necessary but by no means a sufficient condition for the satisfaction of BHN. They argued that it is not enough to raise production by the poor through raising demand for the goods and services produced by the poor, improving their skills, and raising their productivity.

Several Bank papers discussed why these were necessary but not sufficient conditions for eradicating poverty. Many of the measures intended to achieve antipoverty results have simply been unable to alter initial patterns of income; additional income may be spent on nonbasic needs items. Such incremental income may be spent by adult males on themselves, not on women and children whose basic needs would continue to go unmet. The sick, disabled, aged, or orphaned (the destitute) are by definition incapable of earning additional income. Most fundamental, however, was the argument that the income-productivity-output approach, while paying some attention to appropriate technology, has paid little or no attention to appropriate products. In many developing countries the production or importation of inappropriate, oversophisticated, or luxury products has been the principal obstacle to the pursuit of a BHN strategy since it has meant that the economy caters to the demand of a small section of the population. In this view the choice of appropriate products is not necessarily achieved only by a redistribution of income.

Radical Implications of BHN

The BHN view is much more radical than that of *RWG* for it implies larger changes, and perhaps profound ones, in the structure of production and in the role of government in the economy. There would have to be what some theoreticians of the BHN approach have called supply management.

Another in the series of BHN papers produced within the Bank spelled out in more detail some of the radical implications of the approach. It pointed out that there were three policies that flow from a concern with meeting the basic needs of the world's poor. The first two were familiar from the discussion of *RWG*, increasing the productivity and income of the poor by redirecting investment toward them and increasing their access to public services. The third, however, was not present in *RWG* and indicated the latent radicalism of BHN. This is that "the production of nonessential goods (apart from exports) should be tightly controlled, all incentives and market signals should be modified toward the production of basic wage goods and services, the state should stand ready for large-scale market intervention if the existing markets are a slave to the interest of the privileged groups. The opponents of basic needs programs fear that such market interventions will often be inefficient, serve only the interests of the ruling elite, and are probably a soft sell for communism."

Clearly, a great deal of the recent discussion about basic needs failed to realize the thoroughgoing implications of what was being proposed. It assumed that the goal of satisfying basic human needs was unarguable in a sense in which alleviating relative inequality was not. But there are many reasons why producers and importers in developing countries would not want to subscribe to the BHN goal, in particular problems created for the political elite by the empowerment of the poor. The simplest and most common variant of the BHN approach was insufficiently attentive to the political complexity of what was being proposed.

Brief attention was given to the politics of *RWG*. But what about the politics of satisfying basic human needs? This question has gone virtually unexplored. Yet it is immediately clear that formidable problems of political feasibility are encountered. Nothing less than a change in the ownership of productive assets would appear a necessity for the desired changes in the composition of output. The elite would also have to renounce some of its consumption goals. A Bank paper posed the "uncomfortable political question: can all this be done in a reformist fashion? Are the political decisions so fundamental as to require a revolution?" It did not offer a definitive answer. Another Bank paper, however, argued against the idea that BHN is an ideological concept that masks a call to revolution. It maintained that this conclusion simply could not be justified on historical or analytical grounds, and cited such diverse countries as China, Costa Rica, Japan, Korea, Sri

Lanka, Taiwan, and Yugoslavia as among those that had satisfied basic needs within a relatively short time.

It does not appear that a political theory about basic needs attainment can be developed by resort to the traditional argument of reform versus revolution. A more fruitful approach would focus on those countries that historically have met basic needs for their poor citizens. One research strategy would be to assess which countries have actually performed well on a number of social indicators measures. Experience with the PQLI of the Overseas Development Council is instructive in this regard. It has been found that some countries attained PQLI scores considerably higher than what would be expected simply from knowing their per capita national incomes. Examples are Cuba, Grenada, Guyana, Mauritius, and Sri Lanka.[27] These are, of course, deviant cases but of some interest. Countries whose PQLI attainments were considerably lower than what would be expected from just knowing their per capita national incomes were deviant in the opposite direction. Examples of these countries include Gabon, Qatar, Saudi Arabia, and the United Arab Emirates.[28]

The task then would be to explain why basic needs or a decent physical quality of life were attained in some cases and not in others among countries of similar per capita economic attainment. This requires a theory about the principal variables and their interrelationships. Such a theory is totally lacking at present. The Bank was aware of this problem. It lamented in one of its papers that "little analysis has gone so far into the political, institutional, and administrative framework required to make a successful attack on poverty and to remove obstacles to fulfilling basic needs. Some interdisciplinary studies in this field must be organized soon." A workshop on the Analysis of Distributional Issues in Development Planning held in Bellagio, Italy, in April 1977 was attended by some of the Bank's big thinkers. The observations of the workshop were thoroughly tepid when it came to the question of the politics of satisfying basic needs. A summary of the sessions indicated that "the discussion on political aspects raised a number of questions but provided no answers as to how a congenial political climate can be created for successful implementation of redistributive policies." While focusing, as did *RWG*, on the necessity for a reformist coalition, it pointed out that "little, however, is known as to the process of coalition formation."[29]

It is well beyond the scope of this study to elaborate a political theory of basic needs attainment. It would appear, however, that the political aspects of the recommended interdisciplinary studies should include a systematic assessment of the relationship between such attainment and type of political regime. But the typology for differentiating types of regimes would have to be more sophisticated than those commonly found in the political science literature (of which the most common is democracies or polyarchies versus nondemocracies or nonpolyarchies).[30] Attention would have to be given to the many variants of authoritarian or corporatist regimes and to their records on distributional issues. What kind of regime has Tanzania? Sri Lanka? Mexico? Nigeria? Peru? The extant literature generally confines itself to such dichotomies as the existence or nonexistence of political parties, interest groups, legislatures, and the other trappings of alleged democracies and nontrappings of alleged nondemocracies. These common distinctions do not seem to capture anywhere near the full range of diversity among contemporary regimes.

Variables That Affect BHN

What are some variables that, in addition to the macrocharacterizations of the relationship between basic human needs attainment and regime type, might affect the realization of basic needs? Political participation, variously defined and measured, would appear to be one. Have the more participatory countries done better on meeting basic needs? A second variable likely to be of relevance is the extent of governmental centralization or decentralization, again variously defined and measured. Have the more decentralized countries done better (by development from below)? Bureaucratic variables suggest a third type of analysis. Along what dimensions do bureaucracies in developing countries differ, and how are these differences related to basic needs attainment? Another area of inquiry concerns the relationship between basic needs attainment and the structure of political conflict. If the basic political divisions in a society are class based, what does this imply for basic needs attainment? Or if they are ethnically based? Or if the society is relatively homogeneous? There are also sequencing questions. Have the countries that have met basic needs met them sequentially and, if so, in what sequence? Or have they done so in a once-and-for-all fashion, moving simultaneously on all fronts? What then are the politics of sequencing? How can support for basic needs attainment be built cumulatively and incrementally through the political process? Can it?

These are only some of the questions that would have to be addressed in any full-blown theory of the politics of meeting basic human needs. The World Bank, however, does not appear to be in the business of conducting this kind of analysis. In this regard the Bank is a nonpolitical institution, as it functions without very much attention to the social and political dimensions of its work.[31] It operates with a very reduced conception of the political.

Some Observations on the Triumph of RWG

Despite the great deal of attention accorded to it in recent years, the BHN approach to poverty alleviation did not triumph within the Bank over the approach identified with *RWG*. Despite the cogent criticisms of the *RWG* approach put forth by some of McNamara's own "brain trust," the income-productivity-output approach remained the central thrust of the World Bank's approach to poverty alleviation. As such, it is helpful to summarize the main tenets of the preferred strategy.

The emphasis under McNamara was on improving the absolute incomes of the poor, not on alleviating relative inequality. The emphasis likewise was on the distribution of income increments, not on the redistribution of existing assets or income. The preference was for market over governmental mechanisms. Helping the poor meant primarily increasing the income, productivity, and output of the poor. Supply management and all of the other implications of a thorough-going BHN approach appeared to form no part of the Bank's strategy for alleviating poverty. Since they might in fact have been very important for that alleviation, part (perhaps a great deal) of the strategy might have been vitiated. For the income-productivity-output approach did not necessarily mean that absolute poverty would be eliminated or that basic human needs would be satisfied. It was a necessary but by no means a sufficient condition for eliminating absolute poverty or satisfying basic human needs. Finally, the successful pursuit of poverty alleviation could not be attained without at least some elements of a new international economic order, but, conversely, such a new order would not be sufficient—it would have to be joined by real commitment on the part of elites in the developing countries themselves, commitment that was not abundantly in evidence.

The strategy of *RWG* should be seen for what it was: relatively modest, eminently possibilist, bedeviled by political constraints, highly tenuous, subject to complex and formidable problems of implementation. In neither a national nor international sense did it seek fundamentally to change the world in which the poor lived; it sought to improve the terms on which they related to it.

Why might the Bank have adopted this approach to poverty alleviation? No doubt part of the answer had to do with its perceived political feasibility. While many of the political regimes in its developing member countries might have found the *RWG* approach politically distasteful and have been not at all disposed to implement it, it was certain that they would have found thoroughly repugnant an approach that focused on changes in relative inequality, the structure of production, the redistribution of assets, and so forth. It would have been politically catastrophic for the World Bank to have been even dimly perceived as soft-selling communism. It was easier to sell redistribution with growth. Who could quibble with the goal of raising the absolute incomes of the poor?

The Bank's preferred approach to poverty alleviation had much to do with the tenacity of its ideology. *RWG* was more compatible with that ideology; it did not represent a paradigmatic shift. The concern with the poverty of the poor majority was an addendum, not a substitute, and as such more comfortably accommodated. Adoption of the thoroughgoing BHN approach would have entailed a head-on clash with some key elements of traditional Bank ideology.

The answer also had to do with who worked at the World Bank under McNamara and what they knew. They were mainly professional economists and technicians schooled in development economics and engineering. Reflecting the professions of which they were a part, they presumably knew more about increasing incomes, output, and productivity than they did about supply management or the problems of the transition. They were not chiefly community developers, specialists in popular participation, knowledgeable about worker self-management, or members of the "Small is beautiful" school. Part of the answer then had to do with sociology and social psychology—the sociology of the World Bank and the social psychology of World Bankers. Both were more congruent with the income-output-productivity approach than with approaches perceived as more far-out.

Another part of the answer was that *RWG*'s approach lended itself nicely to the quantification of targets and the inputs necessary to attain them. It was thus congruent with McNamara's operational style. He was much given to quantification, to the reduction of complex social reality to figures and numbers of target groups, beneficiaries, incremental output, improvements in productivity, changes in incomes, and so forth. Some within the Bank itself referred to this approach rather uncharitably and did not think it sufficient as a measurement of development or of the Bank's contribution to it. It was, nevertheless, the approach adopted, and the penchant for quantification increased throughout the McNamara years.

RWG appeared to have greater operational significance in the short run than any more fundamental approaches to alleviating poverty. The Bank under McNamara had other goals besides alleviating poverty.

One of these, as has been emphasized, was to make loans, presumably the more the better. But worrying about the ownership of the accumulated stock of assets, or a fundamental change in the structure of production, or measures to reduce imports of inappropriate goods took too long and did not jibe well with the Bank's functions as a money mover.

Thus the adoption of the preferred theoretical rationale was a function of many factors, including the constraints under which the Bank operated, the dictates of political feasibility, McNamara's organizational and managerial style, the kinds of people recruited to work for the Bank and the socialization process they experienced, the prevalent ideology of the Bank, the necessity to increase the number of loans, and so forth. The adoption of *RWG* only partly changed the nature of the institution. The adoption of the main alternative approach to poverty alleviation would have completely transformed it.

Poverty-Oriented Rural Development

The most celebrated feature of the World Bank's poverty-oriented work under McNamara was its rural development projects. In his Nairobi speech of 1973 he summarized the conditions of subsistence farmers in the contemporary developing world and outlined a Bank program whose goal was "to increase production on small farms so that by 1985 their output will be growing at the rate of 5 percent per year."[1]

What was the extent of rural poverty in the developing world at the time McNamara spoke? Estimates varied. The Nairobi speech estimated 100 million families or 700 million individuals as living in absolute poverty conditions in the rural areas of developing countries.[2] According to the Bank's rural development sector policy paper about 550 million people in such rural areas were in conditions of absolute poverty—an annual per capita income equivalent to $50 or less—in the mid-1970s.[3]

Income data from rural areas of developing countries are subject to notorious statistical inadequacies, however, and, when converted into dollar values for purposes of crossnational comparisons, distorted by overvalued exchange rates and other problems of international comparisons. Nevertheless, a World Bank publication provided data on rural per capita incomes for selected developing countries for some years in the early 1970s. In Pakistan, for example, in 1972 the rural per capita income was estimated at only $43; in Indonesia in 1971, $47; Kenya in 1971, $58; India in 1971, $62; Egypt in 1973, $101; Brazil in 1970, $141; the Ivory Coast in 1972, $143; Korea in 1972, $171; and Mexico in 1970, $219.[4] More recent data are not available, but it is certain that rural incomes in such countries remain abysmally low.

Another indicator for measuring the quality of life in rural areas is the percentage of the population with reasonable access to a safe water supply or waste disposal facilities. Regional data from the World Health Organization indicate that, in Africa, only 21 percent of the rural population had access to such a water supply, and only 28 percent to waste disposal facilities. In Central and South America the comparable figures were 32 and 25 percent, and in Southeast Asia, 19 and 6 percent. For all developing countries the figures were 22 and 15 percent, respectively.[5]

McNamara's goal intended to alleviate these kinds of conditions implied a commitment by developing countries to making poverty-oriented rural development projects the hallmark of their agricultural development strategies. This commitment had to go beyond the merely rhetorical to the provision of financial resources for the alleviation of rural poverty. The resources required were substantial indeed. One analysis of the investment required to achieve McNamara's goal of a 5 percent annual output increase for small farmers by 1985, conducted in 1975 using a simple model and data from Bank experience, indicated requirements of between $70 and $100 billion.[6] A $10 billion annual investment in rural development ($100 billion spread over 1975 to 1985) might have appeared modest in comparison with the $170 billion total investment in all developing countries in the single year 1974, but it appeared extremely large compared to the total investment of $25 billion in that year in the lowest-income countries where the desperately poor were concentrated. The Bank estimated that its own lending for agriculture and rural development from 1975 to 1979 would supply only one-fifth of the total investment needed to increase the production of the rural poor by 5 percent per year over the period.[7] The other four-fifths would have to come from other bilateral and multilateral agencies and, more important, from the developing countries themselves.

For its part the Bank attempted to address the appalling features of rural poverty highlighted by McNamara by undertaking many of its rural development projects in rural regions of recipient countries that were not only extremely poor when compared with national averages but were also poorer than other rural areas in the countries as well. In a Bank-financed rural development project in the Brazilian northeast, for example, the level of project-area income averaged about $80 per capita per year at the time of project inception. This was only about 50 and 72 percent, respectively, of the average incomes in the two states where the project was located, and was only 65 percent of the average per capita income level for all of northeastern Brazil. In the state of Funtua in Nigeria, the site of the Bank's first rural development project in that country, the rural population had the lowest per capita income of any state in Nigeria (about $40 per year). In the Kigoma region of Tanzania, the site of the Bank's first rural development project in Tanzania, annual per capita income in the project villages was only around $20 at the time of project inception. (This contrasted with a nationwide per capita income of $160 in Tanzania in 1974.) The average rural household income in Korea at the time of the inception of the Bank's first rural development project was about $1,300 per year, but the average income of an average-size farm under the project was about $1,100, or 15.4 percent less than the overall rural average. The fact that the Bank undertook much of its rural development work in areas of truly extreme poverty and in areas considerably worse off than other rural areas had an important implication in terms of the success or failure of project implementation. It meant that many of the projects had one or two strikes against them before they began. But the stark data on rural poverty in the areas where it implemented projects provided the basic justification for the Bank's rural development activities.

Definitional Problems

What is meant by rural development? According to Albert Waterston, "rural development is generally conceived of as a multisectoral activity that includes, besides agricultural development and rural industry, the establishment or improvement of social overhead facilities or infrastructure (schools, clinics, roads, communications, and water supply) and welfare services or programs that could be for disease control, improved nutrition, widening adult literacy, or family planning."[8]

There was, however, no consensus on the definition of a rural development project within the Bank itself. To the contrary, there was considerable dissensus. With its well-known penchant for statistics, the Bank formulated a quantitative definition of a rural development project. A staff unit within the Bank's Agriculture and Rural Development Department defined a rural development project as one in which at least 50 percent of the direct benefits would accrue to individuals within poverty target groups (defined by absolute and relative poverty criteria). The benefits were the increases in output and income expected to result from the project. What percentage of the incremental output stemming from a project would be accounted for by the poverty target group? What percentage of the incremental income would accrue to the target group?

Many within the Bank were highly skeptical about the utility of this definition, however. They pointed out that it was virtually impossible to estimate with any precision what percentage of the direct benefits were in fact going to members of the target groups. Furthermore it was extremely difficult to sort out direct from indirect benefits which could in any event be more important. The 50 percent figure was seen as arbitrary, and the data employed to generate the calculation of benefits were held to be suspect. As a result there was considerable reluctance among many Bank staff to take the quantitative definition very seriously or to attach much importance to it in their daily work.

As a practical matter rural development projects were not limited to those in which a certain percentage of direct benefits accrued to certain groups. There were also nationwide or "functional" projects that, while not specifically targeted on the rural poor in a specific geographical area, nevertheless contained a substantial component for small farmers or low-income producers. Several nationwide agricultural credit projects in Mexico and a nationwide agricultural extension and research project in Brazil were examples. There were also more general agricultural development projects of a traditional type that might indirectly benefit the poor (rural roads, loans for the production of a specific crop that might in some measure be grown by the poor, and so forth). Project officers in charge of such functional or traditional projects asserted that they were engaged in rural development every bit as much as their colleagues in charge of projects in which it was estimated that more than 50 percent of the direct benefits would accrue to rural poverty target groups.

There was another distinction among various kinds of rural development projects that was frequently encountered at the Bank. In the Bank's terminology, there were "simple," "integrated," and "multisectoral" rural development projects. Simple projects were those that involved a restricted set of actions carried out by a single line agency in the recipient country. Integrated projects were those where successful implementation depended upon specified actions and investments being carried out in a particular sequence, and failure of one component or by one agency would prejudice or undermine the entire project. One agency was usually responsible for coordination. Multisectoral projects were those where a number of discrete activities were supported, but failure in one or more elements would not prejudice the success of the whole. Most of what the Bank called "new-style" rural development projects were generally integrated or multisectoral. New-style projects were defined as projects that (1) benefited large numbers of people, with 50 percent or more of the direct benefits going to low-income individuals and families, (2) were comprehensive in their approach, and (3) had a low enough cost per beneficiary to allow wide replicability.

The response here to these definitional problems was unabashedly pragmatic. For the purposes of the following discussion, it is not crucial whether a given project is, strictly speaking, a rural development project according to any of the above definitions. The principal interest is in rural work designed to assist the rural poor that takes place within new-style projects, but there is also an interest in such work taking place within functional or more traditional projects. The interest is in all kinds of rural projects intended to benefit the rural poor, whether these projects are simple, integrated, or multisectoral. The interest therefore is in rural poverty lending in whatever project guise it occurred. It is thus similar to the interest of those in the Bank who sought to develop a way of measuring the antipoverty impact of all rural and agricultural projects, not only the impact of those projects officially called rural development projects according to the 50 percent definition. In this approach agriculture and rural development projects would be ranked from 0 or 1 to 100 percent rural poverty lending. The approach, however, ran into formidable obstacles within the Bank's bureaucracy and was not adopted. Many of the objections were couched in methodological terms, but it appeared that the real problem was that the many agricultural development projects with very small antipoverty components would have been obvious for all, including McNamara, to see.

In the case of the new-style projects, these focused their benefits upon a specific target population in a specific microregion of the recipient country. They involved the provision of an integrated package of inputs (credit, extension, other agricultural support services, roads, and so forth) designed to increase the output and incomes of small, mainly owner-operator farmers. These kinds of projects were particularly prominent in the Bank's rural development work in Latin America. This inquiry, however, is also extended into the rural poverty components of other kinds of projects that were less overtly and self-consciously new-style. The inquiry is by no means limited to the Latin American experience. A complete list of the rural development projects surveyed is contained in appendix C. These included projects in such diverse countries as Korea, Malaysia, Nigeria, the Philippines, and Tanzania as well as in Brazil, Colombia, and Mexico.

Components of Rural Development Projects

The Bank's new-style projects typically contained a range of input components. Provisions for agricultural credit channeled relatively small loans to small-scale producers who ordinarily had little or no access to institutional credit channels. (It is notorious that the bulk of agricultural credit in most developing countries goes to the large producers.) Collateral demands were small or even nonexistent. The credit was for modest amounts of working capital (to purchase seeds, for example) or was for on-farm investments (fencing, machinery, and so forth). The Bank strongly preferred a positive rate of interest on loans to even the smallest producers, but as a practical matter this was difficult to enforce in many countries. The credit component frequently involved the establishment of branch offices of the official banking system in areas where their presence was minimal or nonexistent before the inception of the project. Credit might be part of a larger integrated or multisectoral project, or there might be separate Bank loans for agricultural credit projects exclusively, and these might include a certain proportion of the credit for low-income or small-scale producers. A good example of the latter was the sixth agricultural credit project in Mexico, for which the Bank stipulated approximately one-third of total project funds to go to low-income producers.

Agricultural extension was another common feature of these rural development projects. Extension services in developing countries tend to be financially and technically weak and, even where moderately competent, they generally fail to reach the small farmer with appropriate production packages. The Bank's projects were intended to overcome this situation. This could be done through an extension component of integrated or multisectoral projects or, as in the case of recent loans to Brazil, Malaysia, and Thailand, through nationwide loans to agricultural extension agencies. The aim was to reach the small farmer with integrated production packages (such as seeds, fertilizer, and new varieties) designed to increase yields.

Before there could be extension, however, there had to be something to extend. This meant provision for basic agricultural research on such matters as crops, cropping patterns, effectiveness of fertilizer application, and irrigation requirements. As in the case of extension this research was provided either in the context of a multisectoral project (it was, for example, the main emphasis of the Bank's first new-style project in Brazil) or in a separate loan to a state agricultural research agency (such as, again, in a loan to Brazil for this purpose). The Bank has customarily been more knowledgeable about irrigated farming than about rainfed farming. A major challenge currently confronting the Bank is the development of production packages for small farmers in areas of rainfed agriculture. The bewildering variety of farming conditions in such areas militates against the adoption of general packages, obliging the necessity to tailor them to local requirements.

In many integrated projects there was a large allocation for roads. This could involve primary access roads, but more usually it involved secondary and feeder roads. In some projects the roads component was the most significant feature. It was a key aspect of the Bank's projects in Nigeria. It was likewise important in some of the Brazilian projects. In the Brazilian state of Ceara, for example, the roads component was credited by Bank project officers as the chief developmental feature of the project. The supply of roads was critical on both the input and output side; they facilitated previously unavailable inputs, and supplied a previously unknown marketing channel. Some Bank project officers thought it might be unnecessary in the future to include a separate marketing component in rural development projects. In their view it was only necessary to provide roads; the small farmers themselves would see to it that marketing occurred (perhaps by pooling resources and buying a truck). In especially poor and isolated rural areas the provision of roads was often the single most important input of projects.

Many of the projects also contained components for such social sectors as education and health. These included the construction of facilities and the provision of staff (such as paramedics and community health workers). The aim was to provide basic education and preventative health care. Until recently, the Bank did not finance health projects per se. Virtually all Bank lending for health took place in the context of rural development projects. Much Bank lending for education also occurred within the context of such projects. The inclusion of such soft sectors within projects principally designed with concrete productive purposes in mind generated an internal Bank debate in the McNamara years about the utility of integrating such diverse features into one project.

The Bank's new-style projects contained some directly productive investments. These included irrigation works, livestock development, and soil and water conservation, designed, as the name implied, to contribute directly to the expected increases in output and incomes. An example was the first nationwide rural development loan to Mexico, of which 17 percent was earmarked for irrigation, 10 percent for livestock development, and 5 percent for soil and water conservation.

If the project was a simple one, it provided funds for only one aspect of rural development, notably credit for low-income producers. If, however, it was an integrated or multisectoral project, it contained a great many different input components. There were 442 agriculture and rural development projects financed by the Bank from fiscal 1974 to 1979. Of these, water supply facilities were included in 119 (or 27 percent), health components in 86 (or 19 percent), and education in 62 (or 14 percent). Among infrastructure categories road components were most prevalent, included in 50 percent of the projects. This was followed by rural electrification components in 42 projects, or 10 percent of all projects approved in the six-year period.

The Goals of Rural Development Projects

What goals were these components of the Bank's rural development projects intended to achieve? In accordance with the general rationale for the Bank's poverty-oriented work, the goals of the projects were to "make the poor more productive," to raise the income and output of small-scale rural producers and make subsistence or near-subsistence farmers into commercial ones.

In many of the Bank's new-style projects large income and output gains were expected to accrue on behalf of the intended beneficiaries. Examples may be given from recent Bank projects, using as the basis for the projected income and output gains the estimates found in the project appraisal reports on these projects.

In a project in the state of Rio Grande do Norte, Brazil, net family income of participating farmers was expected approximately to double as a result of the project. This increase would occur within six years. In a Colombian project per capita income on small farms was projected to increase from $67 to $247. In the Bank's first rural development project in Mexico, income was expected to rise from an average of $440 to $700 per farm in rainfed areas and $1,100 per farm in irrigated areas over a period of approximately eight years. In the second project incomes of about 45,000 farmers would approximately double. In irrigated areas farm incomes were expected to triple.

In the Bank's first rural development project in Tanzania, the goal was to double the annual per capita income in the project villages over a five-year period. (To introduce a sobering note, it should be recorded that this increase would be from $20 to $40.) In a project in Nigeria income of a typical 2.5 hectare farm was expected to increase from $580 to $920 per year. In a nationwide project in Korea the net income of an average-size farm would be $1,820 after seven years of the project compared to $1,100 at its start. In a project in the Philippines net farm household income would increase between 100 and 400 percent, depending upon the location of project-area farmers.

The Bank therefore was expecting extremely dramatic increases in income among the intended beneficiaries of its rural development projects. The diverse implications of a situation in which incomes of the beneficiary population were increasing twofold, threefold, or more in a short span of years deserved considerably greater attention by the Bank than they received. In large measure these substantial income increases were expected to result from increases in agricultural yields and output. The Bank's appraisal reports offered projections about such production increases.

Among the Latin American projects the Rio Grande do Norte project in Brazil was expected to double the annual production of cotton in the project area. In the Colombian project yields were projected to increase by only 10 percent by 1985 without the project. With the project, however, yields were expected to increase by 45 to 88 percent, depending on the crop. In the Mexican projects substantial annual production increases of certain crops were also projected in absolute terms.

In Africa the Bank's first project in Tanzania was expected to dramatically increase per hectare output of four key crops over the eight-year project period (such as an increase from 600 to 1,460 kilograms per hectare in the case of maize). In a project in Nigeria total production of maize in the project area was to increase from 5 million tons per year at project inception to 66 million tons after completion of the project.

In Asia the nationwide Korean project was expected to produce a noteworthy increase in rice production. Incremental rice production attributable to the project would total 26,000 tons (or 10 percent of all Korean rice imports in 1974). In the Philippine project incremental production of rice would total 17,000 tons after five years; of corn, 13,000 tons; of sugar cane, 78,000 tons.

The Bank's projects were expected therefore to be principal contributors toward resolving the agricultural production problems of many developing countries. In having as their primary justification increases in the incomes and output of the target groups of the rural poor, the Bank's rural development projects begun under McNamara illustrated that helping the poor at the World Bank mainly meant increasing the incomes, productivity, and output of the poor. The rural development projects were not intended as welfare programs. They were justified in terms of traditional pre-McNamara emphases on production and growth.

Components + Goals = "Causal Model" of Rural Development Projects

The Bank's "causal model" contained two principal dependent variables—the incremental output and incremental incomes of the target groups of rural producers. The principal independent variables, assumed to produce the variation in output and incomes, consisted of various project inputs—agricultural credit, extension, social infrastructure, and the like. To assess the impacts of projects therefore, the most direct way to proceed would be to measure output and income following project implementation over several years and compare them with output and income levels at the time of project inception (or "baseline" data, as they are called). The project either did or did not attain the figures projected at the time of appraisal.

For various reasons, however, it is often not possible to engage in such straightforward impact analysis. The baseline data may not be very good to begin with, or they may be nonexistent. It may be too early in project implementation to measure incremental output and incomes deriving from the project. The Bank's monitoring and evaluation of project implementation, increasingly provided for in the loan itself, may be far from perfect. These difficulties mean that it is often necessary to resort to less direct forms of measuring the impact of a project.

An alternative suggestion is to take the implementation of the input components of the project as a proxy for the output variables that ideally should be measured. If, for example, there are substantial difficulties in the supply of agricultural credit to small farmers, or if there are difficulties in the provision of technology packages to small farmers on the part of agricultural extensionists, or if the construction of social infrastructure lags—even though the causal model is reasonably correct—then it may be presumed that there will be serious difficulties in attaining the projected output and income goals. Conversely, the expeditious delivery and use of the inputs should lead to favorable developments on the output and income front. That is why, in the interviewing about project implementation, questions were asked not only about the attainment of the output targets in specific projects but also about the progress in the delivery and use of credit, extension services, and other inputs.

The components and objectives of the Bank's rural development projects made a further assumption about the relationship between agricultural production and size of farms. They took note of the considerable evidence that output per unit of land is inversely related to land size. This was one of the principal conclusions of the series of studies on Latin American agriculture undertaken during the 1960s by the Inter-American Committee for Agricultural Development.[9] A more recent report compared data on the per hectare output on farms smaller than five hectares with that on farms larger than 20 hectares and concluded that the smaller units showed higher gross productivity in many countries (such as Brazil, Colombia, India, Iraq, Liberia, and Pakistan).[10] Another study conducted for the Bank investigated six countries in depth—Brazil, Colombia, India, Malaysia, Pakistan, and the Philippines. It concluded that national agricultural output could be increased by 19 (in India) to 49 (in Pakistan) percent if there were a transition in each of these countries to uniformly small, family farms.[11] Another farm survey conducted for the Bank in the Brazilian northeast showed significant declines in the utilization of land as farm size rose. The findings led to the conclusion that a redistribution of land from large estates into family-size units could produce an agricultural output increase of 25 percent. The conclusion was that there was no necessary trade-off between assistance to small-scale farmers in Bank projects and increasing agricultural production in developing countries.

The Beneficiaries of the Projects

In the vast majority of the Bank's rural development projects the principal beneficiaries were to be small-scale farmers who owned and operated their own properties. Virtually none of the projects were designed to reach the rural landless at all, nor were they principally oriented toward tenant farmers, sharecroppers, or squatters. This focus on small owner-operators as the principal target group meant that the projects were not likely to assist the "poorest of the poor." The small owner-operators, while poor, were still comparatively better off.

The Bank acknowledged that it was extremely difficult for it to assist the temporary agricultural workers, sharecroppers, squatters, and other poor in rural areas. A good example of the nature of the beneficiaries in a new-style project was the Rio Grande do Norte project in Brazil, a project that attracted much attention since it was the Bank's first such project in that country. What the Bank labeled the "directly reachable" target population consisted of about 15,000 farm families, largely owners, representing less than 20 percent of the total project-area population. Approximately 35 percent of the project-area rural population were temporary agricultural workers, but, in the words of the Bank's appraisal report on the project, "they can be expected to be only indirect beneficiaries." Furthermore, again according to the Bank's own report, "sharecroppers, representing almost 20 percent of the total rural population, will also be difficult to reach directly by the project."

This situation was not at all atypical of other projects the Bank undertook. The poorest of the poor in rural areas of developing countries were extremely difficult to find and, once found, to assist through Bank projects. The owner-operators were more locatable, and thus project benefits could be more readily targeted upon them.

The notion of targeting was extremely important in understanding the Bank's approach under McNamara to the question of project beneficiaries. The projects focused their intended benefits on what the Bank was fond of referring to as the "target population." This assumed, to continue the analogy, that the target could be readily identified and that, once identified, it could be "hit" with the intended benefits. But these could be difficult assumptions to fulfill in practice. There was always the distinct possibility of benefit deflection, of benefits moving away from intended beneficiaries and toward unintended ones as the implementation of the project proceeded. Who really benefited from the implementation of a Bank rural development project? The rural poor of the target group? Or the contractors who built the project works? Or those who marketed the incremental output? Or those producers (not poor) on the products of whom the beneficiaries spent their incremental incomes? Or those (certainly not poor) who simply bought up or usurped the improved lands? Was it really possible to target in any precise fashion?

Even if targeting was difficult, and even if the Bank's projects were not reaching the poorest of the poor, they were reaching people who were not benefiting from the Bank's previous agricultural projects. (Much early Bank lending for agriculture in fact provided foreign exchange for the importation of expensive agricultural machinery.) According to a report for the Subcommittee on Appropriations of the U.S. House of Representatives, only 28 percent of the Bank's agricultural lending in 1972 could be classified as going for projects oriented to the poor. By 1977 this had risen to 63 percent—categorized as "a dramatic shift in a five-year period."[12] The Bank planned to lend $4.4 billion for agricultural projects in fiscal years 1974 to 1978 (compared, for example, to only $872 million in fiscal years 1964 to 1968), and 70 percent of these agricultural loans were to contain a small-holder component. Was the Bank's rural development work since 1973 to be evaluated in contrast to its past agricultural work? Or was it to be evaluated by some absolute standard of the extent to which it benefited the poorest of the poor? Utilizing the first criterion, its work earned very high marks. Utilizing the second, the record was of course more mixed.

Rural Development and Land Tenure

The almost exclusive focus on the small owner-operators and the practical difficulties with targeting benefits were obvious limitations of the Bank's rural development projects. A related limitation stemmed from the fact that the projects accepted the existing land tenure conditions in the areas in which they were located. Although land reform was briefly mentioned by McNamara in his Nairobi speech, such reform played little part in the Bank's rural development work begun under his direction. The projects made little or no attempt to deal with the basic fact about rural poverty in developing countries—the inequitable distribution of land. They largely accepted the existing land tenure situation as a given and accommodated themselves to it.

This was particularly detrimental to projects in Latin America with its notoriously inegalitarian land distribution patterns. In Brazil, for example, 9.3 percent of landholders held 76.4 percent of the land; at the other extreme, 51.4 percent of landholdings comprised only 3.1 percent of total acreage. In Colombia 1.7 percent of landholdings comprised 55 percent of the total farm land; in contrast, 76.5 percent of landholdings comprised only 8.8 percent of the acreage.[13] The record was not noticeably different in other Latin American countries.

Unequal land distribution was also a problem of great and increasing relevance in Asia. This was highly in evidence in the distribution of land ownership in seven Asian countries that accounted for about 70 percent of the rural population of the nonsocialist developing world. In India, Pakistan, and the Philippines the Gini concentration ratios of the distribution of landholdings were estimated around 0.6.[14] According to one report, "the continuation of the highly unequal ownership of land during a period of rapid demographic growth has resulted in increased landlessness and near-landlessness."[15]

These data concerning national agrarian structure in some of the Bank's principal recipient countries were reflected in data at the level of project areas as well. In a project in the state of Ceara in Brazil, for example, 2 percent of the farms in the project area had more than 200 hectares each and controlled 44 percent of the land. Conversely, 52 percent of the farms in the project area had fewer than 10 hectares each and occupied a total of only 6 percent of the land. Conditions were much the same in the Paraiba project in Brazil. There, 5 percent of the farm owners in the project area, with more than 50 hectares each, controlled 61 percent of the cultivated land. Conversely, 57 percent of the farmers in the project area had less than 5 hectares each and occupied only 10 percent of the cultivated land. The situation was by no means limited to Brazil among the Latin American countries where the Bank has undertaken projects. In a Colombian project, 4,300 small farms, comprising 36 percent of all farms in the project area, accounted for only 7 percent of the total farm area. Conversely, 600 farms, comprising only 5 percent of all farms in the project area, accounted for 44 percent of the total farm area.

In some countries, however, the concentrated structure of land-holding was not as formidable an obstacle to the successful implementation of the projects. This was most obviously the case in countries, albeit few in number, that have experienced genuine agrarian reforms. Korea is an example. The Farmland Reform Laws of 1945 and 1950 imposed a ceiling of 3 hectares of cultivated land per household. The average farm size in Korea is only about 0.9 hectare. Thus the implementation of a rural development project in Korea (a second Bank project is now under implementation) took place in a context in which the appropriation of benefits by the large farmers was less likely, for the simple reason that there were few if any large farmers. Somewhat the same could be said for a country like Tanzania, where much of the Bank's rural development work was in support of *ujaama* villages where private landholding was virtually nonexistent. Roughly the same could also be said for a country like Nigeria. In a project in Funtua state, for example, it was estimated that approximately 70 percent of project-area farmers had only 2 to 3 hectares of land.

"Large" and "small" are of course relative concepts. In Funtua, Nigeria, a large farmer is generally a farmer who has only 10 or 20 hectares of land. In Bangladesh, generally considered a nation of small farmers, it is possible to identify large farmers if "large" is defined in relative terms. There were certainly opportunities for the misappropriation of benefits in countries like Nigeria and Bangladesh (and even in a country like Tanzania), but in principle the problem could be considered less severe than in the Latin American projects which the Bank began in the McNamara years.

The Size of Projects

An additional limitation of many of the Bank's rural development projects stemmed from their relatively small size. With several exceptions, the Bank's projects tended to be quite small in terms of both resources committed and number of projected beneficiaries. This was most clearly the case with the new-style, regional or area-specific projects which are the principal focus of this study. The exceptions were apparently some of the larger nationwide projects such as those in Mexico, but this was more apparent than real since the benefits were spread thinly over numerous intended beneficiaries in numerous project regions.

More typical than these nationwide projects was a regional project begun in the Bolivian altiplano, which was designed to benefit no more than 3,600 poor rural families. This was a drop in the bucket given the total of poor rural families in the country. A project in Paraguay was aimed at 7,000 low-income rural families—another drop in the bucket.

The total cost of a Bank rural development project in Brazil was estimated at $11.5 million; of a steel project in Brazil, $2.1 billion. Some indication of the difference between large and small can be gathered by comparing the total costs of these two projects. With a total cost for the rural development project estimated at $11.5 million, and a total cost for the steel project at $2.1 billion, calculation reveals that the steel project "cost" 184 rural development projects. If the steel project had been foregone, and the funds diverted to financing rural development projects in Brazil with an average cost of $11.5 million, 184 such projects could have been undertaken. The example could be seen as fanciful or simplistic, but it does serve to indicate the small scale of many Bank-financed poverty-oriented rural development projects when measured against the enormity of rural poverty problems in developing countries or the magnitude of some of the Bank's own traditional projects.

Bank Projects and Country Policies

To the various limitations of the Bank's work in the field of rural development must be added another concern—the congruence of individual projects financed by the Bank with more general policies in the agricultural sector of recipient countries. There is rather a continuum of congruence. Some of the Bank's developing member countries have made small-farmer development strategies into the cornerstone of their agricultural policies. These include Korea, Sri Lanka, and Tanzania. In many other countries, however, the prevailing agricultural development strategy remains that of large-scale, corporate or quasi-corporate, highly mechanized, predominantly export-oriented agriculture. Brazil is a good example of this type of country. In such countries, the Bank's typical rural development project may appear as an aside, a diversion, a token, a mere symbol, quite likely an irritant. If what needs to be sought are projects that appear to have maximum or optimal impact upon sectoral policies in agriculture, they are unlikely to be found there. This results in one of the many paradoxes with which the development effort is riddled: Bank rural development projects are likely to be most successful in countries that have already had considerable success with rural development (and where the projects therefore might not be so badly needed) and are likely to be most beset by pitfalls and difficulties in those countries where the plight of the small farmer has not been made the object of systematic national attention (and where the projects might be very badly needed).

In every project appraisal report on the Bank's rural development projects, there was a section, frequently quite detailed, on agricultural policy in the recipient country where the project was to be located. An effort was made to characterize the most salient recent features of agricultural policy in the country. The Bank often made an attempt to demonstrate the way in which the project to be financed dovetailed with recently enunciated or implemented agricultural development policies of the country. In many instances, however, this effort to demonstrate such a relationship was not particularly convincing.

In Bolivia, for example, one Bank appraisal report stated that "the Government does not have a rural development program nor a clear-cut policy for rural development, . . . but the present administration has recently begun to channel more financial and human resources to small farmers." The latter development presumably provided the justification for several Bank projects undertaken in the country.

The Bank stated that in Brazil "attempts have been made to change the (northeast) region's highly uneven structure of land ownership but little progress has been achieved. The government's land redistribution program . . . has had minimal overall impact due to administrative shortcomings and inadequate support from INCRA, the land reform agency." Furthermore, "rural services favor large- and medium-scale farmers. Over 1974–76, for instance, more than 90 percent of rural credit granted in the area by the Bank of Brazil and the Bank of the Northeast was for livestock (tending to be on large-scale farms) rather than for crops. Agricultural extension services have had a similar livestock/large- and medium-farmer bias." The Bank claimed, however, that "the current government has moved toward the reorientation and strengthening of the institutions offering the services required to develop more productive labor-intensive, small-scale farming." This presumably provides the justification for the kinds of rural development projects the Bank began in several Brazilian states.

Colombia provided yet another example. While much emphasis was once placed on agrarian reform on behalf of small farmers in Colombia, the Bank asserted that "the agrarian reform program did not meet expectations mainly because of legal interference by powerful landlords in the acquisition of more land and lack of financial support to develop what had been acquired." The failure of attempts at agrarian reform in Colombia led the Bank to search for alternative strategies among which was the integrated rural development strategy in several poor regions. The Bank was ready for assistance to this presumed redirection in Colombian agricultural development policy.

The matter of linkage between individual Bank rural development projects and more general sectoral policies for agricultural development in recipient countries is taken up again at subsequent points in this study. Its importance cannot be overstressed. If there was little or no linkage between the goals of the individual project and the goals of sectoral policy in agriculture, the project was once more the enclave. In such a situation the individual project gave little promise of adding up to an alternative model of a larger process of agricultural development. There were few opportunities for pyramiding the project into something larger and more important. There could be a kulak effect involving the creation of defensive and isolated groups of primary beneficiaries and overwhelming the positive diffusion from the project that might have been anticipated. The circumstances, in short, would not be conducive to the social significance of the project in some larger sense.

Some Limitations within the Bank Itself

Not all of the limitations of the Bank's rural development work were to be found in the unwillingness of many recipient countries to adopt the Bank's approach. Not everyone within the Bank was satisfied with it either. Indeed, many were critical of what they saw as the new theology of the institution on rural development questions. Many project officers, particularly in the African and Asian regions of the Bank, wondered out loud about the necessity for integrated or multisectoral projects. The alleged innovativeness of such projects was openly questioned. So also was the utility of the rural development antipoverty monitoring effort, with its emphasis upon the quantitative assessment of benefits and beneficiaries. Some admitted that they cooked up the data requested by the unit. Conflicts between the "agricultural development boys" and the "rural poverty boys" (as they were described in interviews) were apparent throughout the eight years of the Bank's post-Nairobi rural development work.

The poverty-oriented rural development emphasis of McNamara accordingly occasioned numerous divisions within the Bank about preferred courses for agricultural development in recipient countries. Korea provided an example. When it was proposed to begin lending for rural development in Korea, conflicts within the Bank itself over the planning of the first project were greater than any of those between the Bank and the Korean government. Most of the internal Bank opposition to the proposed first rural development project (1976) came from the country programs staff who 'were considered by other Bank staff as "quite conservative and out of touch." The alleged conservatives argued that the Koreans themselves would prefer Bank lending for industrial projects. (On this their perception was probably accurate.) They also argued that the rural development project would simply be a "make-work" undertaking, "a lot of leaf-raking and pork barrels." But the rural development staff won this particular debate, and, when the Bank in the end "simply told the Koreans that they would have to do some rural development projects with Bank funds as well, the country programs people fell into line, too."

Another country example concerned an internal division of opinion at the Bank as to the relative emphasis to be given to irrigated and rainfed agriculture in Mexico. This became the principal subject of a controversial internal report on the Mexican rural sector. Some Bank staff argued that large livestock holdings in Mexico could be divided up, converted to crop production, and redistributed to farmers in smaller parcels. (They were of course overlooking the political feasibility of this.) Those who made this suggestion within the Bank were attacked by what they described as the "technical types and the irrigation experts who would prefer to continue on their merry way with irrigation-oriented agriculture." As a result of the internal conflicts generated by the attempted production of this report, it never surfaced in its final version.

Similar stories were repeated in other countries on other rural and agricultural issues. Another internal controversy was occasioned by the production of project completion and audit reports on a series of land settlement projects (the FELDA projects) in Malaysia. The projects, ardently defended by those who had seen them through the Bank's bureaucracy from design to completion, were rather vigorously attacked in the final audit report as excessively costly, of dubious social benefit, and at variance with more recent Bank rural development objectives. In Indonesia, the Bank's transmigration approach to rural problems (involving relocation of large numbers of residents from overpopulated Java to the less-populated outer islands) created a sizable bureaucratic uproar within the Bank itself.

Some of the rural development antipoverty emphases also involved the executive directors in decisions on loans to a rather greater extent than previously. There were some examples of the ways the Bank's newfound concern for rural development affected the consideration of agricultural projects brought to the board. A fiscal 1978 loan to Argentina for grain storage appeared to some executive directors to run counter to the Bank's new officially voiced rural development lending policies. It appeared that the loan would benefit large farmers in Argentina and worsen the rural income distribution. Some executive directors objected on the grounds that the proposed loan was inconsistent with the new poverty-oriented rural lending policy. The loan prevailed (perhaps because the regional vice-president for Latin America at that time was an Argentine openly sympathetic to the post-Perón government's economic policies), but the discussion in the board was indicative of the more political nature of Bank debates about poverty-oriented lending in the rural sphere.

These and similar examples prompted one official at the Bank to recall that "the signals came down loud and clear from McNamara, but somehow they didn't always seem to get picked up by intermediate management." There sometimes seemed to be substantial confusion at the Bank about the kinds of achievements that would bring rewards to staff members. Sometimes it seemed that poverty alleviation in rural areas took precedence. But other times emphasis seemed to be placed on the aggregate amount of loans processed or on the aggregate amount of incremental agricultural production likely to occur as a result of the projects' implementation. Such conflicting signals often contributed to internal controversy.

An astute observer of the Bank has suggested an appropriate metaphor for describing these kinds of intra-Bank disputes about rural development occasioned by the McNamara reorientations.[16] The metaphor is that of the Bank as a large ocean liner that previously was heading full-steam down a certain course. The course was that of trickle-down and support for economic infrastructure in developing countries. The "crew" had been instructed in the techniques of this course and were largely content with it. McNamara's Nairobi speech, however, marked the beginning of a somewhat abrupt attempt to engineer a sharp turn of this large, ungainly vessel. The captain's orders did not always make it down to all of the crew members. While there was no outright mutiny, there was considerable footdragging. Many new crew members had to be hired who were more familiar with the liner's new routes. But previous commitments to arrive at certain ports (agricultural projects already committed to certain countries for more traditional undertakings) could not be readily abandoned. Thus the enterprise was bound to engender some confusion. To make matters more difficult, the "waters" were not very cooperative. The context in which the liner had to undertake its change of course was not at all conducive to its arriving speedily at its new destinations. The effort at a redirection of the Bank's agricultural lending was therefore open to diverse interpretations, ranging from those who might argue that the change of course should never have been attempted in the first place to those who would claim that, with renewed efforts and a little bit of luck, the change could be successfully engineered. Like all metaphors, this one can get strained very quickly. But it begins to suggest some of the difficulties encountered by McNamara as he attempted to reorient the Bank in an antipoverty direction in rural areas of developing countries. Many of these difficulties were found within the Bank itself.

Implementation of Rural Poverty Projects

It is one thing to appraise and approve rural development projects. It is quite another to implement them. The implementation experience of some of the Bank's projects is addressed at two different levels of analysis. The first adheres closely to the project appraisal reports. How have the components of the project, as outlined at the time of appraisal, fared? This entails an examination of the performance of credit delivery, extension services, social aspects of projects, and so forth. The second level of analysis departs from the strict confines of the appraisal report and is more contextual and structural. This inquires into such matters as the socioeconomic context in which the project is implemented, unintended or unanticipated consequences occurring as a result of implementation, and project vignettes that make instructive telling from the standpoint of larger issues of development policy.

A detailed analysis of the implementation of the Bank's rural development projects in the McNamara years uncovers numerous problems and some partial successes. A review of documentary evidence produced by the Bank and interviews with Bank project officers revealed the abundant potentialities for the Bank's approach to rural development.[1] If these potentialities are to be realized, however, effective means will have to be found for dealing with the problems encountered in implementation.

Major Obstacles to Implementation

By far the most common way in which the World Bank explains the principal problems of project implementation is by referring to conditions in the recipient country. Serious implementation problems are not usually seen as primarily the Bank's fault; rather they are viewed as chiefly the fault of the recipient country. The Bank's project documents and interviews with project officers revealed an array of underlying problems within the recipient countries, including conditions in the rural sector, national policies for agricultural development, and the institutions charged with agricultural and rural development.

There were numerous examples of the tendency to fault the recipient country. A particularly good example related to Nigeria. The Bank under McNamara approved seven rural development projects in Nigeria, but these had to operate in the context of sectoral policies of the Nigerian government which were not at all conducive to effective implementation. The general policies of the government were a more important factor affecting implementation than problems specific to particular projects. One adverse policy was governmental distribution of fertilizer, taken over by the government about four years ago. The governmental distribution of fertilizer led to black markets, supply delays, and the like. Since fertilizer was the key ingredient of the basic service package in the Nigerian projects, the difficulties with its delivery substantially impeded the realization of the expected production gains from the projects.

Government pricing policies were another problem, especially the low governmentally established prices affecting cocoa and cotton, which have to be sold through government marketing boards. The government also followed a practice of importing low-cost rice in the name of reducing urban food budgets, but this was to the detriment of the high-cost, inflation-ridden local rice producer.

Agricultural extensionists in Nigeria were not particularly well known for their support of small-scale farmers. There was some suspicion and resentment to be overcome on the part of the small farmers regarding the Bank's projects, since these extension agents were to be the key actors in introducing the basic service package in project areas. There also appeared to be little notion of cost recovery in governmental officialdom in Nigeria—credit, for example, was a giveaway at subsidized interest rates, and the tariffs charged for irrigation were perhaps one-twentieth of what they should have been. There was also some reason to question the government's general commitment to small-holders. About 40 percent of the agricultural sector budget in Nigeria has traditionally gone to large-scale irrigation through conventional dams and mechanized government-owned farms of 10,000 acres or more. Even if the Nigerians were to accept to do more on behalf of the small farmer, it is unlikely for political reasons that they would give up on these investments. The implementation of the Bank's rural development projects in Nigeria generally appears to have gone well, but this is largely despite and not because of government policies in the agricultural sector.

Another case of problems within the recipient country concerns Tanzania. The Bank has been involved in almost every aspect of the agricultural sector in Tanzania, not only in rural development projects. There are Bank-assisted tobacco and coconut projects, grain storage projects, and efforts to assist the Tanzanian Rural Development Bank. A prominent issue in Tanzanian agriculture in recent years has involved the respective emphasis to be given to cash- and food-crop producers. The Tanzanian government, consistent with its general policy emphases, has given considerably more emphasis to food-crop producers. The term "progressive farmer," referring to the cash-crop producer, has become a "bad word" in Tanzania. When the process of *ujaama*ization was accelerated, the government abolished the main credit-granting agency on the grounds that it had concentrated too much on cash-crop producers. Now, more agricultural credit goes to food-crop producers. There were also some discernible changes in the terms of reference for agricultural extensionists in Tanzania designed to bring extension to the food-crop producers. These and other policies were part and parcel of an equity-oriented rural development strategy pursued by the Tanzanian government. On equity grounds the policies appeared unimpeachable.

But these policies seem to have had some serious costs. There were food shortages in 1973 and 1974. The progressive farmers suffered, and so did agricultural production. One Bank project officer claimed that visits to rural Tanzania seemed to reveal no noticeable progress for the farming population over the last ten years. The growth of Tanzanian agriculture was unfavorably compared with the growth of the small-holder sector in Kenya during this same period. Much of this is attributable to the lack of private incentives in Tanzania. There were few incentives for private savings and capital accumulation, and very little have in fact taken place. Also very few consumption goods are available, again affecting the incentive to increase incomes. When combined with certain inappropriate assumptions about technical packages, this sectoral context has impeded the realization of production goals in the Bank's three rural development projects in Tanzania.

There were other problems as well. Tanzanian President Julius Nyerere is alleged once to have stated that the entire agricultural extension system in Tanzania could be eliminated with no effect on production at all! One of the principal conclusions of the Bank's experience with rural development in Tanzania was that the entire extension effort would need to be revitalized and reprogrammed to focus on the importance of the local verification of extension packages.[2]

There were also some severe institutional problems affecting Tanzanian agriculture. Innovation in the Bank's first rural development project (the Kigoma project) was supposed to be concentrated on agricultural production. The Bank's original plan was to work through the Kigoma Cooperative Union (KCU), a parastatal organization. The KCU, however, began the project with large accumulated debts. Nevertheless, it was supposed to supply inputs to project farmers and purchase outputs from them, and it was to receive credit from the Tanzanian Rural Development Bank and re-lend the money to the villages. But early in the implementation of the project it was abolished by a chief aide to the president who found it problem ridden. So the institution building planned for the KCU was never implemented, and the functions that were supposed to be carried out by it were transferred to other parastatal organizations. The unforeseen involvement of a host of agencies in the project delayed implementation substantially.

Another example of the way in which the conditions, institutions, and policies of recipient countries impeded the effective implementation of Bank-assisted rural development projects came from Paraguay. Some Paraguayan institutions suffered from corruption and an almost complete lack of technical competence. The National Development Bank, for example, was in bad shape at the beginning of the World Bank's first rural development project in Paraguay—with big arrearages and extremely large loans to high government officials. The Institute of Rural Welfare, another key agency in the implementation of the project, was not in appreciably better condition. One of the main alleged achievements of the Bank's first project in Paraguay was institution building affecting the National Development Bank. The World Bank was successful in having the previous general manager replaced, and it demanded, and received, loan repayments from prominent generals and politicians.

A project implemented in Haiti was another case in point. The project was given the designation of an official Bank "problem project." There were severe financial problems stemming from the lack of adequate funding by the Haitian government. Owing to this, and the necessity for a seemingly interminable round of required bureaucratic clearances, there were difficulties in paying project suppliers on schedule. The underlying financial problem was the virtually complete exhaustion of general government revenues in Haiti; the country was on the verge of bankruptcy. There were practically no viable local institutions in Haiti for civil engineering works. An additional problem was the almost complete lack of qualified personnel for implementing the project. (The project agency was headed by a Haitian, but the six most important people under him were all expatriates.)

The Papaloapan River Basin project in Mexico, a project that preceded the more famous PIDER (Integrated Program for Rural Development) rural development projects, illustrated additional country-specific implementation difficulties. While not officially labeled a problem project, it clearly was one. As of mid-1980 only about 10 percent of the funds of the Bank's loan had actually been disbursed over the five-year life of the project. Much of the problem concerned the main implementing agency, the Papaloapan Commission. This was an existing organization that antedated the project by about thirty-five years. It had a director, his deputy, and apparently little else. It had historically been based on a concern with hydraulic resources and engineering. Its main goal was to develop water resources within the Papaloapan valley, but in fact it was not really that concerned with agriculture, and certainly not with rural development. The Bank project represented a whole new approach for the commission, and the director was, to say the least, not particularly enthusiastic about it. He preferred to concentrate the budgeted funds for the commission on a large dam in which he was more interested. The principal cause of the project's delayed implementation was attributed within the Bank to the competition for funds within the commission. Budgeted funds were spent on other than the components for which the Bank was willing to disburse. The Bank did not see the importance of the director's dam and did not want to fund it.

Agricultural pricing and subsidy policy in Nigeria, the lack of incentives for food production in Tanzania, the weakness of development institutions in Haiti or Paraguay, and conflicts over development priorities in Mexico: such policies and situations in recipient countries constituted the most serious impediments to the effective implementation of the Bank's rural development projects.

A particularly severe group of problems concerned land tenure, land titling, and related issues within the countries that are the focus of the Bank's rural development efforts. It was pointed out in the previous chapter how the Bank's rural development projects accepted the existing land tenure situation in the areas in which they were implemented. It may now be demonstrated how issues related to such tenurial questions affected the implementation of specific projects.

The most illustrative case in this regard was the Bank's experience in Brazil, where it undertook ten rural development projects in the McNamara years. All of these projects involved some thorny land tenure questions in one way or another. In many projects, not only in Brazil but elsewhere, the Bank included a land titling component. It desired that the benefits to be conferred by its projects go to owners of definable parcels of land. In those instances in which squatters or others did not hold definitive title to the land at the time of project inception, such titles were supposed to be provided by the agencies of the recipient country government during the early stages of project implementation.

In the Ceara project in Brazil, however, the state land institute was prevented from granting titles to about 2,000 families in three project municipalities because of claims to 40,000 and 350,000 hectares of land, respectively, by two politically influential individuals within the state. While the matter was in the courts, the families were either completely prohibited from planting their crops or had their usual planting amounts sharply reduced. Threats were even made against the life of the lawyer representing the families in the case. The project was supposed to include an innovative land purchase credit component through which small farmers could receive loans to purchase land. The component, however, was not implemented; no such credit was extended during the implementation of the project.

In the Alto Turi land settlement project in Brazil land tenure issues were likewise one of the key features of the implementation history. The project area in Alto Turi was state-owned land. As a condition of effectiveness of the loan, the Bank required that the land be turned over to the project-implementing agency for distribution to the settlers. A complicating situation stemmed from the great amount of spontaneous settlement in the project area, largely as the consequence of the paving of a major road, and the attendant severe land-titling problems. The Bank estimated that there were as many as 4,000 to 6,000 settler families in the project area above and beyond the 5,200 estimated in its appraisal report. The Bank learned many hard lessons in this project and these contributed to the design of subsequent projects in the Brazilian northeast. The biggest lesson learned, according to a Bank staff member well acquainted with the history of the project, was that "you can't get into the business of land allocation unless you control the land."

Similarly, in the São Francisco Polders project in Brazil there were land tenure problems impeding implementation. This project was unique in the Brazilian context as it provided for the expropriation of private lands.[3] One of the main issues of the implementation history was land reform. An irrigation component in the project raised issues of windfall profits and land tenure, and these consistently bedeviled implementation. Without land reform the windfall profits from irrigation would have accrued to the large landholders in the area. But the project fell considerably behind schedule, in large measure because the expropriation of private lands went at a snail's pace, and the decree providing for such expropriation expired. Less than half of the expropriable land was in fact expropriated.

As the Bank's experience with rural development projects in Brazil evolved, it learned a good deal from these kinds of land tenure issues. The sobering experiences with land tenure and titling questions in the early Brazilian projects led the Bank to take a firm stand regarding a rural development project under discussion in the state of Piaui. This is a state in which fully 80 percent of the farmers are nonowners. In the states of Bahia and Ceara the Bank felt that much could be done for small farmers without the necessity of a substantial land reform. It did not think this the case in Piaui, however, and, before committing itself to a project in the state, the Bank requested some kind of prior land reform. (Because of this request, however, it is doubtful that the project will be undertaken.)

These problems were not limited to Brazil among the countries of the Latin American region. An otherwise successful project in Paraguay suffered from numerous land-titling problems. Only 15 percent of the farms in the project area had titles to land when the project began. The Institute for Rural Welfare was responsible for titling, and there were numerous problems, including the politics involved (notably pay-offs to government officials) in the securing of a title. After repeated Bank insistence on the necessity for definitive titling, the situation evolved to the point where approximately 1,900 of about 2,000 proposed titles were finally issued.

A project in Haiti provided another example. The situation regarding land tenure in the Haitian project area was utterly chaotic. The only certain factor was that the farms were very small—generally no more than 1 hectare. Nobody, including the Bank, really seemed to know who owned the land, titling seemed unheard of, and there was considerable sharecropping even on the smallest of plots. Because of this the Bank did not try to compel the government to do something about titling. It did, however, receive a commitment that there would be no land transactions during the course of the project's implementation. Theoretically, this could be enforced because such transactions were supposed to be registered with a governmental agency, but in practice this commitment was not enforceable at all. The appraisal report called attention to the fact that "land purchases by larger farmers have increased significantly due to growing demand for agricultural products and rumors of infrastructure improvements expected under the proposed project."

While the land concentration issue was particularly glaring in Latin America, issues of land tenure were not absent from projects in other regions as well. An example was a project implemented by the Ministry of Agrarian Reform in the Philippines. The ministry had a very simplistic approach to plot delimitation stemming from its previous work on rice paddy lands, where the prevailing assumption was that simple geometric crisscrosses could delimit equal plots for the beneficiaries. But this approach failed to take into account the great variations in land quality and configurations in the upland areas of the Philippines where the project settlement areas were located. There were, for example, about fifteen complicated procedures that had to be followed for a person to secure a title; as a matter of practical effect, a person had to pay somebody to get title to land. The Bank became involved in a substantial amount of aerial photography and basic data collection on the land tenure situation in the three settlement areas. All of this delayed the implementation of the project.

While these kinds of land tenure issues were undoubtedly a key factor in impeding the effective implementation of the Bank's rural development projects, particularly in Latin America, and while they were also contributory toward the deflection of benefits away from the intended beneficiaries, it seems that the Bank was over a barrel on this matter. If it had elected to undertake projects only in countries or regions where there had been a prior effective agrarian reform (such as Korea), it would as a practical matter not have undertaken many such projects. The Bank had little alternative but to plunge into projects where the land tenure situation was chaotic or titling unresolved, and thus it was faced with seeing its projects slowed down and otherwise adversely affected by the irresolution of these issues. Obviously, in future rural development projects it would have to confront land tenure and titling issues directly during the process of loan negotiation and lay down the conditions whereby the loan would become effective for the recipient country.

The policy and institutional framework that was responsible for land tenure problems in recipient countries also created particular difficulties for the implementation of the social (or soft) components of the Bank's rural development projects. Not unexpectedly, these kinds of components of the projects appeared to experience greater delays and problems in implementation than the infrastructural components. The health component of a nationwide rural development project in Colombia was an example. Following the line laid out in its sector policy paper on health, the Bank adopted a paramedical approach in Colombia. But the professional medical establishment was opposed to the approach from the start. It argued that the procedures called for could be performed only by regular physicians. Doctors in Colombia staged a work stoppage to protest the inclusion of the component, and they successfully prevented its effective implementation.

In Colombia there was also a problem involving the branch managers of the Caja Agraria, the implementing agency for the credit component of the nationwide project. The Bank and Caja authorities in Bogotá proposed substantial changes in the types of guarantees required for small-farmer loans so that such loans would be easier to obtain. Initially, however, these changes were opposed by many branch managers of the Caja, who were unaccustomed to dealing with small farmers and who, feeling themselves on the front line of a major policy redirection, felt that they would bear the brunt of any policy failures. Eventually, they came to support the new procedures, but not without causing some delays in implementation of the credit component.

Credit components of projects experienced difficulties in many countries. In Tanzania this related to the proposed village responsibility for credit repayment. The Bank concluded that it would have to find alternative ways of delivering credit to individual villagers in the *ujaama* villages. In Haiti the main problem was with the branch of the Ministry of Agriculture which was the principal implementer of the credit component. This agency was in extremely bad financial shape, and credit recovery averaged only about 40 percent under the Bank's project. In the Rio Grande do Norte project in Brazil, implementation difficulties resulted in credit being extended to only one-half of the intended number of small-farmer beneficiaries in the first phase of the project.

These examples were far from adding up to a blanket indictment of small-farmer credit components in multisectoral rural development projects. However, institutional reluctance to lend to small farmers even when that was a declared objective of the Bank loan and failure to fulfill collective arrangements for credit delivery and repayment were among the chief problems of project credit components.

An additional problem in recipient countries concerned the interrelated matters of maintenance, recurrent costs, and cost recovery. Policy and institutional deficiencies in the countries raised issues of responsibility for maintenance of project works after they were completed, responsibility for payment for this maintenance, and adequacy of the maintenance of project works. There was some evidence within the Bank that maintenance had not been adequate in some of its rural development projects. An example was a project in Upper Volta which involved the construction of a large number of wells. The Bank found that the great majority of these wells were insufficiently—or not at all—maintained.

In part this was a problem of the failure systematically to involve farmers in the preparation and implementation of projects, but in large part it was also a financial problem. Maintenance and associated recurrent costs are generally the responsibility of recipient country governments. The growing danger in many countries is that such governments will not have sufficient funds to pay these costs. The problem was most apparent in Africa. The West African region of the Bank commented upon the apparently growing inability of governments to finance recurrent costs. It pointed to the danger that countries' expenditures on agricultural and rural development projects were running considerably ahead of general budget allocations for such projects and ahead of what the beneficiaries themselves seemed willing or able to pay. The region's conclusion was that effective cost-recovery systems would be essential if the projects were to have a lasting impact on West African rural economies—but this would, it admitted, require an "unpalatable political decision."

The Bank's geographical divisions recently conducted a series of reviews of the rural development implementation experience. Reference to problems within the recipient countries was common in the reports of all regions. The Latin American and Caribbean region, for example, cited issues related to government polices (phrased as "government intervention") as a prime factor responsible for delays in implementation. Problems in Latin America included agrarian reform issues in the Dominican Republic, interest rate issues in Brazil, and a depressed meat market affecting the implementation of a livestock project in Uruguay. A report of the West African region examined countries' marketing monopolies, subsidized farm inputs, and producer price controls and concluded that the viability and self-financing nature of local institutions could not be guaranteed unless such policies were rectified. These kinds of issues uncovered by the regional divisions led the Bank to issue a stern comment on the necessity for country commitment: "it is essential that the project should have a high and sustained level of national priority for it to have any chance of success."

Problems with the Bank's Project Designs

Another array of implementation problems, perhaps less formidable than those within recipient countries but still important in affecting project outcomes, concerned the Bank's own project designs for rural development. While World Bankers preferred to emphasize the mistakes of others, analysis revealed some instances of problems closer to home.

An example of one such instance which apparently was quite common concerned difficulties with too many components in the Bank's multisectoral projects. The problem appeared particularly common in the Latin American and Caribbean region. A recurring question in the region was whether the project design of a typical integrated or multisectoral project had not overloaded the project with too many components—with resultant problems of coordination during implementation and the likelihood that the project would be implemented at the speed of its least-fast component. A regional report on this argued for the desirability of considering whether a multisectoral feature was really necessary and justified in the first stages of a project; perhaps, according to the report, the determination of the components to be included should be made on the basis of an emerging order of priorities. Projects would not be based on major innovations but would provide opportunities for testing new ideas on a limited scale. This was an argument for simple projects or for more pilot projects.

This argument was echoed by other regions within the Bank. In the East Asia and Pacific region the great majority of projects were simple in nature (irrigation, extension, or credit). Only three multisectoral projects were approved in the period from fiscal 1973 to 1977. The region noted that it "had increased emphasis on 'rural development' essentially by continuing to do the things we were already doing, but in areas with a higher incidence of poverty." The implication was that this was exactly what the region should be doing; it did not want to go overboard with integrated or multisectoral projects.

The inclusion of multisectoral features in the Bank's rural development project designs in turn appeared to give rise to formidable administrative, managerial, and coordinative difficulties in project implementation. In the Latin American and Caribbean region, for example, organizational and managerial arrangements appeared as the most frequent type of implementation problem (cited in 10 of 18 projects under implementation in the region). The region went so far as to question the replicability of such projects on a large scale, given the combination of the large number of components in most projects and the widespread administrative weaknesses in many developing countries.

In the West African region administrative and managerial issues were chiefly discussed in terms of the relative advantages of special project units versus regular line agencies and the use of nationals versus expatriates. Results seemed to be better when responsibility rested with a specially created project unit rather than with an existing government department or agency. This, however, raised the issue of the utility of Bank projects in contributing to the institution-building objectives of recipient countries. The use of expatriates, very common in Bank rural development projects in all regions, raised the same issue. The West African review found that, while comparisons between projects manned by local staff and those manned by expatriates were suggestive, meaningful or conclusive lessons were difficult to draw from the project experiences in the region. It was apparent, however, that the use of an autonomous project unit staffed predominantly by expatriates—common practice in Bank projects—raised very serious questions about the long-term institution-building capability of many Bank rural development projects.

An example was provided by the experience with the Alto Turi land settlement project in Brazil. The autonomous project-implementing agency was COLONE, the Northeast Colonization Company. It was set up at the insistence of the Bank to run the project. But since COLONE was in charge of nothing else but the Alto Turi project, it ran into great institutional jealousies and difficulties with the regular line agencies of the Brazilian government. The situation had many adverse consequences for implementation of the project. COLONE, for example, built many roads under the project (238 kilometers of them, to be precise). But the regular state road agency flatly refused to maintain the roads that it had no hand in building. The example demonstrated some of the difficulties with employing autonomous project units for implementation purposes.

Some materials from Bank documentary assessments indicated that there were cases, albeit few in number, where the Bank self-critically admitted to certain misconceptions in its policy designs for rural development. In West Africa, for example, there appeared to be at least two deficiencies in the design of projects. One was limited involvement of the beneficiary population and even of local-level governmental officials in project design. There was very limited farmer participation in project decision-making. Without such participation there was inadequate knowledge of farming systems, labor availability, farmer motivation, and constraints on farmer behavior. Many project farmers gave greater priority to food security than to the production of cash crops for the market, and this preference was unforeseen in many projects. Thus, "a major lesson learned from the experience of recent rural development projects [in West Africa] is that we [the Bank] knew less about the socioeconomic environment than was required to correctly anticipate its effect on project design, or even respond to it during implementation."

A second finding about project design in West Africa concerned the occasional inappropriateness of some of the technological packages recommended by the Bank. In some instances, Bank-promoted technological packages had demonstrated their feasibility on agricultural research stations but had not been adequately tested in the farmers' own environment. In others the agronomic aspects of project recommendations did not always agree with the farmers' concerns for food security. In still others there was evidence that some of the modern cultivation techniques promoted by the Bank had lasting harmful effects on the environment (such as soil erosion), and the Bank concluded that traditional farm methods were more beneficial than it previously had thought.

In Latin America, too, problems in the Bank's design of projects were apparent. Sometimes there were inadequate feasibility studies during project preparation and appraisal. This was especially true regarding some of the supporting components of multisectoral projects. It occurred in the cooperatives component of a project in the Brazilian state of Minas Gerais and in the health delivery systems of the nation-wide project in Colombia. The region also called attention to the necessity of a more careful analysis and understanding of the nature of the target population to be assisted in the projects. The tendency for benefits to go to other than the intended beneficiaries was not unrelated to problems in the original project design.

Perhaps the most obvious flaw in the Bank's project designs concerned their insufficient attention to some social issues in projects. A number of the projects studied raised difficult social issues that managed to embroil the Bank in political conflicts. A few of these conflicts were not good for the Bank's public image. They served to illustrate that many of the most difficult matters affecting project implementation were sometimes built into the original design of the projects.

The most difficult social issue that received insufficient attention by the Bank in its project designs involved dislocation and resettlement. In many projects people had to be moved, and this movement caused problems for the supposed beneficiaries of the move as well as for the Bank. A good example was the Bank's first irrigation project in the Philippines. Bank project officers were frank to admit that not much thought was given to the relocation issue in this project. Yet approximately 8,000 hectares were flooded by the Bank's new dam. In the words of a project officer, "a whole municipality was going under water; you were drowning a whole municipality and its mayor.

As a consequence they wrote to McNamara, to the Pope, to everybody. The fanatics said that the World Bank was genociding the population of the area. They argued that all the rest of the Bank's irrigation projects in the Philippines would lead to genocide as well. There's no doubt that OED [the Bank's Operations Evaluation Department] will kill us on this." The problem was that the local residents insisted upon being relocated within the existing municipal boundaries. By agreeing to this, the Bank wound up relocating them "up in the hills with no productive base at all." The project taught some harsh lessons from which subsequent irrigation projects in the Philippines learned. Later projects attempted to relocate people within the service area serviced by the new dams.

The Philippines was not the only country where the issue arose. The São Francisco Polders project in Brazil had its own relocation implications. The irrigation component of the project meant the relocation of some small landholders. This brought forth vigorous church opposition to the project in the form of two local bishops and a foreign priest in the area. Not only was the church opposed to the relocation implications of the project; it also opposed the project's expropriation provisions on the grounds that these would expropriate the lands of even relatively small landholders. Bank project officers conceded that farmers who owned between 5 and 15 hectares of land would be affected by the provisions, since the project called for reduction of their holdings to 3.5 hectares. They pointed out, however, that these 3.5 hectares would be irrigated land. Despite Bank efforts to soften some of the opposition that arose during project implementation, the relocation issues in the project were publicized in the international press and attracted attention at high levels within the Bank itself.

In another project in Brazil, the Alto Turi land settlement project, there were problems with the indigenous population in the area. Some Indian tribes resident in the settlement areas would not permit the colonization agency to run engineering lines through a relatively small part of the project area. The problem was, however, resolved to the satisfaction of both parties. In Colombia, too, there were instances of Bank-financed settlement projects encroaching upon the preserve of native populations and thus embroiling the Bank in social and political controversy.

The dislocation and resettlement issue that attracted the most attention concerned the Bank's experience with transmigration in Indonesia. This involved Bank support for projects designed to move about half a million families from the densely populated island of Java to some of the sparsely populated outer islands. There were controversies both within the Bank and in the Bank's relations with the Indonesian government over these projects. One of the principal issues was how much land a relocated family needed to survive on the soil-poor outer islands; another was the bureaucratic capacity of the Indonesian government for carrying out such a huge undertaking; and another was the total cost of the project. A journalistic report argued that "the dispute over transmigration has caused more internal bitterness at the World Bank than most people can remember on any other project. The moving of a population is a colossal undertaking, and some staffers say the Bank hadn't grasped the immensity of it."[4]

Failure to grasp some of the probable social effects of projects before the projects got underway had noticeably adverse consequences for project implementation. It was apparent that the Bank would need to give greater attention to some of these questions if it desired to continue its poverty-oriented rural development work.

Some Consequences of Implementation Problems

The combination of recipient-country problems and problems in the Bank's own design of its rural development projects led to a number of practical consequences that proved somewhat disconcerting for the Bank under McNamara. A major concern of one of the reviews of project implementation was to compare the experience of rural development projects with more traditional agricultural projects (in which at least 50 percent of the direct benefits did not accrue to poverty target groups). One issue receiving attention directly related to the problems discussed here was that of disbursement shortfalls. Rural development projects tended to experience more such shortfalls than the traditional agricultural projects. In the Latin American and Caribbean region 89 percent of the rural development projects under implementation between fiscal 1973 and fiscal 1977 had disbursement shortfalls of 10 percent or more (in comparison with the disbursement schedule set out at the time of appraisal) as opposed to 65 percent for the agricultural projects (both very high figures in any event). In the West African region 43 percent of the rural development projects under implementation had very substantial disbursement shortfalls (of 50 percent or more compared with appraisal estimates). Such shortfalls were higher for rural development projects than for general agricultural projects throughout the project cycle.

There seemed little doubt that the average, or typical, rural development project experienced lags of some significance and therefore troubled the Bank. The lag of disbursements behind commitments, however, was a Bank-wide phenomenon, and it was not certain what proportion of the lag was accounted for by the implementation of rural development projects alone. In fiscal 1978, for example, the Bank and IDA committed $8.4 billion. But they actually disbursed only $3.8 billion.[5] The Bank's annual report for 1978 was forthcoming on the matter: "These disbursements were below expectations. The review [a review of the matter within the Bank] also shows that disbursements in certain major sectors, particularly agriculture, will, for several years, be somewhat lower than would be expected on the basis of past disbursement experience. 'New-style' projects are not only technically complex; they also involve new agencies and institutions carrying out new activities to benefit groups of people previously considered outside the reach of most government programs. Delays in disbursements can reasonably be expected to fade as borrowers and the Bank gain experience in project execution."[6]

Another reason for the lag of disbursements behind commitments was what were referred to as "counterpart funding difficulties" in recipient countries. These were intimately related to the deficient policy and institutional frameworks discussed previously. The 1978 annual report took note of these, as follows: "[I]mplementation of many Bank-assisted projects has been adversely affected as borrowing governments have tried to adjust to inflation, to balance of payments difficulties, and to rising budgetary deficits. In adjusting to inflation by reducing expenditures, and in adjusting to balance of payments difficulties by cutting back on domestic credit expansion, governments have found that counterpart funds needed for the full financing of Bank- and IDA-assisted projects are in short supply; this shortage of course affects implementation."[7] There was no lack of evidence for these difficulties in the implementation of the rural development projects studied. Counterpart-funding difficulties were experienced, for example, with all Bank-assisted projects in Brazil.

Another issue of concern at the Bank stemming directly from implementation problems was that of the supervision time spent on these kinds of projects. The Latin American and Caribbean region of the Bank discovered a very substantial difference between the amount of supervision required in supervising rural development projects compared to that in more traditional agricultural projects. The region found that supervision of rural development projects under its implementation required an average of 18.5 man-weeks per project per year while other agricultural projects required an average of only 10.3. Such data had implications for the productivity of Bank staff and thus for staffing needs. If there was to be a continued increase in the number of Bank-financed rural development projects, and if such projects would require almost double the supervision input, what would the consequences be for the size of the Bank's staff? If the staff could not grow as a result of budgetary constraints, what would the consequences be for the quality of the Bank's supervision work?

In sum, disbursement shortfalls, counterpart-funding difficulties, and the apparently excessive supervision time spent on rural development projects meant that the Bank's experience with such projects was more difficult than with its more traditional agricultural projects. One internal Bank study made an effort to classify projects according to whether they suffered from "minor," "moderate," or "serious" problems. In the Latin American and Caribbean region 15 of 18 (83 percent) rural development projects were considered to fall in the "moderate" problem category, while 16 of 32 general agricultural projects (only 50 percent) fell into this category. About 5 to 6 percent of both rural and agricultural development projects suffered from "serious" problems. In the East Asia and Pacific region 67 percent of the rural development projects under implementation had "moderate" problems compared to 55 percent of the agricultural projects. In the West African region 5 of 38 rural development projects suffered from "serious" problems (only 13 percent) whereas 4 of 19 (21 percent) general agricultural projects had such problems. The differences found in other regions manifested themselves with "moderate" problems, however: 16 of 38 rural development projects (42 percent) had "moderate" problems of implementation, while only 6 of 19 (32 percent) general agricultural projects had such problems. Overall, then, rural development projects tended to experience more "moderate" or "serious" problems of implementation.

Some Achievements in Rural Development Projects

Discussion of the interim achievements of the Bank's rural development projects must be prefaced by a caveat. Surprisingly, the Bank has conducted little in the way of an impact analysis of its rural development projects. The Bank's work in this area could be primarily justified by its contribution to increased yields and output of small farmers, but it has mobilized very little in the nature of conclusions about the projects' output achievements. The relative newness of most of the projects, together with the notoriously cyclical nature of agricultural production in many poor countries, meant that in the majority of instances it was "too early to tell."

The problem was well illustrated in the Bank's fifth agricultural credit project in Mexico. In this project there were substantial difficulties in the establishment of an adequate project-monitoring system to conduct impact analysis. It was very difficult for the Bank to state therefore what the impact of the credit had been at the operating farm level. The Bank did not appear to know with any precision how the loan funds from the credit were allocated in terms of the productive uses to which they were put. There was a rough breakdown between credits that had led to greater livestock production and greater crop production, but there was no differentiation by type of crops. It was therefore impossible to answer the crucial question of whether the project had had any impact on Mexico's notorious supply situation regarding basic food grains.

Similarly, a report of the West African region of the Bank was silent on the question of impact analysis. A report of the East Asia and Pacific region limited itself to the rhetorical statement that "the rates of return, and the distribution of benefits, expected at appraisal in the rural development projects appear well on the way toward being satisfied." No concrete evidence was presented, however, for such a sweeping statement.

The Latin American region provided no data but gave a good deal of attention to the impact of Bank projects. It candidly admitted that none of the projects implemented in the region had yet reached the point where it was possible to assess their impact on the beneficiaries' production or income. A regional report noted, however, that in some projects the apparent increase in income was too meager to lift the beneficiaries out of the ranks of the rural poor. The report concluded that rural development projects would have to be supplemented by other policy actions, such as support for general agriculture and small industries, which would appear to have more capacity in the long run for improving the income-earning potential of the rural population.

Output Gains from Projects

A combination of interviewing and documentary evidence at the Bank revealed more than a few projects where the preliminary results appeared encouraging. A few are cited here.

In some of the Latin American projects, despite the land tenure and titling problems, there were some very favorable output trends. In the Bank's first rural development project in Paraguay, there was substantial incremental production of cotton, soybeans, and tobacco. According to a Bank project officer, the project resulted in production value-added of approximately 150 percent in real terms over the project life and contributed to considerably greater increases in family incomes than were expected at the time of appraisal.

In Colombia a study of the Bank's Integrated Rural Development Program uncovered significant data regarding incremental output in 1978. The production of each crop achieved by the program was in every case greater than that achieved by the local production technology. While most data were compiled from only four Colombian departments, the report affirmed that the yields achieved by the program largely equaled or surpassed the national averages for traditional agriculture. In addition the report stated that in several cases (particularly in crops of corn, rice, sugar cane, yucca, tomatoes, and onions) income per hectare had improved significantly.

In Brazil the midterm evaluation of the Rio Grande do Norte project found that the area planted with credit-supported cotton increased by 78 percent over appraisal estimates. Although the data were limited, it appeared that significant production and income effects had resulted from this expansion in cotton cultivation. The feasibility of estimated increments in cotton yields (from 175 to 300 kilograms per hectare in nine years) was verified through on-farm trials. As a result of this and the farmers' response to credit access and extension services, estimates for cotton and food crop yields were revised upward. The Ceara project in Brazil also saw incremental production and yields that surpassed those expected at the time of project appraisal. Vegetable production especially increased. Some new crops attained unexpectedly high production levels.

In Mexico the first PIDER project had a significant impact upon certain microregional production levels. The main contributory factor seems to have been the project's small-scale irrigation facilities. The Center for Rural Development Research (CIDER) in Mexico noted from a midterm evaluation that irrigation diversified cropping patterns (with emphasis on crops of greater commercial value), substantially increased productivity on previously cultivated rainfed areas (as a result of assured water supplies and improved complementary inputs), and increased the area under cultivation by opening up new lands and introducing double cropping. Figures for the Mexican state of Guanajuato exemplified these trends. Maize production on newly irrigated plots increased by 245 percent, bean production by 660 percent, and chile production by 1,850 percent. As a result of double cropping alone cultivation grew by 22 percent in land area. The survey indicated that the aggregate value of production per hectare of irrigated land increased threefold after the project's initiation. The CIDER report noted, however, that there were significant variations in aggregate production value per hectare both within and between the various microregions. For example, the aggregate value of production per hectare in Misión de Arnedo, Guanajuato, increased 1.5 times while in the village of Vagui, a semicollective *ejido*, it increased 22 times.

In Bolivia an impressive result of the Ingavi project was that of milk production. There were substantial increases in income for small milk producers, who received high prices for their milk in comparison with the prices received for subsistence crops in the altiplano.

Reports of output gains from Bank projects came from other regions as well. In the first rural development project in Nigeria (Funtua), average yields for maize were approximately 50 percent above appraisal estimates. Production of sorghum was approximately 60 percent above estimates. These were impressive figures since, according to one Bank staff member responsible for monitoring and evaluation of the project, the original appraisal estimates for yields and production levels were "nonsense." By greatly overestimating the existing (baseline) production levels, the appraisal reports insured that the production levels attained over the implementation period would never reach the appraisal estimates. Thus, even though the production of maize, cotton, and groundnuts only reached 58, 43, and 54 percent, respectively, of the appraisal targets, the aggregate incremental production represented a very substantial increase from the real baseline situation.

In the Kigoma project in Tanzania project-area sales of the main food crops—maize, beans, and pidgeon peas—to the National Milling Corporation increased over sevenfold in tonnage. The midterm evaluation report on the project stated that increased sales to the corporation were largely attributable to the 55 project villages that in turn accounted for 50 percent of the regionwide surplus in the project area in the 1978–79 growing season. Project village sales were approximately three times those of nonproject villages.

In the South Asian region of the Bank, the Rajasthan Dairy Development Project in India appears to have been spectacularly successful. A survey of 43 producers from seven dairy cooperative societies showed that the quantity of milk marketed during the two-year period 1975–76 to 1977–78 rose by 248 percent. In addition a 1978 survey indicated that family income from milk production had increased by 560 percent since initiation of the project and that this sharp rise in milk income had enabled increased use of agricultural inputs resulting in higher crop yields in the region.

In Nepal there were likewise positive results from a rural development project in which wheat yields rose from 815 to 1,678 kilograms per hectare during the 1977–78 to 1978–79 growing season.

The main evidence on incremental production in East Asia comes from the experience with rice production in the Philippines. Almost all of the Bank's agricultural work in the Philippines has been in irrigation. This was the result of a deliberate decision made about a decade ago that the most important emphasis in Philippine agriculture should be national self-sufficiency in rice production, and that this would entail a substantial amount of irrigation. The projects were apparently successful, and the goal of national self-sufficiency was attained about four years ago.

Examination of the project profiles prepared by the Bank's Agriculture and Rural Development Department revealed additional examples of increased output—though not always up to appraisal targets—in projects in Ethiopia, Liberia, Malawi, Mali, Rwanda, and Upper Volta.

No doubt it is lamentable that the Bank does not yet possess aggregate information across all projects on the actual (as opposed to the projected) incremental production of various crops following project implementation. Lacking such information, recourse was necessary in this study to such piecemeal evidence as now exists. This, however, revealed sufficient instances of sizable output gains so as to dispute those who might argue that the Bank's projects were ineffective from the standpoint of increasing agricultural production in developing countries.

Despite these output achievements, there was a frequent necessity for modesty of expectations about incremental output stemming from Bank projects. This is because many such projects were undertaken in regions not considered very conducive to favorable agricultural production. There were several examples of this in the Latin American projects. In the Bolivian altiplano, for example, there was very limited absorptive capacity. Despite the Bank's approval of three rural development projects for the altiplano, the pace of future development in the region will necessarily have to be moderate. Accordingly, those interviewed at the Bank noted that the Bolivian government has very modest expectations for agricultural development in the region. It recognizes that income increments, while projected to be substantial in absolute terms, might still only yield incomes will below the Bolivian national average. Similarly, the project in Rio Grande do Norte, Brazil, was implemented in a region with serious ecological problems. The Bank and the Brazilian government had to be very realistic about what could be accomplished there. Seen in this light, preliminary incremental output figures of certain crops on the order of 20 to 30 percent looked good.

Some Questions Raised about Output Gains

The quantitative record of output gains, while admittedly limited, raises a number of issues that have attracted attention to the Bank's rural development projects. Two such issues are closely related: the end use of the incremental output and the beneficiaries of the incremental output.

What is the destination of the incremental output stemming from the Bank's projects? Is it consumed by the producers themselves, or is it marketed outside the area where it is produced? Experience varies. Of the incremental production expected to stem from the Ingavi project in Bolivia, as much as 80 percent was expected by the Bank to be marketed in the La Paz market (and thus outside the immediate project area). Almost all of the incremental production from the first Paraguayan project was exported to neighboring Brazil. In Brazil most of the incremental production of the Ceara project was likewise marketed, either in the urban centers within the project area itself or, in the case of tobacco, outside Brazil. In the Nigerian projects incremental output was chiefly marketed within the respective project regions. In Tanzania there were great variations across project villages in their respective percentages of marketed and consumed output.

Some critics of the Bank have made much of the fact that "the so-called marketable surplus (stemming from World Bank agricultural projects) does not get eaten."[8] This is evidently considered very bad. There is, however, no evidence that the marketed portion of the incremental output from rural development projects (or even the totality of incremental output marketed, if none at all is consumed within the project area) means "no food first." If nonfood crops such as cotton are produced and marketed, the proceeds from incremental marketed cotton production can presumably go to buy food. If food crops such as maize are produced and marketed, then presumably the farmers producing the maize and marketing it have already assured themselves of enough maize for local consumption. If not, they have apparently made a choice that they want other things as well as food and are willing to sacrifice a little of the food they need to get these other things. In any event it is difficult to accept the argument that the production of a marketable surplus attributable to Bank rural development projects constitutes prima facie evidence that such projects are not putting food first or not ultimately satisfying the food needs of poor farmers.

The question about the uses to which the incremental output is put is closely related to the question of the beneficiaries of the Bank's rural development projects. Neither Bank documents nor interviews with Bank project officers revealed a great deal about this aspect of project implementation. The Bank's documentary material is for the most part silent on the question of the socioeconomic characteristics of project beneficiaries, while the overwhelming majority of project officers were of the opinion that it was still too early to ascertain with any precision the characteristics of the beneficiary populations.

Frequent concern was voiced, however, about the distribution of benefits. All project officers interviewed about Brazilian projects expressed this concern. Regarding the Rio Grande do Norte project, a special Bank interim evaluation concluded that "the project did not have a sufficiently strong poverty target group orientation and ended up assisting a relatively greater proportion of medium and large farmers than expected." Project officers generally concurred in this assessment. They agreed that the credit disbursed under the project and the benefits stemming from it appeared to have gone disproportionately to farmers owning between 50 and 200 hectares. (There were approximately 6,500 to 7,000 units of more than 50 hectares in the project area and between 15,000 and 20,000 of less than 50 hectares.) In the second phase of the project it was decided by the Bank that none of its loan funds would go to the larger farmers.

While project officers were greatly impressed by the spurt in commercial activity in the Bank's Ceara project in Brazil, an overriding concern was expressed repeatedly throughout the interviews about who among the target population was actually receiving the benefits. In its initial phases, according to one project officer, the project seemed principally to have benefited the "upper-lower" farmers who already had access to credit, extension, and other inputs before the project began. There was reiterated concern about the somewhat larger and already better-off farmers appropriating the bulk of the projects' benefits in almost all rural development projects under implementation by the Bank in Brazil. One difficulty was that of referring to the number of hectares owned as the principal criterion for identifying a small farmer in Brazil. Some apparently small farmers may actually be quite well off. (After its first supervision mission to Ceara the Bank lowered its definition of what constituted a small farmer in the region.)

It was difficult to ascertain the nature of the beneficiaries in the Bank's first PIDER project in Mexico, but there appeared to be a concern similar to that expressed about Brazil. According to the special 1978 midterm evaluation of the project, approximately 75,700 out of 215,000 families in villages of 300 to 3,000 inhabitants had received some type of social and economic benefits from PIDER works. But a report of the Mexico-based project monitoring and evaluation unit concluded that "project benefits have often been excessively concentrated in the hands of a small number of 'wealthier' inhabitants in the project area. In fact, usually no more than 10 percent of the target group in any microregion received income-generating benefits of small-scale irrigation." Project officers were reluctant either to confirm or deny this conclusion; they limited themselves to observing that the nature of the project beneficiaries appeared to vary widely from one PIDER microregion to another.

The nature of the beneficiaries was an issue in non-Latin American countries as well. The issue arose frequently in the course of the Bank's irrigation work in the Philippines. Despite a September 1972 land reform in the Philippines that limited to 3 hectares the amount of irrigated land that beneficiaries of land reform could own, some observers argued that benefits from the Bank's irrigation projects in the country were excessively concentrated on large landholdings. Project officers vigorously challenged this. They contended that the overwhelming percentage of the beneficiaries from the Bank's Philippine irrigation works were small farmers owning fewer than 3 hectares each, although they readily admitted that the Bank's irrigation works were not benefiting the poorest of the poor since potentially irrigable areas in which projects were undertaken were already better off than those rainfed areas where the really miserable were located. The Bank's data indicated that only about 8,000 hectares of land of the approximately 300,000 irrigated under its irrigation projects in the Philippines were farmed by individual owners possessing more than 7 hectares of land.

Analysis of the implementation of the Bank's first rural development project in Tanzania revealed something similar to the PIDER experience in Mexico: significant variations across the affected regions. Figures for 1977 to 1978 showed as high as a fourfold per capita income differential among some of the villages in which the project was implemented. Bank project officers alleged, however, that virtually all of the beneficiaries fell within the project's target group, although there was a question as to whether the beneficiaries were large or small in number. The officer closest to the project thought it possible that benefits mainly accrued to small groups of beneficiaries, but these small groups seemed to be among the poor of the target group.

Another Mexican project illustrated some of the difficulties in assessing the beneficiaries from the Bank's projects. The fifth agricultural credit loan to Mexico included a substantial proportion of funds for low-income producers. The Bank, however, adopted a very generous definition of the low-income producer, enabling many people to qualify for project loans who were not really low-income at all. Mexican data divided the low-income producers into *ejidatarios* (members of *ejidos*, Mexico's *sui generis* communal farming unit, a product of the Mexican Revolution that is sometimes characterized by private landholding, sometimes by collective, and sometimes by a bewildering array of intermediary forms) and *pequeños propietarios*, or small private farmers.

Data on the distribution of credit under the fifth agricultural credit project's "low-income producers' subproject" had to be interpreted with care. They showed that approximately 94 percent of the borrowers were *ejidatarios* and only 6 percent small private farmers. But the average loan to the small private farmer, who was generally better off than the *ejidatario*, was about $10,000 while the average loan to an *ejidatario* was only about $1,000.

Furthermore the lack of an effective project monitoring and evaluation system designed to provide impact analysis meant that the Bank did not know with any precision (indeed, did not appear to know at all) what the breakdown of low-income beneficiaries was in terms of income levels. The upper limit for defining the low-income producer under the project was an annual income of 1,000 times the daily minimum rural wage, with this wage varying greatly by region within Mexico. Anyone earning less than 1,000 times the minimum was classified by the Bank as a low-income producer. It was possible, however, that most of the low-income beneficiaries were close to the 1,000 times limit. This would be quite a different situation from that in which the beneficiaries were concentrated near the 200 or 300 times level. These experiences under the Mexican credit project were illustrative of the difficulties of definition, measurement, and targeting in establishing the beneficiaries of the Bank's rural development projects.

Not all projects were marked by the deflection of benefits away from intended beneficiaries in the target population. Limited data from Colombia and Nigeria, for example, indicated significant increases in labor use resulting from the implementation of the Bank's projects, suggesting benefits for the smaller labor-intensive farmers. In Bolivia virtually all of the beneficiaries of the Bank's Ingavi project were small farmers, with typical farm size ranging between 2 and 6 hectares. Almost all project officers interviewed, however, either saw the deflection of benefits as a major problem in projects under implementation or saw it as a large potential problem. Almost all agreed that it was inevitable that large farmers as well as small farmers would benefit from the Bank's projects, the exact proportions being impossible to discern. Almost all were quite philosophical about this, as perhaps best summed up in the words of a project officer on Nigerian projects when discussing the issue of large and small farmers: "In Nigeria, you bring everybody up or you bring nobody up" (without including some benefits for the larger farmers, the rural development projects in Nigeria never would have gotten off the ground).

One of the main difficulties was related to the direct and indirect beneficiaries of projects and the practical dilemmas in attempting to disentangle the two. The point was illustrated in the Rio Grande do Norte project in Brazil. One project officer suggested that "the real beneficiary of the project was the textile industry in Brazil." A second officer confirmed this observation and offered some explanation. The principal crop in the project area was cotton. The success of the project was thus dependent upon the governmentally established price for domestic cotton. Naturally, the domestic textile industry wished to hold this down as much as possible, and in this it was quite successful. There were also some matters related to how the industry operated. Much of its production was exported and eligible for export subsidy payments; these payments were made to the exporting industry by the government immediately upon exporting; but, in sharp contrast, payments to cooperatives or private cotton ginners could be often delayed for up to 120 or 150 days. These features supported the assertion that the project had benefited the Brazilian textile industry more than anything else. No one at the Bank argued that this was bad, but it did illustrate the difficulty of any quantitative exercise focusing on the attribution of direct benefits.

Second- and Third-Round Effects of Projects

The first-round effects of projects refer to those things expected to happen as a direct result of the projects' implementation, such as the output and income effects with their increased consumption, increased marketing of additional crops, and array of beneficiaries both within and without the project area. But these are by no means the whole story of the projects' effects. There are also second- and third-round effects—other things that happen, some decidedly unintended and unanticipated, as a consequence of the projects' implementation. Since it was admittedly early to assess even the first-round effects of the Bank's projects, it was even earlier to evaluate these second- and third-round effects. Nevertheless, it appeared that a number of such effects were prominent as a result of implementation.

One such effect was the apparent escalation of land values. In Colombia there was a substantial inflation of land values after implementation of the nationwide rural development project. As a consequence the monetary benchmark figure for identifying the small farmer included in the Bank's project appraisal report rapidly became outdated. Similarly, in the Ceara project in Brazil no land purchase credit was extended, but there was considerable land speculation in the project area. Land values in the area more than doubled in two years. The typical pattern, according to a Bank project officer, was that urban people from the nearest big city to the project area would buy up 100 hectares or more at a time and then rent it out to those able to pay for it.

There did not seem to be enough evidence to justify Ernest Feder's fears, but they were relevant. In Feder's opinion, "it is improbable that the lucky small-holders, beneficiaries of World Bank assistance, will be able to retain for long any advantages they might enjoy from the McNamara scheme. If projects are located in or near areas with large landholdings . . . , every effort will be made by owners of the latter to get control over land in which funds for long-run improvements have been sunk and whose land productivity and commercial value are increasing. Sinking money into the small-holder-sector land is like waving a bone before a hungry dog: the entrepreneurial spirit of the large landowners or other rural real estate investors will seek and find ways to get a hold of it."[9] It remained to be seen whether this would be a familiar consequence of the Bank's small-holder-oriented projects, but it was certainly a very real possibility.

Another second- or third-round effect concerned the use to which the expected incremental income was put by project beneficiaries. Once again it was too early to reach conclusions; there were both favorable and unfavorable signs. Initial developments in the first Paraguayan project, which project officers claimed to be "not only the most successful rural development project in the Latin American region of the Bank but perhaps the most successful rural development project in the entire Bank," were not terribly encouraging. There were substantial incremental incomes as a result of the project's implementation, but these led to hideous displays of conspicuous consumption and behavior on the part of project beneficiaries. It was "a common sight to see project farmers walking around with money wrapped around their ears and hanging from their necks."

Another rural officer at the Bank raised the issue of the very successful rice cultivation project (in an unspecified country) in which the incomes of the project beneficiaries rose very substantially in a short period of time, but so did alcoholism, venereal disease, and other social vices. The project raised the issue of the expenditure of incremental incomes in glaring terms, and it was frankly admitted that the Bank had given very little if any attention to this question.

The question was more fully addressed in an audit of three loans to the Federal Land Development Authority (FELDA) in Malaysia. These were for various land settlement projects in an area known as the Jengka Triangle. Although criticized within the Bank for their high per settler costs, and thus open to question on replicability grounds, the loans were extremely successful in raising the income levels of the target beneficiaries. By 1975 the income of settlers producing oil palm had risen to about three times the officially established poverty line in Malaysia. The Bank's audit report noted that "FELDA has a reputation for providing relatively high earnings, for creating a rural elite out of a small favored group of the poor, and for running the risk of the social problems that implies."

Because of income increases well over half of the Jengka settlers made substantial modifications to their original homes, adding one or more rooms and enhancing their outside appearances. Almost every family purchased at least one motor vehicle. FELDA was also successful in designing and popularizing a voluntary settler savings scheme. It claimed 77 percent participation by the settlers in the Jengka Triangle by mid-1977. Although savings per settler were small, FELDA expected continued growth.

There was evidence of nascent capital accumulation in other Bank projects as well. After the initially discouraging instances of conspicuous consumption in the Paraguayan project area, things turned around. There was increasing evidence of rudimentary savings and capital formation among project area farmers. Many personal savings accounts were opened with the National Development Bank. Similarly, in Haiti, small organizations of project area farmers began some small-scale capital accumulation. The Bank estimated that about $2,800 in savings had occurred in the first year of project implementation as a result of the activity of these new organizations. The Malaysian, Paraguayan, and Haitian experiences were the merest straws in the wind, but they did serve to indicate the previously unrealized potentialities for savings and capital accumulation, and thus for reinvestment and further production gains, among the small farmers who were intended as the principal beneficiaries of the Bank's rural development projects.

In the Haitian case the primitive capital accumulation came from approximately 100 small associations of project farmers formed during project implementation. This illustrated another second- or third-round effect. A number of the Bank's projects appeared responsible for increases in farmer organization and participation. In Haiti the emergence of an entirely new style of farmer organization was one of the un-anticipated consequences of the project. These were organizations of eight, ten, or twelve farmers who pooled their resources for small joint ventures (like buying some farm implements). In Colombia village committees came into existence at the municipal and departmental levels after the implementation of the Bank's project. Given the past history of the politicization of rural organizations in Colombia, this was a touchy subject. But it did not prevent the emergence of the committees that offered advice on allocative priorities of rural development funds. In Bolivia groups of farmers emerged that agreed to take collective responsibility for credit and the delivery of technical assistance. In the first Bank-assisted project in Korea there was re-inforcement of the Saemaeul movement (a nationwide popular action movement with religious overtones). The Saemaeul organizations within project participating villages selected their highest priority project for the upcoming year and oversaw the implementation of the project within the village. In a project in the Philippines increasing farmer participation was the major unanticipated consequence of implementation. The participation was not so much in the organized form of cooperatives and farmer groups, as in the sense of discernibly more farmer initiative and more demonstrable farmer willingness to co-operate with local governmental officials. This was considered by Bank project officers to be "the most beneficial side effect of the project to date."

In Tanzania an unanticipated consequence of the implementation of the Kigoma project was the success of its self-help efforts. As a result of a mass mobilization compaign initiated by regional authorities, there were impressive results in the self-help construction of village roads and school buildings. The villages contributed unskilled labor and produced some of the materials used in construction. The input of the villagers comprised approximately 40 percent of total construction costs. "Frequently," according to the Bank's special midterm evaluation of the project, "the volume of village contribution has been such as to overwhelm the capacity of the regional authorities to respond either with material inputs or with adequate supervision."

There were some larger, structural consequences of Bank projects as well. A particularly unanticipated one occurred in Tanzania. The Bank's first rural development loan for a multisectoral project in Tanzania was intended to support the socialist objectives of *ujaama*ization. While in some respects *ujaama*ization clearly benefited from the implementation of the project, there was an extremely interesting second-round effect. Implementation of the project appeared to increase social differentiation within project villages. Some villagers bettered their shelters, others didn't. The size of block farms (communal) apparently decreased, and the land people now farm is as likely as not to be nonblock farm. It might have been of some concern to the Tanzanian government that a Bank-financed project in the country had increased rather than reduced social differentiation within *ujaama* villages. This appeared to run counter to the socialist objectives of the regime and could be perceived as having introduced elements of "insidious capitalism."

Another example of an unforeseen consequence came from Bolivia. There, the project farmers were not initially interested in the production components of the project, which the Bank considered very important. But they were interested, to an unexpectedly high degree, in the social infrastructure components. The latter provided tangibles (such as schools) the farmers wanted, and the provision of these by the project considerably heightened the interest of the farmers in subsequently participating in the less tangible production components of the project. (A possible lesson from this was that such tangibles should have been provided early in the implementation of the project in order to awaken interest in the other aspects. The nondirectly productive components might have important, indirect, unanticipated, and positive effects.)

In the first PIDER project in Mexico, other effects of the project arguably outweighed its contributions to production and income. Some of the unanticipated effects included the decentralization of expenditures to the state level (rare in the highly centralized Mexican system), the strengthened coordination of investment activities at both the central and state levels, institution building with positive effects on the project's participating agencies, the systematization of project monitoring and evaluation (virtually unheard of in Mexico), and the training of specialized staff in the techniques of rural development. These were extremely important for bureaucratic development in Mexico.

There were also some longer-run issues stemming from one of the avowed aims of the projects—making subsistence farmers into commercial ones. Some Bank project officers were quite explicit about this. They freely admitted, for example, that the main goal of a project in the Bolivian altiplano was to make subsistence farmers into commercial ones. That is why about 80 percent of the incremental output from the Ingavi project was marketed in La Paz, the national capital. The subject, however, aroused some debate as the Bank examined the medium- and long-term effects on the social structure of the altiplano likely to result from this intended achievement, and therefore a sociologist in the Bank's Central Projects Staff was charged with studying the project's social implications.

In Brazil the medium- and long-term social effects of commercial farming on small-scale and subsistence farmers also became a concern. Although it was obvious that there had been a tremendous increase in commercial activity in the Ceara project area after the project's inception, it was not clear what effects this had on the social structure and behavioral patterns of the area.

Preliminary evidence on some of these questions apparently led in conflicting directions. On the one hand, there were examples of increasing social differentiation such as in Tanzania and heightened popular participation such as in Colombia, Haiti, and the Philippines. On the other, there were instances of few noticeable social effects; this was the case of Paraguay, where the social structure of the project area, described as "totally amorphous, even nonexistent" when the project began, did not seem to change very much as the project was implemented. Project officers in Paraguay were disappointed that the community centers at the heart of the project did not go well at all. The officers were not able to offer any convincing explanation as to why this had not occurred.

Many of these second- and third-round effects were not technical or economic but were contextual, structural, social and political. Incremental incomes brought with them some highly differential patterns of spending and thus highly differential effects on the production and distribution systems within the recipient region or country. Depending upon the distribution of the benefits from the project, there would be widely varying political consequences, notably in the stability of the rural areas in which the projects were located. Even if it could be shown that some or most rural development projects were effective in helping the poor, it also had to be shown what else they did besides helping the poor.

Additional Achievements of Projects

There were at least two other positive achievements of the Bank's rural development projects. One concerned the way in which later projects learned from previous projects in what has aptly been called "learning by doing." The other is the impact some Bank projects had on a country's national or sectoral policy goals.

The incremental accumulation of knowledge about processes of rural development was an important Bank contribution in a number of recipient countries. In the Ingavi project in Bolivia, a project that initially had a somewhat dismal reputation within the Bank, there were major difficulties with the irrigation component of the project, technical deficiencies relating to drainage problems, and major input supply deficiencies. These included difficulties in the supply of seeds, fertilizers, agricultural chemicals, and particularly of dairy cattle. Many cattle were brought up to the altiplano from the low-lying areas of Bolivia and collapsed at the higher elevation. There were also institution-building difficulties. A semiautonomous project unit was created and placed under the Ministry of Agriculture, but this unit initially did not interact well with the farmers in the project areas.

Rather than scrap the entire project in the face of seemingly insurmountable obstacles in the early going, it was decided by the Bank to be as flexible as possible in the redesign of the project. The emphasis on flexibility was a persistent theme. As a result the irrigation component was reduced to a pilot scheme. A special input supply fund was created, and this facilitated the delivery of needed inputs. An acclimization center for dairy cows was established, significantly improving the dairy production program. Difficulties of relating to project area farmers were resolved by building an office for the farmers within the area. Not only was the Ingavi project itself redesigned, two subsequent Bank projects in the altiplano profited from the lessons of Ingavi. For example, the credit delivery system in the latter projects took greater cognizance of the individualism of the farmers. Individuals drawn from the local population itself were employed as dispensers of project inputs and technical assistance. The input supply systems, training programs, and cattle acclimation centers of the latter projects were built on the lessons of the Ingavi experience.

Learning by doing was not limited to the Latin American region of the Bank. Later projects in Tanzania learned from the experiences with the first project (Kigoma). The Kigoma project was seen as too ambitious in its assumptions about what could be achieved by technical packages for rainfed agriculture in Tanzania. As a result of the experience with the Kigoma project there was an increasing realization by the Bank of the need for basic infrastructure in the poor rural regions of the country. (This was also the case in Nigeria.) Basic infrastructure meant especially roads and water supply. The second project (Tabora) had a much heavier emphasis on such basic infrastructure and in addition there was as an experimental pilot production program, with less stress on social components of the project. The third project (Mwanza-Shinyanga) was even less ambitious. Incremental production and income goals were scaled down because there had been little relevant agricultural research before the project began.

Another development in the Tanzanian projects was the Bank's increasing recognition of the necessity of working with local administration. The Tabora project was more integrated with the work of the regional planning agency than the Kigoma had been. In Mwanza-Shinyanga there was an attempt to work with the existing line agencies in the region. The village self-help program of the Mwanza-Shinyanga project represented an increasing emphasis on participation. There was also an increased recognition of the need for in-project training as a result of a substantial training component included in the Mwanza-Shinyanga project. In addition, there was considerably greater emphasis than in Kigoma on project monitoring and evaluation.

In Asia all subsequent Bank irrigation projects in the Philippines learned lessons about how to deal with dislocation and resettlement issues from the experiences of the first project begun in 1969. The solution adopted—to relocate the affected population within the area of the major dam—was an important Bank example of learning by doing.

Many other projects and countries experienced learning by doing; it was more than mere rhetoric. The Bank profited from some of the mistakes of its earliest ventures, and the lessons learned were incorporated into the design and execution of subsequent projects.

Despite much that has been made here of the frequently insufficient relationship between the goals of Bank projects and national or sectoral policy goals within recipient countries, the Bank sometimes made significant contributions to the larger agricultural policy debate in some countries. While a great many examples of projects having larger impacts were not found, there were potentialities in this regard.

In Colombia, for example, changes in public sector investment planning for rural development were brought about by the Bank's nationwide project. Such changes were both substantive and procedural. There was a clear reorientation of credit toward small farmers, reversing a trend that had been evident since 1973. A new credit manual prepared by the Caja Agraria revised the types of guarantees required for small-farmer loans. The Colombian government instituted five-year budgetary planning for rural development as well as a procedure for carrying over unspent balances into a subsequent fiscal year.

In Paraguay the success of the Bank's first rural development project led, according to Bank project officers, to the adoption of its approach in the development of the entire eastern region of the country.

In Brazil there were several aspects of this process. The most important, but most difficult to measure, was the legitimization role the Bank's rural development projects seem to have played. They legitimized the concept of assistance to the small farmer; they made small-farmer-oriented agricultural development strategies politically feasible in Brazil in a way in which they were not only several years ago. In the opinion of Bank project officers, the Brazilian government became much more seriously involved with the problems of the small farmer than it had before the Bank's efforts.

Beyond this legitimization role, and the way in which it put the large landowners of the Brazilian northeast somewhat on the defensive, Bank project officers referred to other aspects of the projects that extended beyond specific project features. The federal agricultural research agency in Brazil, for example, began to generalize the extension approach adopted from the on-farm research trials in the Rio Grande do Norte area to most other areas of the northeast. The demonstration of what could be accomplished in assisting small farmers with credit contributed to work on a proposed agricultural credit project that would incorporate thirty *Polonordeste* projects in the northeast. (*Polonordeste* is the name given to the Brazilian government's general program for agricultural and rural development in the northeast.) This was still far from completely turning around the basic directions of Brazilian agricultural policy, but these developments were considered by Bank project officers to have been some of the larger achievements of the Bank's work in Brazil.

In Africa project officers pointed to some larger impact from projects in Nigeria and Tanzania. In Tanzania they claimed that the Bank's projects had been responsible for considerable institution building, most notably the strengthening of the Tanzanian Rural Development Bank. (They argued moreover that such institution building had been more effectively pursued by the Bank in the context of functional projects, such as in grain storage, than in the context of more diffuse multisectoral rural development projects.) They maintained that the experience with the Bank's projects in Tanzania had led the government to place somewhat greater emphasis on agricultural production goals instead of only rural equity goals. Changes in governmental marketing and pricing policies also seemed in some measure attributable to Bank efforts through its projects.

In Nigeria the problems with agricultural policies which became so apparent as a result of the Bank's rural development projects were addressed in a comprehensive agricultural sector survey. Since the preliminary drafts of the survey were the subject of intensive discussions between Bank staff and Nigerian government officials, the staff hoped that the result would be some policies that were more supportive of the Bank's efforts in rural development in the country.

In Asia several examples were found in which, paradoxically, projects were apparently so successful in achieving their intended objectives that this very success compelled governmental reexamination of policy alternatives. In the Philippines the Bank seems to have reached the limit on its primary irrigation work. In what directions could it now move? According to a Bank project officer, one would be toward financing communal irrigation systems, which would involve the Bank in a host of sociopolitical issues for which it is not well prepared; another would be toward efforts to increase the productivity of already irrigated areas. The productivity issue, however, runs into the problem of increasing income disparities since farmers in irrigated areas already tend to have higher incomes than those in nonirrigated areas. Since the principal approach employed by the Bank to date has reached its limits and can only lead to two irrigation alternatives which would involve more problems than encountered previously, the Bank and the Philippine government gave increased attention to the possibilities of rainfed agriculture. The generalized success of a sequence of projects led to consideration of a whole new program.

This phenomenon was at work in Malaysia as well. The experience with the FELDA land settlement projects was eminently successful in terms of achieving the intended output and income results. But it was realized, first by the Bank and subsequently by some quarters of the Malaysian government, that the approach was too expensive to replicate on a nationwide scale. It was not applicable to the very poor state of Kelantan, with its acidic soils and rough topography. This realization led in two directions, one toward a sixth FELDA project which was lower-cost and in which the projected income levels of project beneficiaries were only about 70 percent of that of current FELDA settlers, and the other toward the undertaking of a multisectoral rural development project in Kelantan. This and the Philippine example were cases illustrating the limits of success in rural development projects. Once these limits were reached and perceived, the Bank and the recipient countries attempted to formulate alternative development strategies.

The Inaccuracy of Sweeping Generalizations

The available evidence marshaled for this study indicates that the implementation of the Bank's rural development projects in the McNamara years confronted some major problems within the recipient countries of Bank funds. Some problems, perhaps a bit less major, had to do with faults in the Bank's project designs for rural development.

But there is evidence—albeit limited at this early stage of the implementation experience—of some significant project achievements, both direct and indirect. From all of the foregoing observations and reflections, can there be agreement with the following pungent observation by a severe critic of the Bank's work?

Our analysis of the Bank's intentions and plans in developing a rural development strategy finds little substance in the Bank's analysis in terms of promising and feasible approaches that are likely to reach the poor effectively. For the time being, the Bank can only offer its willingness to experiment at the financial and political expense of recipient countries. Although the Bank advocates major policy changes necessary for an effective rural strategy, it will suspend lending if political turmoil accompanies a movement leading to change in a country's internal distribution of power and influence. Given its institutional and structural position it is unable to behave otherwise. The contradiction between what the Bank says should be done, and what it can or does do, makes it a singularly unsuitable institution to practice what it now preaches.[10]

Almost everything previously argued here, from the normative stance emphasizing varying shades of gray in chapter 1 to the multifaceted discussion of the problems and potentialities of rural development projects in this chapter, leads in the direction of rejecting this macroscopic set of assertions. The answer to the question "Has the World Bank been effective in helping the rural poor?" cannot be a simple yes or no. What is meant by "effective" (or "promising" or "feasible")? Effective in what countries (Korea or Brazil)? In what aspects of its rural work (roads or health)? Over what time period? Effective with what segments of the rural poor? Effective at doing what—increasing rural output, increasing rural incomes, creating rural jobs, or contributing to rural stability and peace in the countryside?

Because of the relative newness of the Bank's rural development work, the analysis in this chapter cannot be definitive in answering these kinds of questions. The comparative excursions into project behavior offered here, however, reveal the most salient factors impinging on the current status and likely future of that work. They reveal the need for sensitive disaggregation and differentiation of both questions and answers and thus the prematureness of overarching generalizations that allegedly reveal why the Bank's rural poverty work begun under McNamara was good or bad.

Poverty-Oriented Urban Work

The turning point on rural development was the Nairobi speech of September 1973, whereas the turning point on urban development was McNamara's annual address of September 1975. On the urban poverty issue McNamara referred to these basic facts: The proportion of developing countries' populations living in cities will greatly increase from now until the end of the century. Over 1.1 billion people, most of them poor, will have to be absorbed by the cities of the developing world in the next twenty-five years. The four largest countries in Latin America, for example, will be overwhelmingly urban by that year. Projections suggest that Argentina will be 89 percent urban; Brazil, 76 percent; Colombia, 78 percent; and Mexico, 78 percent.[1]

In the developing world the urban poor exist in thoroughly squalid conditions, afflicted by malnutrition, devoid of rudimentary sanitary facilities, lacking employment, possessing minimal shelter if any at all. Adopting an absolute poverty measure based on the local cost of minimum nutritional and nonfood requirements, the World Bank estimates that 25 percent of the urban populations of the Bank's developing member countries are in conditions of such poverty.

The glaring dimensions of urban poverty are even more apparent from data on specific countries in which the Bank began projects during McNamara's tenure.[2] In Jakarta, Indonesia, the site of the Bank's most famous slum-upgrading projects, 65 percent of the people had no private toilet facilities before project inception. Eighty percent had no electricity, and 90 percent had no piped water connection. Permanent houses comprised only 24 percent of the total city housing stock. In the Calcutta Metropolitan District of India, the site of the Bank's main institution-building project in urban development, 5.5 million people, or 57 percent of the population, live totally without basic urban services. In the Philippines, a country with three urban projects financed by the Bank, about 30 percent of the urban population, or 3.2 million people, live at or below the minimum subsistence level. In La Paz, Bolivia, about 62 percent of the population, or more than 400,000 people, live in substandard housing along the periphery of the city or in downtown slum areas. In Colombia 25 percent of the urban population does not have direct access to public water supply. About 60 percent does not have direct access to sewerage services. Thirty-one percent of the urban population of Peru lives in squatter settlements on the outskirts of cities. In a recently formed settlement near Lima only 43 percent of households have running water. About 40 percent of the dwellings have electricity. Health facilities are minimal, and the incidence of respiratory disease is exceptionally high.

What was to be done? Until recently, there were two principal schools of thought about the problem of burgeoning urbanization and accompanying urban poverty in the developing countries. One stressed policies designed to lower out-migration from rural areas, policies to mitigate the "push" factors responsible for migration. This was one of the principal justifications for the Bank's rural development policies. It seemed unlikely, however, that such policies would have more than a minor impact on the problems of hyperurbanization. Even if such policies succeeded in increasing rural income growth rates significantly above historical rates, urban–rural income differentials would probably not narrow. With an annual rural per capita income growth rate of 4 percent, per capita rural income in Brazil would still be only $340 in the year 2000 (the national per capita income was $1,030 in 1975) and in Mexico would be only $437 (the national per capita income was $1,050 in 1975).[3] The "push" factors are likely to continue.

A second policy response was urban decentralization. A number of countries adopted decentralization policies. The most common instruments were fiscal incentives designed to alter the location of investment and the subsidization of urban infrastructure in smaller cities. Such efforts were frequently undertaken, however, with little systematic rationale. The goal of industrial decentralization sometimes appeared costly in terms of loss of national output. There were conflicts between regional equity and national efficiency. Economies of scale were neglected.

The doubts that rural development or industrial decentralization policies could solve the fundamental urbanization problems in the developing world led to the Bank's conclusion that large urban agglomerations were a fact of life. They would not go away. The only realistic question was what to do about their poorest populations. What was needed in urban areas were integrated policy packages analogous to those of rural development projects. Facing up to the fact of hyper-urbanization meant, among other things, improving urban housing, generating urban employment, and introducing urban water supply, sewerage, and other public services.

McNamara outlined this strategy to reduce urban poverty: (1) increase earning opportunities in the informal sector, (2) create more jobs in the modern sector, (3) provide equitable access to public utilities, transport, education, and health services, and (4) establish realistic housing policies.

Some Aspects of Urban Work

Basic Urbanization and Housing

Issues relating to urban housing are especially illustrative of the problems and new solutions proffered by the Bank. There had been no absence of assistance geared to developing countries' housing needs, particularly in Latin America. The problem, however, was that the vast majority of housing units financed could only be afforded by middle- and upper-income groups. A Bank study of housing conditions in six cities of the developing world concluded that from 35 to 68 percent of urban residents were unable to afford the cheapest housing units produced by the public sector.[4]

Therefore a principal emphasis of the Bank's urban development strategies under McNamara was on housing for lower-income groups. Most typical were sites-and-services projects, whereby land parcels outfitted with rudimentary urban services were provided to poor people who then either constructed their own dwellings or contributed to their construction. Another emphasis was on upgrading existing urban settlements, also employing self-help methods. The essential argument about these approaches was that unrealistically high standards for urban housing had to be lowered. The basic reorientation was one of redefining criteria for appropriate housing. It attempted to get away from the traditional approach of making calculations of the investment required to meet the present and prospective housing deficit. According to the Bank's sector policy paper on housing, "This approach is basically unsound. [I]t suggests that the housing problem is a bottomless pit."[5]

While the Bank's basic urbanization projects were principally directed at the shelter needs of the urban poor, they frequently entailed other components as well, including employment. There was no hard and fast definition of a basic urbanization project. As will be seen, however, most such projects tended to have a fairly uniform list of components.

The Bank's basic urbanization projects were the most publicized of its urban lending. A whole new department was created to implement them. Some were rather controversial, and much was made on behalf of them. From fiscal 1972, when the first such urban project was approved, through the completion of fiscal 1981, fifty-two of these basic urbanization projects were undertaken. Bank loans or IDA credits for these projects totaled $1.6 billion.[6] The projects were implemented in greatly diverse regions of Africa (Botswana, Egypt, the Ivory Coast, Kenya, Morocco, Senegal, Tanzania, Upper Volta, and Zambia), Asia (India, Indonesia, Korea, the Philippines, and Thailand), and Latin America (Bolivia, Colombia, El Salvador, Guatemala, Jamaica, Mexico, Nicaragua, and Peru).

Industrial Policy
Strategies for developing the existing and growing urban areas also implied redirections of industrial policy. The outlines of the basic critique of import-substituting industrialization are well known. In many countries much urban industry is capital-intensive, and this has meant insufficient absorption of the increments to the urban labor force. For the noncommunist, less developed countries as a whole, it was estimated that new jobs in manufacturing industry absorbed no more than 10 to 12 percent of the surplus rural labor force in the period from 1960 to 1970.[7] In Latin America the share of industry's contribution to the nonagricultural labor force actually fell from 1950 to 1970.[8]

These facts about the urban labor force gave rise at the Bank to a renewed concern with the development of small-scale enterprises (SSE's in the Bank's jargon) as an integral part of its urban development strategies. The general presumption was that small-scale industry would tend to be more labor-intensive than its technologically sophisticated competitors. Its regional location might be more flexible; it might be located on the periphery of the large urban areas or in smaller provincial localities. Another advantage, not to be slighted in an era of increasing nationalism, was the prevalence of national capital in small-scale industry, in marked contrast to the subsidiaries of multinational corporations.

Obviously, a problem with the Bank's attempt to reorient much of its industrial lending toward SSE's was that not all industry was in urban areas, and especially not all small-scale industry. But there was a high correlation, and lending for industrial projects was mostly urban lending. A large proportion of the Bank's industrial lending was to development finance companies (DFC's, in the Bank's jargon) within recipient countries. These DFC's then re-loaned or "on-loaned" the money to industrial establishments within the country.

Other Urban Lending

Lending for urban services of one sort or another primarily included water supply and sewerage projects, education projects, and transport. When the Bank's urban work began under McNamara, it was intended to reorient urban lending so that one-third of it would go for direct assistance to urban poverty target groups. (This figure roughly corresponded to the proportion of the urban poor in the cities of the developing world.) This meant that one-third of Bank lending for water supply and sewerage should go to these target groups, one-third of Bank lending in urban areas for education, one-third of Bank lending in urban areas for industrial development, and so on.

A unit was created within the Bank's Urban Projects Department to monitor the implementation of this effort. The unit used a concept of urban poverty lending that differed from the measurement technique of its analogous counterpart on the rural side. In dealing with the consumption side of the urban monitoring effort (such as the provision of water supply, sites, and shelters), the principal computation involved the percentage of the costs of project components that produced benefits accruing to the urban poverty target groups. (It did not measure the percentage of the benefits accrued to the poor, as was done in the rural-monitoring effort.) What percentage of project costs would produce benefits accruing to the urban poverty target groups? The answer to this question was the measure of urban poverty lending in a project. Using this measure, it was possible to make a rough assessment of the antipoverty component of urban projects. Several such projects appear to have an antipoverty component of more than 90 percent. The antipoverty component of a Kenyan project appraised in April 1975 was estimated at 94 percent; a Guatemalan project appraised in July 1976, 92 percent; and a Tanzanian project appraised in July 1977, 91 percent. On the other hand, several projects appeared to have a relatively low estimated antipoverty component: only 11 percent for a project in Thailand appraised in April 1978, only 22 percent for a project in the Ivory Coast appraised in December 1976, and only 38 percent for a project in Zambia appraised in July 1974.

McNamara's strategy to reduce urban poverty was translated into the following Bank emphases: (1) "increase earning opportunities in the informal sector" meant small-scale enterprise development, especially through credit and technical assistance, (2) "create more jobs in the modern sector" meant mainly the encouragement of less use of capital and more use of labor in productive processes, (3) "provide equitable access to public utilities, transport, education, and health services" meant making sure that lending for water supply and sewerage, transportation, and other urban services was increasingly targeted on the urban poor, and (4) "establish realistic housing policies" meant sites-and-services housing projects with reduced standards for the dwelling units, so that they would be affordable by lower percentiles of the urban income distribution, and slum upgrading, rather than demolishing the slums and relocating the thereby dispossessed urban poor.

Much of this was discussed in a document that was a landmark in any analysis of redirections in the Bank's urban work: the Interim Report on Urban Poverty, which appeared in March 1976. The document was the principal product of the Bank's Urban Poverty Task Force established in July 1975 with a mandate from McNamara to elaborate an integrated urban work program for the Bank. This document provided much of the context for the discussion that follows.

The Guiding Task Force Document

The interim report of March 1976 was sharply critical of the Bank's previous urban work. Its conclusion was that "the review of past lending has highlighted a lack of any systematic attention in project appraisal or program development to urban absorption [of the labor force], income distribution, or employment characteristics." It was found that only one-third of the urban projects from fiscal years 1973 to 1975 "provided clear evidence of [generating] substantial unskilled employment." Somewhat less than a quarter of the projects "could be said to have favorable impacts for the urban poor in improving their relative access to urban services." In only about a third of the projects, "some positive impact on urban institutions and/or policies could be deduced." The report also found a "concentration on large infrastructure and industrial projects providing little evidence of direct benefits to the poor or of direct increases in the capacity of the cities to absorb the target populations." This indictment of past Bank urban lending provided the justification for the proposed program the report recommended.

But who were the urban poor whom it was intended to benefit from new kinds of projects? The task force's analysis concluded that there were approximately 190 million people in absolute poverty in urban areas of the developing world. The important point about the target population, however, related not so much to its quantitative numbers as to its lack of differentiation in qualitative terms. The report concluded that "on the urban side we will have no equivalent of the small farmer, i.e., one fairly homogeneous group of producers with access to the basic factors of their production process." This had numerous ramifications: it meant, for example, that targeting was even more difficult in the urban areas than in the rural areas; it meant that in many instances the basic factors of their production process had to be supplied by the Bank; and it meant that the multidimensional characteristics of urban poverty did not lend themselves to one single urban strategy for the Bank.

In proposing to bring Bank assistance to bear on the absolute poor of the developing world's urban areas, the task force report established a number of targets. In the area of shelter, for example, the announced goal was to implement projects by 1980 that would service one-third of the annual increase in the squatter and unserviced slum populations. This was a modest goal; it would not dent all of the increase, and it would not dent the backlog. In the area of water supply the target was to ensure that all people within a given project area would have access to safe water and that by fiscal 1978 at least 50 percent of new personal consumption beneficiaries in any one year of a water supply construction program would be of the target population defined in income terms. The report hoped for a rate of increase in the access of the urban poor to water and sewerage of about 4 and 2 million persons per annum, respectively. Again, this was a modest goal: the report had estimated that 11 to 12 million would be added per annum to the target group, but only 4 and 2 million, respectively, would be served.

The principal conclusions of the report in terms of the impact upon Bank lending merit special emphasis. They were that "the sectoral targeting of Bank Group lending . . . would imply some important changes in the sectoral composition of the overall lending program. The main implication would be the redirection of that part of the overall program that has an urban orientation. The main features of the urban program would be a more rapid expansion of 'new style' industrial, basic urbanization, and water/sanitation lending; and to the extent that overall lending remains at presently planned levels, the holding of traditional-type projects in these sectors and in the large traditional sectors of Bank lending, transportation and power, fairly constant in real terms."

Causal Model?

Did the thinking behind the redirection of the Bank's urban work possess a coherent theoretical framework? Unlike rural development, a question mark is placed behind the causal model of urban projects. This is because the urban projects appeared to be less explicitly production oriented than the rural development projects. The dependent variable therefore was not as clear.

There were two sides to the Bank's urban work. There was a consumption side, the direct provision of shelter, sites, or water supply to the urban poor. A debate ensued within the Bank as to whether such items as shelter were really consumption goods, or whether they were not more appropriately seen as production goods, in the sense that, indirectly to be sure, they contributed to increasing the income, output, and productivity of the urban poor (assuming, of course, that they had jobs to begin with).

The unit created to monitor the implementation of the Bank's new-style urban work tended to focus on consumption. One report, for example, argued that the sites-and-services approach (the main feature of the consumption side) "was founded on the assumption that the provision of secure tenure to a plot, selected infrastructure, selected social or community services, and certain incentives to house construction would lead to improvements in the environment, the construction of better housing, some opportunities for added employment and, as a result of all these, improvements in the welfare of the affected populations." The focus was very much on welfare, with little said about income, output, or productivity.

Others at the Bank, however, strongly argued that the various components of sites-and-services projects could be expected to have a major, albeit indirect, effect upon the productivity, output, and ultimately the income of the urban poor. Community services such as health clinics could lead to improved health of workers; more healthful workers would be more productive. The same could be said for access to a safe water supply or sewerage system. The construction of dwellings could create jobs and augment incomes during the construction phase. An upgraded slum could stimulate commercial activity among the poor. All things considered, however, there did appear to be a consumption side to urban projects that was not as apparent in rural development projects. Certainly, the contribution to income, output, or productivity was decidedly more indirect.

But there was also an income side to the Bank's urban work, as implied by the relatively greater lending to sectors that tended to generate more gainful employment opportunities and by greater attention to the employment implications of specific projects within sectors. Many projects in fact were intended to create jobs. Here the contribution of a project to income, output, and productivity was direct: unemployed poor became employed, underemployed became more gainfully employed.

Impact analysis of urban projects therefore had to run in several different directions. On the consumption side the measurement of the actual delivery of sites and services and shelter could be taken as a proxy for the measurement of an increase in the welfare of the urban poor and also, very indirectly, as some measure of their increased contribution to national output. On the income side measurement was made of the employment impact of projects. The effort, however, was much more roundabout than in the rural sphere, where the measurement of incremental output, for example, appeared conceptually and analytically tighter.

Principal Features of Urban Projects

There was considerable evolution in both the consumption and production aspects of urban projects undertaken between fiscal 1973 and fiscal 1981. The earliest projects had a sites-and-services emphasis. This was followed by somewhat less emphasis on sites and services and somewhat more emphasis on slum upgrading. Then followed increased attention to the employment-generating components of projects. Today there seems to be an emphasis on some movement away from the isolated project toward more general urban programs. The interested observer investigating a typical urban project undertaken as a result of McNamara's initiatives will find the following improvements.

Sites and Services
In many of the projects sites and services was by far the largest component as a percentage of total project costs. In the first Bank project in Dakar, Senegal, for example, the sites-and-services component represented 59 percent of total project costs. In a project in Jamaica the corresponding figure was 65 percent; in the first project in Tanzania, 61; in the first project in Kenya, 52; in a second project in El Salvador, 55; and in a recent project in Thailand, 57.

Sites-and-services components were integral parts of Bank urban projects in all regions. In Africa, for example, a project in Zambia provided for the preparation and servicing of 4,400 residential plots in six sites. A project in Egypt provided about 4,600 serviced plots benefiting a population of approximately 23,000 people. A project in Tanzania prepared about 19,000 surveyed plots to be allocated to low-income applicants in five towns. In Asia a project in Thailand offered sites and services in Bangkok for about 3,000 housing units. A project in Calcutta provided residential lots and rental units for a target population of about 45,400 people. A project in Madras, India, provided 13,470 serviced plots and constructed 9,760 core units. In Latin America a project in Colombia provided 7,300 sites in secondary cities. A project in La Paz, Bolivia, developed an estimated 5,525 serviced sites with core dwelling units. In a project in El Salvador there were about 7,000 serviced lots and 3,500 basic dwellings.

There were different kinds of site options provided. These ranged from a surveyed plot only (the cheapest option, evidenced by a project in Tanzania), to a plot with a sanitary core, to plots containing various housing options. Options differed according to size of plot, size of basic dwelling, and the balance of community versus individual services. Obviously, the different options would be affordable by different percentiles of the urban income distribution.

Depending therefore upon the array of options in a given project, there would be homogeneity or heterogeneity in the social composition of the sites. Where only a surveyed plot or a plot with a sanitary core was provided, there would be little heterogeneity among site occupants. Such was the case in Tanzania. Where, however, there were more diverse offerings, there would be more heterogeneity. Such was the case in a project in the Ivory Coast.

Another difference across projects related to their varying reliance on self-help, mutual-help, or contract labor in site preparation and house construction. Some projects relied heavily on self-help and mutual-help schemes, especially after construction of the basic frame of a dwelling; others used more contract labor to meet employment objectives.

The sites-and-services component of urban projects confronted the Bank with a host of issues. One was not unfamiliar from the previous discussion of rural projects. It concerned land acquisition and titling. The land for a project usually had to be acquired from private land-holders by the government, and this frequently led to great delays and difficulties. There were also more general issues of urban land use, such as whether the project fit in with zoning regulations in the recipient country. In some instances, national building codes did not accommodate the lower-standards dwellings favored by the Bank. Institutional questions abounded, such as whether traditional housing agencies or new, perhaps nongovernmental, agencies should implement the projects. There were questions about the socioeconomic charac- teristics of the intended beneficiaries and about whether they could really afford the housing and other services provided by the projects.

Slum Upgrading

Partly because some of the earlier sites-and-services projects proved too costly for the urban poor, partly because the number of beneficiaries in sites-and-services projects tended to be small, partly because it fit better with the Bank's emphasis on realism and lower standards, there was a tendency in later urban projects to include more components for slum renovation.

This tendency was evident in some of the countries where the Bank has undertaken more than one project. In its first project in Tanzania, for example, the slum-upgrading component accounted for only 16 percent of total project costs. In the second project, approved three years later, the percentage of total costs accounted for by this com- ponent rose to 32. In the first project in Calcutta (approved in August 1973), the slum-upgrading component was only 3 percent of project costs. In the second Calcutta project (approved in December 1977), this component rose to 18 percent. In the first project in Kenya (ap- proved in April 1975), there was no slum-upgrading component at all. In the second Kenyan project (approved in April 1978), the upgrading component accounted for 19 percent of project costs.

Just as there were some prototypical sites-and-services projects, there were also some prototypical slum-upgrading projects. Most fre- quently mentioned by officials within the Urban Projects Department were two projects in Indonesia and a project in the Tondo slum area of Manila, the Philippines. The kampong improvement program in Jakarta was much celebrated by Bank officials. It represented the Bank's largest commitment by far to the concepts of slum upgrading. The level of effort entailed upgrading about 1,000 hectares per year, benefiting approximately 450,000 people annually. Jakarta, according to a Bank project appraisal report, "is the first major city which, with Bank assistance, has been able to mount a long-term program at a level sufficient to catch up with need within a reasonable period of time." In the second Bank-assisted project for the improvement pro- gram there was provision of basic urban infrastructure including water supply, human waste disposal, drainage, footpaths, and roads to 3,000 hectares of densely settled neighborhoods. This infrastructure was intended to benefit directly about 1.2 million low-income residents. Primary schools and health clinics were also provided in the neighborhoods, and a pilot program of community health and nutrition was undertaken. In the Tondo project similar components were expected to provide benefits to about 160,000 slum dwellers occupying an area of about 180 hectares.

The rationale for this was straightforward. Upgrading was seen as economically, politically, and socially less costly than slum demolition and resettlement of the affected individuals. Everyone would presumably be better off. The poor would take great pride in their upgraded neighborhoods. The government would be happy with a less costly solution to the staggering housing problems. There might be some political payoffs since the government takes credit for improving the lot of the slum dwellers (this occurred in the Philippines). The World Bank was happy; it was benefiting more of the urban poor than it could reach with sites-and-services projects. Upgrading projects also tended to be larger in terms of total project costs, thereby achieving the not unimportant goal of moving money better than sites-and-services projects.

All of this did not mean, however, that there were no issues and problems for the Bank regarding slum upgrading. There were occasionally severe relocation issues. If streets were to be widened or paved, if footpaths were to be installed, if waterborne sewerage facilities were to be constructed, some people would have to be moved to make way for the improvements. How they were moved and with what compensation were big issues. As with sites-and-services projects there was the issue of tenure and titling. The Bank did not ordinarily like to assist a project for improving people's community facilities and private dwellings unless the people had title to the property. In Brazil the Bank opted for sites and services over upgrading because, in the words of a project officer, "upgrading in Brazil is a political bombshell." In proliferating shantytowns with sometimes incredible population density, the plot demarcation that was a prerequisite of successful titling was considerably more complicated than in rural areas. An expensive, time-consuming cadastral survey was often needed. Even the entire underlying concept of land ownership was not so simple in some places; there was, for example, a highly complex system of land tenure in Indonesia, with about six kinds of tenure, not just ownership and nonownership.

Questions of community participation loomed large. There were apt to be many more community organizations in urban areas than in the rural hinterland, and they wanted some role in the determination of what was upgraded, where, how, and when. There were, in addition, issues of maintenance and recurrent costs. These were among the most contentious issues in upgrading projects, where maintenance of the upgraded facilities was crucial and where the local agencies charged with maintenance were frequently starved for funds. Another problem was that some recipient-country governments had trouble accepting the slum upgrading approach. They could see a payoff with nice new shelters, even if modest; they did not see a payoff with modest upgrading of a slum that to them still appeared grubby. Many governments wanted modernization of urban areas, and to them this implied new houses in neat rows along nicely perpendicular streets.

Urban Employment

Compared to sites-and-services and slum-upgrading components of projects, the employment components tended to be small. This applied both to funds committed and number of beneficiaries. There was, however, a trend toward the increasing importance of this component. In the Bank's first 11 urban projects, there was no component for assistance to small-scale enterprises. Such a component did not appear until the Tondo project in the Philippines (approved in May 1976), and even there it accounted for only 1 percent of total project costs. Subsequently, a component for aid to small-scale enterprises was added to 15 of 18 projects. Only in Korea (approved in January 1975) was the employment generation component the largest single component of a project (at 47 percent).

Of what did an employment generation component consist in the Bank's urban projects? In a project in Egypt (approved in June 1978) there were loans for small businesses, technical assistance and training for such small businesses, and some vocational training. It was estimated that about 1,100 jobs would be created. In a project in Tanzania (approved in June 1977) there were serviced sites for about 150 workshops, as well as credit for equipment and technical assistance to selected small enterprises, cooperatives, and artisans. The Bank's second project in Calcutta (approved in December 1977) prepared and serviced 10 hectares of industrial land and 3 hectares of commercial land and provided 50 industrial sheds. There was also a loan program of 200 to 400 loans for small-scale entrepreneurs. A program of productivity credits to small-scale businesses in a Colombian project (approved in April 1978) was expected to create about 3,800 new direct jobs. A project in Bolivia (approved in October 1977) provided for approximately 142 commercial and industrial plots to be used for artisan activities, small-scale industry, and small-scale service enterprises. These sites, all for labor-intensive, nonpolluting, and simple-technology enterprises, were expected to provide about 900 new employment opportunities for the project area residents.

Despite these features, however, all of this was the merest drop in the bucket considering the urban employment needs in the Bank's recipient countries. It was all well and good to plan to create about 9,000 new jobs in the Madras metropolitan area of India, but when it was considered that the total population of that area was about 3.5 million, the scope of the effort paled in the face of the scope of the need. The Bank's urban projects were therefore first and foremost housing projects. Employment creation was a decidedly secondary feature of such projects.

Community Facilities

Another aspect of many urban projects was a component providing various kinds of community facilities. Most common were schools and health clinics, but there was also a diversity of other features including vocational training and day care centers. The percentage of total costs devoted to such community facilities was quite high in some projects: as high as 25 percent in a project in Dakar, Senegal, and as high as 20 percent in a project in Colombia. In half of the urban projects implemented between fiscal 1972 and fiscal 1980, provision for community facilities ranged between 10 and 20 percent of project costs.

Institution Building

One of the primary goals of some projects was to strengthen the financial and managerial capacities of the institutions that were responsible for the supply of low-cost housing and general urban services.

The best example of this was the Bank's efforts with the Calcutta Metropolitan Development Authority. The CMDA was designed to plan a multitude of aspects of urban management in Calcutta, and the first IDA credit for urban development in India went toward financing various aspects of its investment program. But, according to a Bank staff member who worked on the project, the CMDA was basically not a development institution. It was rather uncharitably described as "a bunch of public works engineers out of control; all they wanted to do was build." In the intervening years, however, the Bank contributed to a significant reorganization of the management structure of the CMDA. The second IDA credit for urban development in Calcutta was intended to move into those areas of the CMDA investment program which "really appeared to form part of a system of policy, to move into those areas where the Bank could effectively disburse." This meant building up the administrative, financial, and managerial resources of the CMDA in those areas. It also meant improving the "legislative framework for urban planning." This framework was greatly improved following the passage by the government of a number of pieces of new legislation.

There were many other instances of Bank efforts at institution building in urban projects. In El Salvador there was the story of how the Bank came to be associated with a private foundation as implementing agency. In Brazil there were efforts to persuade the National Housing Bank to strengthen its capability for making loans for low-income housing. In Colombia there were Bank-induced changes in a semi-autonomous decentralized agency that acted as the country's national urban housing authority. With Bank assistance the agency moved toward the construction of social interest housing and toward an innovative loan program for upgrading in secondary cities. In Kenya there were Bank efforts to bolster the capabilities of the Nairobi City Council in this field. In the Philippines there were efforts to improve the capabilities of the National Housing Authority and, more recently, to defend it against the incursion of the newer Ministry of Human Settlements, which appeared to favor more traditional housing approaches.

Issues Raised by Basic Urbanization Projects

Out of the implementation experiences of the Bank's basic urbanization projects arose a number of issues that were closely analogous to some of the structural issues posed concerning rural development projects. One issue that figured very prominently in the assessment of these projects by observers both inside and outside the Bank concerned the basic justification for undertaking them. As in the case of rural development projects, basic urbanization projects were not seen as welfare projects by the Bank, so they were justified in terms of such hard-headed notions as affordability, cost recovery, and replicability. Every appraisal report included a section on these aspects of a project. As the director of the Urban Projects Department explained, "affordability is the key to cost recovery, and cost recovery is the key to replicability. It's as simple as that." Was it? What did this mean?

Affordability—Cost Recovery—Replicability
Since the Bank's principal justification of the new-style urban projects was that they would be more affordable to lower percentiles of the

urban income distribution than was the case with more traditional housing programs, every appraisal report on urban projects included affordability estimates. The percentile of the urban income distribution expected to be reached by varying housing options depended on the sophistication of those options. In projects with more than one option, then, there was more than one affordability estimate.

Some projects had widely varying estimates. In the first Bank project in Tanzania (Dar-es-Salaam), for example, the least expensive option was estimated to be affordable by the 14th percentile of the urban income distribution. (All such estimates assumed a certain proportion of the residents' income to be spent on shelter.) The most expensive option in the project, however, would only be affordable by the 79th percentile of the urban distribution—hardly the poorest of the poor. In other projects there was much greater uniformity in the options and thus in the percentiles reached. Such was the case in Madras, where all three options were intended to reach between the 8th and 9th percentile.

But estimates made at the time of appraisal were based on income distribution data that were not always reliable and on assumptions about the percentage of income to be spent on shelter that might not be accurate. One of the questions during project implementation therefore concerned the real affordability of the housing constructed under these projects. If the projects were in fact affordable by low percentiles of the urban poor, then project costs could be recovered. In this sense affordability was described by project officers as the key to cost recovery. The Bank desired full- or near-full cost recovery. There were mortgage payments for shelters, rental payments for leases, and user charges for services, such as water supply, provided by the project. In practice, however, there could virtually never be full cost recovery. This was certainly the case with indirect costs. There were many departures from the hallowed principle of full cost recovery. An example was a project in a very poor area of Cartagena, Colombia. There, since cost recovery measures had to be tailored to the low capacity to pay of the beneficiaries, the Bank expected only 55 percent of project costs would be recovered. Nevertheless, the goal remained full- or near-full cost recovery. The aim, frequently reiterated, was to avoid subsidies. Why?

Because the Bank associated cost recovery with replicability, projects could not be replicated if they required outright subsidies from the public treasuries of developing countries. The countries, of course, did not have the resources to finance the Bank's projects. For the Bank to be ensured cost recovery, the very poorest could not be the target group of these projects.

Urban Income Distribution

As with its rural development projects, which failed to come to grips with the issue of land tenure and suffered accordingly, the Bank's urban projects were in many ways second-best initiatives; they failed to deal with some of the main problems of the urban poor in developing countries. Although the data on the concentration of urban landholdings were not as precise as on rural land tenure, there appeared to be many roughly analogous features.

The urban income distribution, for example, is notoriously skewed in developing countries, more skewed than the rural distribution. One reason why urban land ownership is concentrated is because investment in urban real estate is a favorite speculative activity. In some countries such concentration reaches truly impressive levels. Among the countries in which the Bank has undertaken urban projects, El Salvador was perhaps the best example. Urban land-use policy moreover favors the rich. Zoning regulations in developing countries are frequently copied from developed countries and may exclude the poor from residence near industrial, commercial, and high-income residential zones that could provide them income-earning opportunities. Property taxation policies likewise favor the rich. A good example of this was in Jamaica. There, total property tax receipts in a recent year amounted to only one-fifth of 1 percent of the tax base. Over 400,000 of Jamaica's more than 450,000 landowners were completely exempted from the payment of the property tax except for a flat 30 cent payment. There were many such "Proposition Thirteens" in developing countries implementing the Bank's urban projects.

These features of urban life in countries where the Bank undertook projects had great implications for its work with the urban poor. It was difficult to escape from the world of the second best, the best solution being significant income redistribution in urban areas. With meaningful income redistribution better housing for the poor (better than sites-and-services housing) could be provided, though not necessarily on a par with more developed countries.

Bank Projects and Country Policies

Another issue raised by the Bank's project work in urban areas concerned the relationship of its programs with more general urbanization policies in recipient countries. This again parallels the discussion in the rural sphere. Were the principal emphases of the Bank's urban projects congruent with overall country policies in the countries where the projects were undertaken? The limited evidence from urban projects showed highly divergent country experiences.

In Egypt, according to the Bank, "no adequate development plan for low-income housing has been formulated, nor has the [Low-Income Housing] Fund financed such operations, nor developed a financing strategy." In Kenya, "little real progress has been made. [There has been] past preoccupation with 'acceptable standards' costing too much for the people or the economy to afford on any scale. . . . [There is a need to] find realistic solutions to problems of unauthorized settlements and actually to implement a lower standard urban shelter program on a meaningful scale." In Jamaica, "most Government houses built to date are certainly not low-income ones. Two-thirds or more of Kingston's population would not be able to service the mortgage or rental payments required on the government-constructed houses without considerable subsidization." In Calcutta, "the existing housing programs of the Government of West Bengal are small and serve mainly middle-income groups. The role of the informal business sector . . . is not well understood." In Madras, "existing . . . programs in the housing sector are primarily aimed at middle-income groups. The approach has been far from successful. Focus on costly slum clearance instead of inexpensive improvement and a lack of any significant housing programs for the lowest-income families have contributed to the continuing increase in the slum population." In Morocco, "costly design standards eroded budget provisions prematurely and rendered many housing schemes unaffordable by urban low-income groups."

To judge from other observations, in some countries, once the Bank began urban projects, this commonly described situation apparently started to change. In Morocco, for example, the new development plan for urban areas supposedly "reflects a remarkable reorientation in planning and technical approaches to urban development." Policy was also alleged to be improving in Madras. The Bank detected "a major shift in government emphasis from its highly subsidized slum clearance/resettlement program to environmental improvement in situ at a fraction of the cost." In Thailand it found "a new approach to solving housing problems in Bangkok." The National Housing Authority was alleged to be reviewing its program in order to reduce subsidies by adopting lower-cost housing solutions. In Colombia the Bank hailed "a major departure from previous government approaches to urban poverty." This consisted of a national program to alleviate urban poverty that sought to raise the living standards of the poorest 50 percent of the urban population through combined measures in various sectors.

It remains an open question, however, whether these announced changes in governmental urban policy were more than merely rhetorical. In some cases the Bank seemed to have fallen into one of its familiar habits, that of equating a country's willingness to undertake a poverty-oriented project with a wholesale change in sectoral policy in the country. The issue, however, was whether developing countries really desired to replicate these kinds of projects, whether they really wanted to translate one or two sites-and-services or slum-upgrading projects financed by the Bank into a nationwide program of popular housing options for the urban poor.

It appeared that genuine desire for this kind of replication varied greatly from country to country. The Bank pointed with pride to Indonesia and the Philippines, especially the former. But there appeared to be foot-dragging, especially on slum upgrading, in countries as diverse as Brazil, the Ivory Coast, Morocco, and Thailand. If Bank projects appeared genuinely to reorient urban development policies in recipient countries, if there was progress from a project to a program, this could be considered a real achievement. If they did not, this was, once again, the "enclave" and the "island of sanity."

The Bank's Other Urban Work

Two additional areas of Bank work were earlier identified as integral to its efforts under McNamara to assist the poor in the urban areas of developing countries. These entailed employment creation and increasing the antipoverty impact of its more traditional urban projects. No comprehensiveness is claimed in dealing with these aspects of the Bank's work here. Rather, the approach adopted is to focus on the Bank's efforts to formulate employment-creating guidelines for urban and industrial projects and to reorient its traditional water supply and sewerage lending.

The Employment Debate in Urban Poverty Lending

How should the Urban Projects Department monitor the employment-creating impact of the Bank's urban work? This question was asked within the Bank during the latter McNamara years. It led to an internal debate that was illustrative of the tensions that the movement in an antipoverty direction at the Bank entailed.

In September 1976 the Urban Projects Department issued a memorandum designed to guide the employment-generating aspects of its urban poverty program. It attempted to define concepts such as "job," "employment creation," "capital spreading," and "capital availability." Bank urban projects were supposed to create jobs, but what was a job? After much discussion back and forth within the Bank, a "job" was defined as "fifteen man-years of employment." Projects were to be labor-intensive in order to economize on the use of capital. The urban poverty monitors attempted to formulate capital/labor ratios for specific projects. The capital cost per job of a given project was to be obtained by dividing the total capital cost of the project by the number of jobs created. The ratio for an individual project was compared with a national capital/labor ratio for the entire economy. Projects qualified for urban poverty lending if the capital cost per job created was less than twice the national ratio.

The chief economists in the regional divisions of the Bank took issue with the proposed enterprise. Many conceptual and methodological objections were advanced. They argued that the proposed criteria represented sloppy economics. They alleged that the criteria ignored employment of the poor at low wage rates in processes with high average capital cost per job per year, neglected indirect employment effects, said nothing about the way in which creation of a new capital-intensive job could free a poor job somewhere else in the economy, and reflected an arbitrary definition of low capital cost. They suggested some alternative approaches for assessing employment creation. Bank management eventually requested an end to a debate that had reached diminishing returns.

A revised procedure was adopted that estimated the investment available in each country by multiplying the gross national product per capita by the investment rate that was considered normal for countries having that level. The estimated investment was divided by the country's total labor force, and the resultant figure gave a norm or index of the capital available to sustain a man-year of employment. This was then multiplied by 15 (the number of years of duration of a job) to obtain a national figure for what constituted a labor-intensive production process. The urban poverty monitors in fact attempted to formulate country-specific targets for poverty-oriented, employment-generating lending. The estimated amount of capital required to generate a job in different countries was used as the baseline for creating a job in a Bank project that was poverty oriented and labor-intensive.

There were great variations in national norms. In East Africa an Ethiopian project was to aim at creating a job with an expenditure of no more than $440 in capital. For Zambia, however, the figure was $3,170. In West Africa the range was from $410 in the Sahelian states of Mali and Upper Volta to $4,100 in the Ivory Coast. While the job-creating figure for Bangladesh was only $380 in capital, that for Korea was $6,270. In Latin America some countries had very high norms: Argentina, $16,560; Brazil, $15,290; Mexico, $13,190.

But this experimental exercise in quantitative specificity did not halt the internal debate. A subsequent memorandum evaluating the experience referred to "continued and widespread unease with the general approach to urban poverty alleviation implicit in this procedure." Program coordinators in the Bank's regional divisions were supposed to provide data on lending for employment creation to the central monitoring staff, but this obligation met with substantial resistance. Partly because the debate surrounding the various uses of the capital/labor ratios had generated a widespread conviction within the Bank that the approach represented bad economics, the reporting obligation on employment impact was never taken very seriously by staff in the regional divisions. Moreover the information available did not permit definitive conclusions about employment generation.

A Bank internal study designed to explore these questions produced extremely disappointing results. The study evaluated the extent to which fifty industrial projects financed during fiscal 1977 and 1978 had met the urban poverty program criterion, namely, the extent to which a concern about capital spreading had been articulated in the projects. It found that only one industrial project had a capital/labor ratio below a country's national norm: only one out of fifty projects qualified as meeting the monitoring goal. This was despite the fact that many of the projects were in sectors that were generally considered relatively labor-intensive. Most of the projects had capital/labor ratios that were twice or more the national norm; almost half of the projects' ratios were more than ten times the national norm.

The Bank concluded from this study that there was no evidence that employment concerns had influenced project design or choice of technology in industrial projects. "In short," according to one Bank assessment, "the analysis . . . reveals a picture that shows great preoccupation with the financial rate of return of the project and little or no concern for relative capital-intensity in either the project design or appraisal stage."

It was not clear how to account for these disappointing findings. One possible explanation was intrabureaucratic. The director of the Urban Projects Department was of the opinion that two of the Bank's six geographical regions had simply rebelled against the department's monitoring effort. This rebellion might have had something to do with the apparent failures to attain the targets.

Could something, nevertheless, be said on behalf of the monitoring effort? A senior adviser in the Bank was loath to defend the capital/labor norms of the monitoring unit on theoretical or methodological grounds. But he argued that they should be viewed primarily as a management tool. Seen in this light, their justification was functional in nature. They represented a somewhat crude attempt to move the Bank's urban poverty activities along toward their general goals. In his view they served to prod and cajole, not to prove a convincing theory.

The director of the monitoring effort was also of the opinion that at least some of the furor had been generated because the targets that were established as a result of the exercise gored the ox of many people in the regional divisions of the Bank. The findings "showed them up." They showed the great discrepancy between what should be accomplished and what was being accomplished in capital spreading and employment creation. The legitimacy of the targets had therefore to be impugned by those whose work was revealed as inadequate in terms of the stated goals of the urban poverty program.

What the Bank apparently needed was an employment paper—a Bank-wide, Bank-produced document that would clear away some of the conceptual and methodological clutter, spell out some of the principal issues, set some reasonably simple goals, and discuss some simple operational means of attaining them. It also needed to give attention to the possibility of implementing some of the recommendations of its Research Advisory Panel on Income Distribution and Employment. This panel of external experts filed with the Bank's executive directors in June 1978 a report that recommended a concerted effort to assess the direct and indirect employment impacts of the Bank's projects. The panel made the seemingly obvious observation that "it is important to find out what has been successful in reducing the pool of the jobless and partially employed and to analyze the reasons for failure as well as success." Yet the Bank had done surprisingly little in this regard. The panel also made the point that Bank research, "instead of perfecting and adapting what is a dominant mode of academic analysis, might encourage a fresh look at the heterogeneity of urban employment opportunities." These kinds of observations seemed more relevant to practical, project-specific questions of employment generation than some of the work of the Bank's urban poverty monitors or many of their critics within the Bank.

The Impact of Water Supply and Sewerage Services
The third aspect of the Bank's urban poverty work was its effort to increase the antipoverty impact of allegedly more traditional sectors

of urban lending. Some case materials·were selected from the Bank's work in urban water supply and sewerage to illustrate how an effort was made to ensure considerably more direct benefit to the urban poor than was the case before the inception of the urban poverty program. These case materials largely stem from an internal Bank assessment of all of its efforts in this regard. Preliminary results were brought together in a report that was examined for this study.

As of fiscal 1979 approximately 7.5 percent of the World Bank's total lending was estimated to be for water supply and sewerage. About 29 percent of urban water supply work was poverty-oriented (according to the percentage of the costs of such lending directly benefiting the poor), and the water supply sector contributed about 23 percent to the Bank's urban poverty program. In both fiscal 1978 and 1979 the percentage of project beneficiaries accounted for by the urban poor was approximately 42, roughly proportional to the percentage of poor in the cities in which such water supply projects were undertaken.

Personnel in the Urban Projects Department became involved in a number of interrelated efforts. These began in mid-1977 in two preappraisal missions for Bank water supply projects to Indonesia and the Philippines. These missions identified the urban poverty areas in the cities where the projects were to be located. The Bank then selected from each region a number of projects for further assistance in water supply lending for fiscal years 1977 to 1981. This produced 27 projects, distributed across all Bank regions, for urban poverty analysis and targeting assistance.

Criteria and processes for identifying the urban poverty groups and their water and sewerage needs were systematized into guidelines. Staff on a water supply mission were (1) to determine the number of people in the urban poverty group and their proportion of the population in the proposed project area, (2) to identify the location of these urban poor within the project area, (3) to identify among the urban poor who had adequate access to basic water and sanitation services and who were in need of services the proposed project could provide, (4) to estimate the impact of the project on the urban poor, including the percentage to be served by the project and the percentage and absolute number remaining unserved, (5) to indicate the amount of the proposed project loan or credit that would be attributable to the urban poor as well as the percentage of all project beneficiaries who were poor, and (6) to determine future actions required to satisfy the unmet needs of the urban poor, including future levels of Bank investment. These urban poverty guidelines and procedures were applied to several water supply prototype projects chosen by the Bank's regional divisions.

Much of this urban poverty analysis was conducted by consultants for the Bank. One of the chief tasks of these consultants was the mapping of the urban poverty population in need of access to water supply and sewerage. The effort was particularly thorough in Brazil, where maps showing the numbers and locations of the urban poor were matched with maps of existing and planned water distribution networks to determine the urban poverty impact of a proposed project. Other consultants' studies revealed that there was considerable variation among water supply and sewerage projects in terms of the percentage of project beneficiaries who were in the urban poverty population. In ten projects approved in the first half of fiscal 1979, this percentage ranged from a low of 11 (India, eight towns in Punjab) to a high of 70 (in Monrovia, Liberia). It appears that the emphasis on service to the urban poor has improved in the Bank's water supply projects in recent years.

What were some of the measures that seemed necessary to reach the poor? They were both technical and financial. The technical questions concerned alternatives to individual household connections (another example of lower standards). Additional study was needed of alternative technologies for water supply and waste disposal for the poor. The need was for project design innovations, including shared yard connections and standpipes. If the assumption was made that the technical problems were not insurmountable, there were still some difficult financial issues. The Bank seemed hoisted on its own petard here: it wanted financially viable water companies in recipient countries and cost recovery from users of water supply services, but it also wanted safe water for the poor.

The Bank under McNamara failed to face some of these contradictions head-on. If the urban poor were really to be included in a wholesale way as the beneficiaries of its water supply projects, then it was likely that governments in recipient countries would have to be persuaded to cover some water charges out of general government revenues. Or they might have to implement cross-subsidization programs, in which the rich would pay considerably more for water than the poor, and the surplus from the rich would be used to subsidize the water needs of the poor. They might have to experiment with preferential credit arrangements for the lowest-income groups, or they might have to provide subsidies to those groups for water supply and sewerage. How to reconcile the twin goals of safe water for the poor and financial viability for the water companies was probably the most difficult issue facing the Bank in its poverty-oriented water supply work begun under McNamara.

There was another familiar issue as well: in many recipient countries the public water companies were organizational disasters. This was the case with the Municipal Water Company of Lima, Peru, which was described as 50 percent of the implementation problem in an urban development project in Peru. In the Bank's first sites-and-services project in El Salvador, otherwise considered a success story by Bank staff, the agency charged with delivering the water supply for the sites was said to be guilty of "gross inefficiency."

Some of the difficulties in recipient countries that had to be confronted by the Bank's urban poverty personnel were well illustrated in connection with water supply work in Brazil. The Bank made five loans for water supply and sewerage to Brazil beginning in 1971. The latest of these loans was poverty-oriented and consisted of the expansion, improvement, and construction of water supply and sewerage systems in three capital cities, 80 medium-size cities, and approximately 300 villages—all in the extremely poor northeast. Sixty-one percent of the water supply beneficiaries and 56 percent of the sewerage beneficiaries were to be members of the urban poverty target groups in the project areas.

There were many features of the water supply sector in Brazil that did not appear conducive to the project reaching the poor. The state water companies in Brazil were not in good financial condition. As a consequence there seemed to be little incentive for them to design projects to serve the urban poor, since the poor generally would not be able to pay the full costs of the water investments and would thus require cross-subsidies from other users.

In addition water supply guidelines of the state water companies in Brazil specified individual household connections as the appropriate physical standard for urban areas, and traditionally no investment funds were provided for projects involving lower standards. As a practical matter much water supply work in the urban areas of a country like Brazil would have to be undertaken in areas of illegal squatter settlements. The state water companies were not supposed to provide water service until the local municipality legitimized the squatter community. This meant that water service generally followed the provision of electric power and a road plan, resulting in an anomalous situation whereby the state water companies would wait until roads were provided in an area and would then go in and tear them up to put in water and sewers. The state water companies historically refrained from providing water to communities before these communities appeared permanent because the companies were sensitive to the charge of institutionalizing slums. Most state agencies in Brazil required some settlement of land tenure issues before providing services. Since it was obvious that land tenure questions take a long time to resolve (recall the earlier examples from the Brazilian rural scene), it seemed equally obvious that many urban poor in Brazil would be without safe water for a substantial period of time in the future.

Such issues emerged in virtually all of the water supply projects that received detailed attention from urban poverty personnel. In Cameroon, for example, the Bank's proposal for shared yard connections was not accepted by the National Water Supply Company. The company argued that social differences in the neighborhoods of the project areas precluded the acceptance of such shared connections. In Colombia, despite a rhetorical commitment by the water supply company to implement a system of cross-subsidization on behalf of the urban poor, the government apparently did little to further this approach.

Such examples caused urban poverty personnel at the Bank to conclude that "in cases where a given government's water supply standards are too high to be affordable to the poverty group, for example, when house connections are the only method acceptable in the recipient country, Bank leverage should be employed to obtain agreement on at least an interim basis. . . . The project development period is the most pragmatically immediate point at which pressure can be brought to bear. If the project officers [the Bank's water supply project officers] are unable to exert the necessary influence on governments, then other Bank officials . . . should be called on to do so."

This implied that not all problems connected with poverty-oriented water supply work were to be found within the recipient country. Some of the more traditional water supply experts at the Bank appeared to have resisted the poverty policy emphasis. They contended, rather vigorously, that a satisfactory water supply system should be provided for an entire city—and that, if this were done, the poor would likewise benefit. Some of these traditional water supply personnel saw the "urban poverty boys" (as they called them) as somewhat woolly-headed; after all, they had never laid a pipe. Much the same tension surfaced between the urban poverty staff at the Bank and staff in traditional sectors. In one of the interviews conducted with him for this study, the director of the Urban Projects Department lamented how long implementation of the antipoverty impact goal had taken and how many difficulties had been encountered within the Bank in implementing it.

On an appraisal mission to the Philippines which received assistance from the urban poverty staff, the principal project officer in charge of the mission estimated that he spent about 20 percent of his time answering questions of the staff "because the urban poverty staff, not being engineers, required considerable explanation of the [technical] proposals. In his view [in the view of the water supply project officer], if a project officer reads all the material on poverty put out by the Bank, and if he is familiar with the Bank's philosophy, he should not need a special poverty study." On the other hand, "the water supply project officers cannot do the poverty analysis themselves. They have neither the background nor the time during the short duration of their missions to collect the necessary information and assess it."

Perhaps that is why a water supply project approved for metropolitan Manila caused a conflict between staff in the Bank's Urban Projects Department and staff in the Bank's Water Supply Department. Some of the urban poverty staff questioned whether the project did not run counter to some of the antipoverty goals of the department's slum-upgrading projects. The Manila-wide water supply project, designed by the Bank's Water Supply Department, provides "bulk supply." According to one project officer unfavorably disposed toward it, the project had "tied up a tremendous amount of the financial resources of the metropolitan government." As a consequence there was competition for resources with the Zonal Improvement Program (upgrading component) of the proposed third Bank urban development project in the Philippines. This created a sizable resource constraint for the new upgrading project. Moreover, "since they're bringing so much water in, they'll need a separate sewerage project to get it out!" In the view of some staff all of this water supply work in Manila could have been done better, especially on behalf of the urban poor, for half the cost. The debate was illustrative of the differing points of view between staff in the Urban Projects Department and staff "out in the regions."

Another part of the problem at the Bank was that some of the water supply officers had over the years developed rather cozy relationships with water supply officials in recipient countries. There had been fairly substantial agreement on the definition of the "formal city" to be served by water supply projects, the technologies to be employed, and appropriate rate structures and returns on investments of the official water supply agencies. Brazil was again a case in point. For some time the Bank and the state water companies of Brazil had agreed on a standard 8 percent annual rate of return as the appropriate return on assets for the companies. Serving the poor population in the northeast, however, required a reluctant change to acceptance of only a 5 percent annual rate of return on these assets. The poverty analysis, with its implied redirections of water supply lending, could only rock the boat. It called into question a whole institutionalized pattern of relationships between the water supply people at the Bank and in recipient countries. It was not surprising therefore that there were many sharp internal battles at the Bank over the proposed redirections.

Implementation of Urban Poverty Projects

Most of the Bank's new-style urban projects were approved after mid-1976. No project, not even one of the eleven approved before 1976, can yet offer conclusive judgments about the realization of longer-term objectives of the Bank's urban work. Nonetheless, the Bank recently engaged in a comprehensive review of its urban operations in an effort to lay the groundwork for the next five years of urban project lending. Its own assessment is that the urban development projects have had an impact at four distinct levels: (1) In some countries they have affected (favorably, in the judgment of the Bank) national urbanization policy. (2) In some the projects have had an impact on what the Bank labels "project design, planning, and investment programming." (3) In many countries there was a noticeable impact on institutional development, particularly the strengthening of agencies of municipal governments. (4) There was a more concrete impact on policies and programs in specific cities. In some instances there was a citywide impact across numerous sectors, in others such an impact in one sector.

Bank Assessments of Urban Impact

It is obviously difficult to make judgments about the impact of the Bank on national policy—in this or any other sector. But the Bank's assessment concluded that its urban lending had "changed the terms of the discussion" on urban policy in India, Nigeria, the Philippines, and Bolivia. "Impact on the policy thinking of governments has been noticeable in many countries," including Indonesia, Botswana, and Senegal. The most obvious manifestation of these changes is held to be that "publicly constructed housing, the model of the 1950s and 1960s, has given way to private investment through self-help, thereby reducing the role of the public sector." According to the Bank, a move in this direction can be discerned in Thailand, Mali, Ecuador, Brazil, Kenya, Tanzania, Morocco, Jordan, Lesotho, and Burundi. The Bank's general conclusion from this is that "many governments are now aware that, if existing obstacles such as unaffordable building codes or zoning regulations are eliminated and tenure assured, households will respond to less regulated environments by investing in urban shelter, often to an extent far beyond what their income levels would suggest possible."

The Bank's impact on project design, planning, and investment programming is more measurable. Changes in design standards have brought shelter costs way down. For example, in Nigeria in 1978 at the time of appraisal of a Bank sites-and-services project, the cheapest house financed by the public sector cost $40,000. The shelter unit in the project was estimated to cost only $1,600. In slum-upgrading projects the Bank review asserts that projects in Brazil, Botswana, Thailand, and Tanzania, among many others, have demonstrated that it is possible to design projects that reach the first decile of the urban income distribution. In Tanzania, for example, the Housing Bank has loaned about 60 percent of all its loan funds under a sites-and-services project to households with monthly incomes below $120, of which 75 percent are to those below $85. In some instances, although apparently not as many as the Bank would like, it has been demonstrated that costs can be recovered. The best example of this seems to be Indonesia, where the low investment cost of the upgrading program ($37 per capita) and the use of citywide tax revenues to finance the program have facilitated cost recovery. The Bank also claims considerable success in the matter of land tenure through its insistence that existing settlements improved by its projects be legalized. According to the Bank, "this process has occurred in almost every one of the projects having shelter components." Implementation of the Bank's approach to urban development has also allegedly resulted in some changes in the design *process*, particularly the introduction of more comprehensive urban planning.

The goal of institutional development in urban projects is that previously discussed in chapter 2, the strengthening of organizations that can act as efficient "retailers" of Bank funds. In a number of countries— including Indonesia, the Philippines, Peru, Nigeria, India, Thailand, Korea, and Brazil—the Bank is assisting municipal agencies to identify, prepare, and sometimes even appraise potential components of future Bank-assisted projects. Nevertheless, the Bank candidly admits that "it is certainly premature to evaluate the impact of urban operations on institutional development."

Impact in specific cities of the developing world is easier to see. The Bank through its projects has contributed to improved urban planning, investment programming, and urban management in two cities above all others: Calcutta and Manila. The Bank's projects, according to its own assessment, have resulted in citywide improvements that cut across sectors (housing, transport, urban services). Thus in its judgment, "The Calcutta Metropolitan Development Authority has developed as an effective investment agency," and, in Manila, the Bank's operations "have given birth to concepts such as the Capital Investment Folio which is intended to coordinate investments in the Metropolitan Manila region." Another kind of city-specific impact— what the Bank calls a "citywide, single sector impact"—is most apparent in Jakarta and Madras (India). The housing sector is the principal beneficiary in these instances. The housing impact goes far beyond Indonesia and India, however, and the estimated total number of households served by the Bank's shelter projects throughout the developing world from fiscal 1972 to 1981 is estimated at 1.9 million.

These relatively "upbeat" assessments of the impact of the Bank's urban poverty work do not imply that all is rosy. The record of interim successes is counterbalanced by a record of interim disappointments. Moreover, even when success has been attained, it has come only after a long history of struggle. The experience in fact parallels that of the Bank's work since 1973 in the field of rural development. As with the implementation history of rural development projects, that of urban poverty projects reveals many problems largely attributable to the policy and institutional frameworks within the recipient countries themselves. In other cases, as in rural areas, the Bank could perhaps be faulted for insufficient sensitivity to some issues that should have been addressed more thoroughly when the projects were being designed. The ensuing discussion, based on the Bank's own internal documentation and extensive interviews with Bank staff overseeing the implementation of urban projects, chronicles some of the main aspects of the implementation history that lie behind the Bank's partial successes and failures in alleviating urban poverty.

Major Features of Project Implementation

Problems with Agencies, Conditions, and Policies
A Bank document reviewing implementation came to the conclusion that "institutional problems persist in almost all the projects under

review and must be expected to continue to do so for a considerable time as the programs are expanded and amended." According to the report, "the institutional problem addressed by these projects is in practice much wider than the functioning of the principal implementing units or the agencies primarily concerned with program development. Important new bureaucratic routines have also to be conceived and established." These observations were abundantly borne out in interviews with Bank project officers supervising urban projects.

The Bank's work in Calcutta was a case in point. It was noted in the previous chapter that the Calcutta Metropolitan Development Authority was not a development institution at all but a loose coalition of public works engineers out of control, wanting only to build. This had a serious effect upon the implementation of the Bank's first urban development project in Calcutta. By 1976, in the words of a Bank project officer, "there was a pile of uncoordinated, unoptimized investments all over the place. The CMDA had spent $200 million without making a dent in anything." There was insufficient knowledge of how to cope with municipal growth. The legislative framework for urban planning was antiquated, and the local fiscal base inadequate. The redefinition of the project in 1976 did not really correct the fundamental problems of the CMDA, although it did make some improvements in the coordination of the investment programs. "Even today, however, the attitude around the Bank is just to get it over with, get the disbursements made, cut losses, and wrap it up. The only way that you could ever label the project a 'success' was in the sense that it was a ticket to start a dialogue to get in."

Some things about the CMDA improved under a second IDA project, others did not. A significant reorganization of the management structure of the CMDA meant that the planning directorate of the authority functioned better. The authority gave more attention to water supply work, and this proceeded fairly well. The slum improvement aspect of the second project was also considered to be proceeding well. Still, there were continuing problems with the organization; the transportation directorate of the authority was still performing poorly, as was the sewerage and drainage directorate.

The CMDA in India was not the only agency in a recipient country that presented an institutional problem. The inability of the National Water Authority of El Salvador to deliver water to project sites seriously delayed the Bank's first urban project in that country, and in the end the private foundation that was the main implementing agency for the Bank project had to build its own wells and transfer them to the water authority. Similarly, the schools, health clinics, and other community facilities of the project were all to be built by the regular line agencies of the Salvadoran government. While these were underway, they were running way behind schedule because of the formidable operational problems of these agencies.

In Jamaica problems with the main implementing agency of the sites-and-services project (the Jamaican Housing Ministry) were a major factor delaying project implementation. The project unit was short on managerial ability and not capable of adequately supervising the project's implementation. Similarly, the Municipal Water Company of Lima was described as "50 percent of the problem" with the implementation of the sites-and-services project in the Peruvian capital. It was continually in arrears to the Housing Bank in Peru, and the World Bank was skeptical about its abilities to perform under the project. In Colombia the Secretariat of Popular Integration, the main implementing agency for an urban development project in twenty-three cities, seemed mainly a political agency with inadequate technical expertise.

In Bolivia and Guatemala the agency with the official mandate for popular housing was not really up to the task. Staff turnover was a big problem. In both countries the people who appraised and approved the projects were not those in charge of implementing them. In Bolivia, for example, there were five different housing ministers in three years. Two project management units appeared and disappeared. Some of the original designs produced by the principal project-implementing agency were considered unacceptable by the Bank. They were too expensive and did not meet Bank appraisal estimates.

These kinds of problems were not only found in Latin America. In Tanzania, the site of the lowest-cost solution of all of the Bank's urban projects, the Tanzanian Housing Bank initially failed to carry through on a program of loans for building materials. As a result the intended residents could not build on the surveyed plots. The Tanzanian bank was not accustomed to making such high-risk or small loans. Nor was it initially accustomed to the kind of house to be built under the project. Another key governmental agency involved in implementation of the project was never staffed at more than 50 percent of the requisite level. This was in part attributable to the extremely low salary levels in the Tanzanian public sector and in part to the irrational allocation of manpower within the agency.

In the Philippines there was a different kind of institutional problem. The National Housing Authority, the original implementer of the slum-upgrading project in the Tondo, was formed at about the time the Tondo project was first appraised, and its director (a general in the armed forces) was seen as broadly sympathetic to slum upgrading.

Subsequently, a Ministry of Human Settlements was created which apparently had to do with the furtherance of the political career of an official close to Imelda Marcos, wife of the president of the Philippines. As a consequence the National Housing Authority was relegated to a subordinate position and acted principally as the national home mortgage authority in the Philippines. Since it was no longer autonomous, it was reluctant to push its point of view in favor of upgrading within the newly created ministry. The minister of human settlements leaned in the direction of more conventional housing options, and there were conflicts between this new minister and the general who remained the head of the National Housing Authority.

The problems in the recipient country were not always related to specific agencies. The Bank's characterization of the sites-and-services project in Peru could be voiced for other country experiences: "This is not a problem project; it is a problem country." The remorseless decline of the Peruvian economy after the approval of the project in 1976 created a host of financial problems for the implementation of all development projects in the country. The severe constraints upon government spending imposed by an IMF stabilization plan occasioned problems for local counterpart funding, and the Bank had to resort to making a program loan to Peru to provide counterpart funding for on-going development projects (not only those financed by the Bank).

The same road was lately traveled by Jamaica. Problems in the general economic and fiscal environment in Jamaica over the past several years were at the heart of the implementation difficulties regarding the Bank's sites-and-services project there. These had a devastating impact upon an already weak local construction industry. That industry, central to the implementation of the project, was characterized by no funds, no supplies, no working capital. It was little wonder that the project came to a grinding halt just before the Jamaican presidential election of 1976, that it moved on to the Bank's official problem project list, and that it was the subject of a highly critical report by the Bank's Operations Evaluation Department. Jamaica was subsequently the recipient of a Bank program loan to facilitate the implementation of development projects stalled not only by the incompetence of a particular agency but also by more general financial malaise.

"Recognition of the inherent difficulties of institutional development in this field and appreciation of the need for flexibility both in seeking immediate solutions and in developing longer-term institutional frameworks does not of course mean that the difficulties are readily overcome." This conclusion of an internal Bank report on implementation of urban projects was well supported by the case materials

stemming from interviews with project officers. The interviews reiterated the most common Bank explanation for the manifold problems
of project implementation—chronic, endemic, seemingly intractable
problems with the general conditions, development policies, and implementing agencies in the recipient countries with which the Bank
must deal.

Political Problems Affecting Implementation

A special kind of problem in recipient countries mentioned more
frequently by urban than rural project officers concerned political
developments during implementation. Urban officers were more inclined to view political factors as impinging upon implementation.

In Morocco the political issue could be phrased as "the king changes
his mind." Previous urban policy in Morocco had led to large-scale
slum demolition and relocation of slum dwellers. Moreover the housing
programs of the government were not affordable by the poorest urban
dwellers. The Bank assumed that the Moroccan government's willingness to undertake a sites-and-services project in Rabat marked a
real change in government housing polices. The king, it was thought,
had been "sold " on the concept of slum upgrading, and there was
even talk of replicating the Rabat project in some of Morocco's secondary cities. But after appraisal and approval of the loan for a project
in three settlement areas of Rabat, the king decided that the largest
of these areas would be razed instead of upgraded. This was described
by project officers as a bombshell for the Bank. The issue eventually
made its way to the Bank's senior vice-president for operations, and
a threat was apparently made to discontinue the Bank's entire lending
program in Morocco. The king relented, and the project is now under
implementation.

A decidedly unanticipated event also occurred in India. This was
the election of a communist government in the state of West Bengal
(site of the CMDA) in mid-1977. At first many of the members of that
government saw the World Bank as a capitalist, imperialist institution.
It appeared for a while as if the second IDA credit for urban development in Calcutta might be in jeopardy. But discussions between
several Bank missions and authorities in the new government apparently convinced the government of the worth of the project. Not only
did the communist government wish to implement a project financed
by the Bank; it wanted to redefine the project toward even more slum
improvement. It wanted in fact to redefine the project in a direction
the Bank wanted to move anyway. At first, a political development
involving a wholesale change of regime threatened the implementation

of an urban project. Later, it actually seemed to have contributed in a positive way toward implementation.

In Peru there was also a regime change, but this time with adverse consequences for project implementation. The Bank's first sites-and-services project in Peru was conceived at a time when the government of General Juan Velasco Alvarado was committed to policies on behalf of the *pueblos jóvenes* ("young towns," the name given to the squatter settlements of Lima by the revolutionary government). An agency called SINAMOS had been created in 1971 to oversee the delivery of urban services to the squatter settlements, assist in community development and organization, engage in a limited amount of consciousness raising, and, not incidentally, serve as a conduit for government policy directives so that the mobilization of the squatters would remain under effective governmental control.

Following approval of the project, there was an abrupt change of political regime in Peru. This saw the overthrow of Velasco by a segment of the military decidedly more conservative and with policy orientations not as congruent with the previous regime's emphases on agrarian reform, workers' control, social property, upgrading of squatter settlements, and the like. The result was that political support for the World Bank project in Peru diminished badly. SINAMOS was disbanded. The project unit was disbanded. The commitment to upgrading of the *pueblos jovenes* greatly declined. This abrupt political change was called responsible for 30 percent of the implementation problem in the project, according to the project officer most knowledgeable about it. It was also intimately linked to the technical difficulties that allegedly accounted for an additional 20 percent of the problem.

As the project proceeded to limited implementation, there was a deterioration of the technical infrastructure. This infrastructure had been largely maintained by SINAMOS and its associated network of community organizations. SINAMOS, for example, had been heavily involved in water distribution within the squatter settlements. Following its demise, much of this distribution reverted to the use of unsafe water trucks. The infrastructure of the project declined to the same extent as community organization had with a change in political regime.

The Bank's two sites-and-services projects in El Salvador raised interesting questions about the relations between the private foundation which was the chief implementing agency of the project and the Salvadoran government, not particularly known for its antipoverty policy orientations. The foundation desired that the low-income population of El Salvador "be charged with a zeal to change the hierarchical structure of Salvadoran society." From time to time the government attempted to gain control over the foundation's board of directors, but with no success. In the past several years, however, relations between the foundation and the government entered a very difficult phase. For a proposed third urban development project in El Salvador, which would be considerably larger than either of the first two, the government recommended its own Institute of Urban Housing as the implementing agency for sites and services. The government did not want any part of the foundation'in the project because of the foundation's refusal to become involved in the government's *Bienestar para Todos* ("Well-Being for All") program, which was candidly described by a Bank project officer as the government's "antipoverty publicity effort for the next five years." Some in the Bank were of the opinion that the government would probably move to scuttle the foundation altogether. The foundation is run by what was described as "the liberal wing of the local bourgeoisie" and thus a likely casualty of the increasingly deteriorating political situation in El Salvador. Such a development would be ironic, since preliminary evidence gathered by the Bank's monitoring and evaluation team in El Salvador indicates that "the low-income population seems so far to be departing from the desired result. . . . Once they have attained their more immediate goals of better housing, they seem at present to be more occupied with consolidating their gains than aiming at even higher goals."

While some nasty political developments might lie ahead for the implementation of the Bank's urban projects in El Salvador, some nasty occurrences have already taken place during the implementation of the sites-and-services project in Jamaica. Despite the problems occasioned by the general financial situation of the country and the manifest deficiencies of the main project implementing agency, overtly political problems seemed to be the main factors delaying implementation of the project. The location of a site in the Marcus Garvey area of Kingston was widely perceived by the Jamaican opposition as having a political orientation; the opposition thought that the government was elbowing into "their" area. The location of another site in Montego Bay was also in an opposition area. It suffered from chronic vandalism and "hire us!" demands by opposition young thugs. There were sporadic disturbances, including organized violence, on all project sites. Two of the sites were eventually ringed with barbed wire and turrets were placed around them. The incidents seriously tarnished the image of the Jamaican Ministry of Housing.

Meanwhile the Bank, with its preferred commitment to economic explanations for the difficulties of projects, was at a loss to account for the causes of rioting on its project sites. It hypothesized that maybe the Jamaican contractors were not paying their help, maybe the groups were organized by the political opposition, maybe the violence was attributable to very high levels of youth unemployment in Jamaica, or maybe the violence on the Bank's sites was simply a reflection of endemic violence throughout Jamaican society. While the Bank grappled with these alternative explanations, and while some residents finally moved into three of the project sites, it was undeniable that this was one project whose implementation was beset by political difficulties.

In commenting upon implementation, a Bank report stated that there were "some important limitations to the program," and added that "in large part these spring from limitations in local administrative capacity and the constraints of existing sociobureaucratic-legal frameworks." The report did not spell out exactly what it meant by these constraints. The discussion of the unilateral decision of a Moroccan monarch, the emergence of a communist government with a nominally anti-Bank ideology in an Indian state, an abrupt change of political regime in Peru, conflicts between the private and public sector in El Salvador, and an unusual degree of unexplained violence in connection with the implementation of a Bank project in Jamaica: all provided concrete examples of what might have been meant by the constraints of such frameworks.

Popular Participation in Project Implementation

In some projects the dominant political issue was that of community participation. This was an area where the Bank's own designs for urban development could perhaps be faulted. It could be argued that some of the Bank's urban projects were not sufficiently attentive to the need to involve the intended beneficiary population in all stages of the projects. Popular participation was especially an issue in connection with the frequent necessity for relocating inhabitants. The various ways in which the issue arose may be illustrated with reference to projects in El Salvador, Indonesia, Morocco, and the Philippines.

Although the king of Morocco was defeated in his bid to raze one of the settlement areas in the Rabat sites-and-services project, the project did entail a considerable amount of relocation of squatter inhabitants. The percentage of project area residents to be moved— about 30 percent—was higher than in any other Bank urban project. There were highly contrasting viewpoints in Rabat about how relocation should proceed. One was that of the national government, the other that of the elected, somewhat left-of-center municipal council embracing the squatter areas. The approach of the national government to relocation questions was described as "overly bureaucratic." The government simply wanted to inform the inhabitants in a high-handed fashion of when and where they should move. It was alleged to have done "a very poor job of public relations" with those people who would have to be relocated. The municipal council objected to this approach of the national authorities. It desired a more participatory approach in which the residents would be fully consulted on their relocation needs and desires. To further complicate matters, the municipal council was headed by a prominent opposition politician (a sociologist by profession). Conflicting approaches to popular participation in relocation were the principal factor delaying the implementation of the project.

Such participation was also an issue in the implementation of the Bank's projects in El Salvador. There were numerous agencies operating in the project area. There were two government and one private, foreign social-action organizations, plus the project-implementing foundation and the World Bank. A project officer supervising the project lamented that "the Bank had to try to organize the local residents while all of these other outfits were also doing the same thing." He referred to "tremendous institutional jealousies" among the various organizations in the project area, all of which desired to organize the squatters' participation. The multiplicity of organizations impeded efficient implementation. From the standpoint of some at the Bank, it appeared as if it would have been preferable if the issue of the participation of the beneficiaries had never arisen. In their view, it only served to "mess up" an otherwise efficient implementation process.

It was in the Philippines and Indonesia, however, that the main issues arose in connection with popular participation. The participation issue dominated the implementation of the Tondo project. There were several community participation debates in the Tondo. One concerned a subject familiar from the Salvadoran experience, competing organizational claims to representation of the residents. Organizations called *barangays* were created by the Philippine government following the imposition of martial law. In effect they served as the "king's eyes and ears." A *barangay* might contain between 500 and 800 families, grouped on a neighborhood basis. Leaders could be appointed or elected, but they were not part of any formal decision-making structure within the government. Since the Tondo area contained about 160,000 inhabitants, there were approximately 50 *barangays* within the project area.

The other side of the community organization story within the Tondo was ZOTO, the Zone One Tondo Organization. This was a popular, grass-roots organization widely perceived by the Marcos government as "antiregime and a troublemaker." It had considerable influence beyond just Zone One of the Tondo and beyond the entire Tondo area.

As the time came to implement the Tondo slum-upgrading project, of which so much had been made both within the Bank and in the Philippines, the question became: Who represented the community, ZOTO or the *barangay* leadership? The National Housing Authority, official government agency and principal implementing agency for the project, naturally claimed the latter; ZOTO, of course, claimed itself. After the Bank's annual meeting was held in Manila in September 1976, the ZOTO-*barangay* conflict got progressively worse. ZOTO organized a series of marches against a program for the widening of drainage canals. These resulted in numerous arrests of ZOTO and other leaders. There was a national uproar and the Bank "had to do all it could to harmonize the views of the conflicting sides." It even became necessary for the Bank to prepare a special report for the executive directors following the 1976 annual meeting.

While the competing organizations espoused ostensibly different approaches to slum upgrading in the Tondo, implying different priorities for the upgraded facilities and different approaches to the relocation of the inhabitants, Bank project officers were frank in alluding to the essentially political dimension of the community participation issue in the project. The real issue was competition for the political loyalties of the squatter settlers in the area. It was the antiregime ZOTO versus what were, in effect, government representatives, and the squatters were merely pawns in a game of political competition.

The Bank's approach was described as that of "leave it to the residents. Don't rely on either ZOTO or the *barangay* leaders." But leave what to the residents? The issue was that of plot demarcation or, as it came to be known within the Bank, the reblocking issue. Upgrading of communal facilities, while not involving mammoth relocation of inhabitants, involved a certain amount of moving of existing structures within blocks of the Tondo. The question concerned the extent of such reblocking; depending on the alternative upgrading methods chosen, there would be more or less reblocking. This question was to be left to the residents.

The government of the Philippines initially preferred a much more orderly approach to reblocking than that favored by the Bank. The government desired street layouts to be as regular as possible, and there were sharp differences with the Bank on this issue. In the event the decision on alternative approaches to upgrading with their associated reblocking implications was left to the individual neighborhoods within the project area. Three radically different plans for plot demarcation were presented to the neighborhoods in a voting process. (To be concise, they were: use existing layouts, use existing layouts with slight modifications, or adopt the government's plans for neatness.) Curiously enough, all of the neighborhoods picked the most conventional (and most expensive) alternative, the one with the straight streets. "Leaving it to the residents" resulted in their acceptance of the desire for neatness; this in turn meant a greater amount of moving of structures within blocks than had originally been planned, which in turn meant an increase in the costs to the residents. A project officer at the Bank lamented that this is what happens when the Bank "goes overboard" on community participation.

In the Indonesian case it did not appear that anyone "went overboard" on community participation. A project officer working on the projects in Jakarta and Surabaya, projects deemed by the Bank as virtual models of slum upgrading, admitted to significant differences concerning community participation between the Tondo and the Indonesian experiences. In Indonesia the alternative choices for upgrading were not put to the residents as formally as they were in the Tondo. Physical works were undertaken by private contractors under general directives from the municipal authorities. There was some ad hoc consultation with residents on the location of streets and toilets, but by and large the approach was relatively top-down. The Bank's designs for slum upgrading in Indonesia were faulted for this.

Allegations arose about some of the supposedly adverse consequences from such a top-down approach. Maintenance of the upgraded facilities was alleged to be poor because, owing to lack of participation, the residents felt no sense of responsibility for them. The dismissal of community input allegedly meant that physical plans were not always well formulated. Physical improvements were allegedly not coordinated with socioeconomic programs. It was claimed furthermore that the residents who had to move as a result of upgrading almost never received any compensation for the value of their homes.

In response to such allegations, the Bank took a somewhat unusual step. It dispatched a consultant to Indonesia in June and July 1978, specifically to examine community development and popular participation in the Kampong Improvement Program (KIP). The consultant's report created a stir at the Bank because it seemed to give substance to the charges. Among its contentions were the following: "The Kampong Improvement Program has been almost totally a top-down operation. . . . Neither the residents nor their elected neighborhood representatives have had any appreciable say. . . . The community participation . . . involved . . . the residents' donating labor or money for the implementation of some project which was determined from above. No input from below was obtained in the planning stages — no options were presented as to level of services, location of facilities, or timing of construction. No choice was even given as to whether the neighborhood wanted KIP or not; and in many cases the residents and their leaders were not even informed that there would be a KIP program in their area . . . there is no incentive to share power or involve local people. . . . Since the people were never involved or consulted from the start, they see the project as an imposed package and take a passive stance in terms of preserving its components."

Bank officers reacted vigorously to these assertions. While it was generally agreed that the approach to participation in the project was top-down, it was felt that the consultant had overstated the case by a considerable factor. The officers did not feel that the problems were anywhere near as serious as the consultant alleged. Even if they were, however, it was considered a highly debatable proposition that more community participation would serve to alleviate them. The consultant was merely offering textbook remedies.

The point here is not to resolve this particular debate between Bank staff and one of the Bank's consultants. The point rather is that community participation should not be simplistically viewed as either a panacea or an obstacle to the implementation of urban projects. The experiences recounted from Bank projects in Morocco, El Salvador, the Philippines, and Indonesia indicate that the Bank could stand to give more attention to questions about the preconditions, strategies, and consequences of community participation in its urban projects.

Land Tenure, Titling, and Acquisition
A Bank report on implementation gave rather short shrift to the interrelated issues of land tenure, titling, and acquisition. "Unexpected difficulties in completing land acquisition" were briefly mentioned in conjunction with a number of factors impeding the implementation of projects. In fact the matter was much more serious than this. Land-use issues were almost as prominent in histories of the implementation of urban projects as in histories of rural development projects. The Bank did not adequately foresee the importance of urban land ownership issues for the effective implementation of its urban projects.

In a sites-and-services project in La Paz, Bolivia, 20 hectares of land were supposed to be acquired by the government. But a thoroughly unexpected development was the proposed expansion of the La Paz airport, which took away about half of the originally intended land for the project. This necessitated purchases of land by CONAVI, the implementing agency for sites and services, to a totally unforeseen extent. The problem of land acquisition continued well into project implementation.

In El Salvador land acquisition ranked with the provision of water supply as the major problems of the implementation experience. Land in El Salvador generally, and in San Salvador in particular, was extremely concentrated. In the project areas of the first Bank urban project, only a few individuals owned the land required for the sites. They did not want to part with the properties, which were excellent speculative investments. As a result of the sobering land acquisition experience with the first project, it was stipulated in the Bank's loan agreement for the second project that the Salvadoran government would acquire all project sites. In the San Salvador metropolitan area, at least 40 of the 100 hectares required were to be purchased by May 1977 and the remainder by the end of the year, "if necessary by expropriation."

In an earthquake reconstruction project in Guatemala, there was a "horrendous time" with land acquisition. Likewise the land acquisition for the sites in a three-cities project in Brazil was an unresolved issue; "they're still negotiating in São Paulo." The Brazilian government was extremely reluctant to adopt a slum-upgrading approach on any significant scale because, with upgrading, "the biggest issue is land tenure." This was why upgrading in Brazil was earlier referred to as "a political bombshell."

In the Tondo project, "land tenure was always the key issue; you had to deal with it." Approximately one-third of the inhabitants of the Tondo had titles to their properties at the time the project began. The land was all government-owned land that had been reclaimed from the sea, but the majority of the inhabitants did not have titles to it. The project was to provide titles to all those present and "tagged" in the project area as of 1974. The plot demarcation necessary in the titling process was a tough issue. Titling was still not complete at a very late date in the implementation of the project. Indeed a very distinctive feature of the Tondo project was that physical works proceeded without the definitiveness of land titles for many of the inhabitants. The residents were simply confidently assuming that titles would eventually be forthcoming. If they were not, the Philippine government would have on its hands an enormous case of frustrated expectations.

Africa also provided its examples of these kinds of issues. Land acquisition problems were the first to confront the implementation of the Bank's urban project in Morocco. It was prescribed by the Bank that there would be no disbursement on its loan until the government acquired the necessary land. There was a land expropriation decree in Morocco, but it entailed extremely complex adjudication procedures. Land problems were not limited to acquisition. After acquisition came plot demarcation with its demands for costly cadastral surveys. The project established a threshold size for a viable plot (25 square meters). This was one of the reasons why a large percentage of project area residents had to be relocated during implementation.

In a project in Abidjan, the Ivory Coast, similar issues substantially delayed progress. It took two years for the project to resolve the many problems of plot demarcation. The Abidjan project involved an unusual social aspect to the demarcation issue. Many of the immigrants to Abidjan in the decade preceding the project were non-Ivorians, mainly former residents of the impoverished countries of the Sahel. As a consequence there was a very large non-Ivorian population in the slum areas to be upgraded under the project. This raised the issue of whether to award permanent title to urban property in the Ivory Coast to someone who was not even a citizen of the country. The debate over this thorny question also contributed greatly to a slowdown in project implementation.

The examples indicated that the Bank would have to exercise greater leverage over recipient countries on land acquisition—perhaps making such acquisition a condition of loan effectiveness, if necessary by expropriation. It would also have to provide larger amounts of funds within its urban project loans for technical and other forms of assistance to official land agencies in recipient countries, for cadastral surveys, perhaps for pilot land-banking arrangements—in short whatever was required in the herculean task of acquiring land and equitably distributing it for the intended beneficiaries of its urban projects.

Dislocation and Resettlement of Inhabitants

Just as some rural development projects entailing irrigation required that area inhabitants be moved, slum-upgrading projects involved a certain amount of dislocation and resettlement. The widening and paving of roads, the installation of footpaths and drainage canals, and the construction of other community facilities inevitably disrupted existing housing.

The extent of this varied greatly from project to project. In Rabat approximately 30 percent of the residents of the squatter areas had to be relocated. Either the size of their plots was below the threshold for plot viability established by the project, or they were in the way of a proposed road through the area. In Abidjan relocation involved less than 10 percent of the total project area population. Relocation was relatively small because most of the existing grid network was already in place at the time implementation began. In the Tondo the Bank was successful in requesting the government of the Philippines to scale down original plans which would have involved considerable relocation. Only about 2,000 families had to be completely uprooted and relocated. In a project in Cartagena, Colombia, relocation was expected to involve about 7 percent of the total number of families in the area. Bank staff considered this a more or less standard percentage for the Bank's urban projects.

The matter may be discussed in more detail with reference to the Bank's large slum-upgrading project in Indonesia. While providing no quantitative evidence on the extent of the phenomenon, a consultant's report dealing with this matter pretended to find some prevalent difficulties. Cases were discovered in which people's homes were to be totally removed owing to the widening of a road or the construction of a school or other public facility. According to the consultant, the number of people to be displaced in this manner was grossly under-estimated: there was no community involvement in the locational decisions regarding roads or other facilities and no opportunity for dissent among those affected by relocation. It was further alleged that the affected families almost never received any compensation for the value of their homes, and ended up moving to kampongs of much worse quality nearby or on the urban periphery.

There were also alleged to be problems occasioned by space reduction of homes due to road widening. It was deemed "a very common occurrence" in all kampong improvement projects for houses to be reduced by one to three meters in front as access ways were widened and canals installed. According to the consultant, there was to be no compensation for this on the grounds that the increased value of the owner's property as a result of the improvements would balance out any cost or inconvenience of rebuilding their front walls and reducing the internal space. What distressed the consultant was that many families thus affected had allegedly never been informed of what would be entailed with upgrading or even of the intention to undertake the project at all. "Many learned about it the day the bulldozers appeared at their front door." This may have been hyperbole. Bank project officers claimed that there was compensation in cases of total dislocation, although they did not challenge the assertions about no compensation for space reduction due to road widening.

Affordability and Related Issues

Much of the documentary evidence produced by the Bank in assessments of project implementation tended to focus on the question of affordability. There is some evidence that the Bank's project designs may have been excessively optimistic about the ability of intended beneficiaries to afford improvements rendered by the projects. One assessment acknowledged that the speed of housing consolidation and the standards of interior furnishings acquired by the residents raised the question of whether the sites in some projects were in fact occupied by somewhat higher income groups than had been targeted. The report concluded that there was little evidence of a clear pattern in this regard, although "there may be biases toward the upper end of the target group."

Another report, however, was a bit less sanguine. In several of the countries studied, it was found that many of the housing units in the Bank-financed projects had in fact been occupied by families with incomes higher than originally intended by the Bank. In some instances this was an unexpected result; in others it reflected a deliberate decision by the governments to satisfy the demands of middle-income groups. Sites-and-services projects were readily acknowledged by the Bank to be considerably more expensive than upgrading projects, and the report stated that sites-and-services projects "are almost always inaccessible to the lowest-income families." Although in general it appeared that upgrading was more affordable, there seemed to be some initial evidence that even a substantial proportion of families in upgrading projects could not afford the payments for improved service levels. Under many projects surveyed, the costs of the houses constructed appeared to be considerably higher than had originally been estimated.

Evidence from specific countries was skimpy; most of what existed consisted of data on *ex-ante* affordability projections. Some monitoring was done in a few countries, however, particularly in El Salvador. The appraisal report for the first sites-and-services project in El Salvador had expressed a desire that all project participants come from the first to the fifth income deciles. According to information gathered from the Bank's evaluation, it was found that 63 percent of project participants on one project site and 93 percent of those in a second project site fell within this income class. However, only 13 percent of the participants in the first site and 17 percent of those in the second site belonged to the poorest of the poor; the first and second income deciles.

One report exclusively devoted to the question in El Salvador concluded that project costs of a typical family were higher than originally expected by project designers, so that the projects reached down only as low as the 25th percentile instead of the 17th percentile as originally planned. Another report on El Salvador concluded that "the project apparently does not 'reach' the poorest 20 percent of the population."

An additional country considered in some detail by the Bank was Senegal, because Dakar was the location of its first sites-and-services project. There, of the 400 households that had started construction under the project, only 187 had been selected according to the established criteria, the rest having been allotted plots at the "informal discretion" of the implementing agency. Of these 187 households only about half fell within the target population defined by monthly household income.

A third country that was the subject of detailed monitoring was Zambia. The project selection criteria stated that half of those selected for serviced sites would have average monthly incomes of $26 to $90, and half would have monthly incomes above $90. Things were apparently moving reasonably close to the mark; the evaluation team's figures indicated proportions of 42 and 58 percent for the two income categories, respectively.

Three cases—El Salvador where there was a relatively slight departure from affordability estimates, Senegal where there was a more marked departure, and Zambia where there was reasonably decent approximation—did not add up to a trend. They did, however, provide warning signals, and in interviews with project officers additional evidence was sought.

The deflection of benefits away from intended beneficiaries was of considerable concern in the implementation of a multicity development project in Colombia. There was a concern that the middle-income groups in the municipalities would push out the intended lower-income beneficiaries from the day care centers, health clinics, and vocational training centers being constructed. This appeared to be happening with the day care centers provided by the project. Use of these community facilities could not be targeted; Colombian law provided that all such facilities had to be open to everyone in the municipality. There could be no discrimination against the well off.

The core units built under the shelter component of the Bank's first urban project in Korea, which demonstrated that there were viable alternatives to walk-up flats that could be afforded by the poor, proved extremely popular with the residents of the project area. This was reflected in the fact that applications under the project outran the sites and units available by a ratio of three to one. ("Demand has not been a problem," states a Bank report on the matter. "Only in two or three cases of small individual components of the site programs has there been an insufficiency of applicants with the right credentials.") There was a problem with the shelter component, however. The people moving into the houses built under the project had higher incomes than the Bank had planned. The project had a cross-subsidization feature, however. The government bought the land for the project. Forty percent of this land, once developed, was sold to anybody in individual parcels. From the sale of these parcels to anybody, no matter what their income, the entire land development was financed. This translated into developing for free 60 percent of the land for low-income plots. Such cross-subsidization was to be found in some form in many urban projects, but it was a particularly large feature of the Korean project.

Why was it difficult for the Bank to reach the intended beneficiaries? What were some things the Bank did not adequately foresee? One factor seemed to be that in some cases a higher percentage of household income had to be spent on housing and related services than was anticipated when the affordability estimates were established. Another factor was that, where residents had the choice of several different options for plot sizes and dwelling units, they almost invariably chose the most expensive options presented. This was seen in the Tondo, and something similar occurred in El Salvador. There it was apparent that the residents in the project area desired higher standards than the Bank planned on providing or than could be justified on affordability grounds. At one point some of the residents petitioned the president of El Salvador for individual flush toilets for their new residences. A third factor related to the high-standard official building codes in effect in many recipient countries. Such codes were an issue in El Salvador. In Tanzania and some other countries the problem was with official codes prescribing high minimum standards for road construction.

An additional factor deserves mention all by itself. This, again analogous to the situation found in many rural development projects, concerned the escalation of land values as implementation proceeded. In the Guatemalan earthquake reconstruction project the usual land acquisition difficulties were vastly complicated by the enormous inflation in land values after the earthquake. According to the project officer working on Guatemala, "this is a major problem in all sites-

and-services projects, anywhere; it wreaks havoc with appraisal esti-mates of affordability." Other countries provided similar examples. In Brazil, "a key problem . . . will be the expected inflation of land values as people in the area learn that the Bank is coming in." In the Philippines, land value in the Tondo was about five pesos per square meter at the time the project began. Several years later it was estimated at about 270 pesos per square meter. With the delays in titling, and thus in the purchasing of titles, they became considerably more ex-pensive as each day passed. What price, then, would the residents have to pay for their titles? According to one of the Bank's project officers working on the Tondo project, President Marcos agreed to grant title to the land at the original price of five pesos; at this price the land was a giveaway. This appears to be a rare event, however.

Indonesia was once again an illustrative case. There, turnover of properties due to increased value as a result of the Bank's upgrading projects was, in the words of a consultant, "an extremely controversial matter for which there are no reliable data or documentation on either side." Some critics of the projects contended that there had been a massive replacement of the poorest people by wealthier people in the upgraded kampongs. There is no doubt that the installation of new roads, paved footpaths, electricity, and water taps, as well as the de facto recognition of rights to land use, made the upgraded kampongs much more attractive to a higher-income group. One consultant re-ported that rents in some of these kampongs had gone up considerably, allegedly by 13 times in one case and 50 times in another, and that many renters had left. (Bank staffers disputed the evidence.) On the displacement of owners, little definitive could be said. Some reports of the project unit indicated about a 5 percent turnover in home registration as project implementation proceeded, but the data were undoubtedly unreliable since many transfers of property went unrecorded.

While escalation in land values as the result of project works might make controlling affordability problematic, it did have a kind of para-doxical effect in some of the numbers games at the Bank. Escalation of land values after project implementation could, curiously enough, increase the rate of return of a project. A higher rate of return at a sacrifice of affordability remained, nevertheless, a vexatious matter. There were those at the Bank who demanded that poverty-oriented projects show rates of return as high as more traditional projects, and they held firm their position against those who demanded that poverty-oriented projects reach the very poor, especially the poorest of the poor, in urban areas. It did not seem possible to have it both ways.

Cost Recovery

Problems with affordability led to problems with cost recovery. One Bank assessment concluded that "obviously, more needs to be done to improve collections of monthly charges from site occupants and/ or develop alternative financing sources. Otherwise affordability cannot be equated with replicability."

In Tanzania the problem with cost recovery was with the Land Rent and Service Charge Act. Cost recovery was more or less adequate in the sites-and-services areas, but the act completely ignored the squatter areas. It provided for no charges at all in these areas. Consequently, in the upgrading areas of the Bank's first urban project in Tanzania, there was no cost recovery whatsoever. For a second urban project, which was virtually all upgrading, the Bank impressed upon the government the strict necessity for better cost-recovery mechanisms. But the government, despite Bank protestations, refused to adopt a 100 shillings annual charge for each dwelling in the areas being upgraded. Because of the refusal of the Tanzanian government to institute even minimal cost-recovery mechanisms, the Bank refused to proceed with a proposed third urban project. The two parties were at loggerheads on the cost-recovery issue.

In the multicity project in Colombia, a Bank project officer asked: "What are the implications of the project for recurrent costs? Will it require income transfers forever?" In his view, "there is a very large danger of arrearages on loans for home improvements" if at the same time little or nothing was done on the income and employment side. There was little in the way of solid evidence on cost recovery in this project. It was too early to tell. It was also too early to tell in the Cartagena project in Colombia, although it seemed certain that the project would stop short of full cost recovery. This was mainly because of a loan program begun in Colombia in 1976 which provided subsidized loans at an unindexed 12 percent rate of interest. The local bureau of the Institute of Territorial Credit, the main implementing agency for the project, proposed whole neighborhoods as candidates for these loans. Cost recovery on the loans was deemed inadequate, and this clearly had implications for the financial status of the institute. Since it was changing its portfolio more in the direction of these loans, it would have to rely increasingly on transfers from general government revenues.

A project in Bangkok, Thailand, appeared to be another where there could be some difficulties with cost recovery. Project officers were of the opinion that "there are formidable problems with regard to cost recovery and thus replicability." Indeed this was cited as "easily the biggest problem with this project." On the private land in the project area there was no "legal vehicle" for recovering costs. On the public land the residents had a reticence to pay for services they felt were being provided free of charge elsewhere in the city. In Indonesia the Bank attempted to deal with these problems through a betterment tax.

Documentary materials examined at the Bank all reflected some concern about cost-recovery matters. Studies of the monitoring and evaluation units in the Bank's Development Economics Department concluded that there was concern about collections. In some of the projects studied by the monitors there was found to be a high default rate, and the monitors expressed concern that the same could happen in other projects once payments came due. It was their view that "this is potentially one of the most serious barriers to the replicability of the model on a larger scale." Much of the concern seemed to stem from the record on defaults in projects in Senegal and Zambia, particularly the latter.

Not all was amiss with regard to cost recovery, however. Another Bank report called the record on collection of charges "very varied," and pointed to projects in El Salvador and Kenya as examples where bad debts were minimal and well below expectations. Another report, completely devoted to interim findings concerning the first Salvadoran project, found that the foundation implementing the project had experienced a relatively strong collection position, with a very low percentage of arrearages.

Many explanations were sought for recovery difficulties. In some countries there were simply long-standing traditions of the nonpayment of public charges. In others there were staffing problems or poor bookkeeping practices, or opposition from the residents because of the late or partial delivery of certain planned services, or delay in the issuance of formal tenure documents so that the price of the property escalated in value with attendant implications for repayment, or no legal basis for sanctions. These factors, again largely unforeseen when the Bank formulated its designs for its urban projects, had numerous implications for its future work. The Bank would have to devote more attention to clearing away legal difficulties in advance of tenure allocation, the staffing of collection units, and agreements with recipient countries on procedures for follow-up and sanctions (including eviction, if necessary) in cases of nonpayment.

Maintenance
Closely related to issues of cost recovery were some issues concerning the maintenance of the facilities provided, particularly in upgrading

projects. If such facilities were costly to maintain, there was a question of whether the residents or the government would maintain them. According to one report, "experience of actual performance demonstrates that understandings, particularly related to maintenance, are often not fully carried out." According to another report, "although most of the projects are still very new, there is a concern about the future maintenance of infrastructure and community services. Many projects have low levels of services (communal standpipes, open drainage or sewerage channels, unpaved roads, etc.) and rapid deterioration can take place." In an interview with a senior adviser in the Urban Projects Department, he professed to be "very concerned" about this aspect of project implementation.

An example contributing to such concern came from the maintenance of infrastructure, particularly of roads, in the Bank's urban projects in Tanzania. The city administration of Dar-es-Salaam was responsible for the maintenance of roads, but it apparently was not doing its job. The Bank went to the Tanzanian government with a request for a line item in the budget for roads. Failing such a line item, there would be no more infrastructure provided from Bank funds. One of the problems was a legacy from the colonial era known as the Street Adoption Act. Under its terms the city engineer only had to repair a road if the road had been built according to certain prescribed standards. Since the roads constructed under the Bank projects in Tanzania were lower-standard roads not built to the standards of the Street Adoption Act, there was an additional problem for maintenance.

A sites-and-services project in Kenya experienced similar difficulties. Some Bank project officers "suspect that other projects may also be facing this problem." A more technical question arose in Kenya. A lower-standard road implied completely different maintenance requirements from a higher-standard road. Moreover maintenance requirements for the lower-standard road could well be more costly. The Bank did not seem to understand the trade-offs between the low construction costs of low-standard roads and the high recurrent costs of maintaining the roads (and, more important, the prospect of no maintenance at all, thereby leading to the virtually total loss of investment).

Another issue concerning maintenance was the role of popular participation in the process. A Bank report argued that some of the maintenance difficulties in projects had to do with the relatively low level of community participation in them. The problem, according to this report, was that "many communities do not feel a responsibility for maintaining the services." The principal empirical base for this assertion came from Indonesia, where it was claimed by a consultant that the residents in project areas "were never involved or consulted from the start." Because they were not, they viewed the project as an "imposed package" and took a "passive stance in terms of preserving its components." Nor was the government any better at maintenance. It saw its primary task as that of building the project facilities, not maintenance.

Whatever the reasons, the consultant's report painted a dreary picture of the situation in the Indonesian project areas: "One of the most striking features about the Kampong Improvement Program is how poorly maintained the project has been. Drainage canals are filled with garbage and sewerage; footpaths are collapsing around the edges; garbage is uncollected and overflowing; many water stands are broken." Project officers working on the Indonesian projects did not dispute the fact that there were some problems with maintenance of facilities. The main concern of these officers was with garbage. They admitted that there was some evidence that the drainage canals in project areas were getting clogged with garbage. They questioned, however, whether whatever maintenance difficulties existed were really attributable to lack of community participation in the project.

Unanticipated Developments during Implementation

There were many unanticipated developments as the implementation of projects proceeded, but not all of them were consequences of the projects. In this category of developments may be placed the taking of land for a sites-and-services project in Bolivia by airport expansion, the king's changing his mind in Morocco, the entrance of a communist government in West Bengal, an abrupt change of political regime in Peru, and so forth. Other developments were more the consequence of project implementation. Here were found the emergence of political vandalism in Jamaica as the consequence of locating sites in areas of the political opposition, maintenance problems with roads in Kenya and Tanzania as a result of the project's construction of low-standard roads, or the abrupt escalation of land values as people near project areas learned that "the Bank is coming in." Many of these consequences could not have been totally foreseen by the Bank when the projects began.

El Salvador provided a particularly good example of the unanticipated and unintended. The main finding of the monitoring and evaluation effort of the Salvadoran projects is that more hired, contract labor was employed than had originally been expected. In El Salvador much had been made by the implementing foundation and in the Bank's appraisal reports about mutual and self-help. The mutual help aspect of the projects, however, did not go as anticipated. Many families were unwilling or unable to participate in mutual help construction activities. In one site area, for example, 100 of 240 families selected for the project eventually dropped out of it. Nearly two-thirds of these families gave difficulties in participating in mutual help on workdays "as the main or a contributing reason for their dropping out." The opportunity cost of labor in mutual help schemes was evidently far from zero. Many preferred, or were required, to work on weekends rather than engage in mutual help activities. Mutual help also had high time costs. The construction process using mutual help took 20 percent longer than had been planned, occasioned by an average of 15 percent absenteeism, the participation of fewer families than had been planned, and deficiencies in training the mutual help workers.

Another unexpected finding in El Salvador concerned the number of households that had a female household head. In the main site area of the projects, fully 40 percent of participating households were headed by a female. This created certain problems for implementation, since these households tended to have less stable incomes than male-headed households. Also, since female wages in El Salvador were legally lower than male wages in many occupations, and since the range of job opportunities open to women was much more limited, various problems were created for the employment generation components of the projects.

Still another unexpected finding was the lack of competitiveness of project housing in comparison with nearby illegal subdivision housing. In the area of one of the project sites it was found that only 18 percent of families sampled in illegal subdivisions (which contained 30 percent of the area population), and 40 percent of those sampled living in rented rooms (which contained 45 percent of the area population) were willing to participate in the project after the price, size of proposed unit, and mutual help process were explained to them. The others preferred staying where they were. Additionally, families with rural backgrounds appeared to prefer a larger plot size with lower level of services to the reverse option. Both of these findings caused the foundation and the Bank to consider alternative plot and house designs.

Monitoring and evaluation also revealed that participants in the project had a lower level of political consciousness than other low-income families. They appeared to have a lower level of awareness of the existence of social classes and a lower level of identification with a social class than did other low-income families. Perhaps participants saw the project as a way of achieving individual mobility and were decidedly less concerned with class identification. For some people the project was seen as a means of breaking away and identifying with a new group of people. These conclusions about social mobility were of great concern to the private foundation that was the implementing agency of the project, since a basic part of the foundation's philosophy was that the project should be a means to stimulate a process of social and political consciousness raising rather than an end in itself.

All of these unexpected developments had implications for the design of future urban projects, and not only in El Salvador. If contract labor was really more important than mutual help labor in the construction process, and if there was consequently more employment generation during the construction phase than had been anticipated, the Bank might consider imposing employment requirements on local contractors in order to ensure that low-income persons, and especially project participants, receive positions during this phase. Alternatively, some of the features of the mutual help process, such as the requirement for mandatory work on weekends, could be modified. Regarding female heads of households, special attention would have to be given to developing small-scale enterprises tailored to the special circumstances of these families. The apparent lack of competitiveness of project housing required greater attention to alternatives to serviced sites — in particular rented rooms or larger plots with fewer services. If consciousness raising was really desired, there would have to be much greater attention to local community development organizations, the use of social promoters, the preparation of informational materials, and so forth.

From Projects to Programs

Some rural development projects seemed to have had an impact beyond the confines of the individual projects with respect to goals congruent with national or sectoral policy. Some similar observations can be made regarding urban projects.

Bank project officers rated Indonesia and the Philippines as clear success stories. According to them, the fundamental concepts of slum upgrading became widely accepted in Indonesia. In this acceptance the implementation of the first two Bank projects played a key, if not determinative, role. The projects followed policies already undertaken in Jakarta since 1969, but they helped to tilt the whole national low-income housing effort of the Indonesian government in a desired direction.

Project officers claimed much of the same achievements in the Philippines. The third Bank urban project in the Philippines, a large upgrading project for much of the rest of Manila, was taken by the Bank as evidence that the Philippines was going national with slum upgrading, much as Indonesia had done. The situation was not as unambiguous as it apparently was in Indonesia, but the achievement was nevertheless claimed—doubtlessly with some justification.

There were certain less obvious examples of the phenomenon. In Korea, the shelter component of the Bank's first urban project demonstrated the viability of an alternative to walk-up flats. Such flats had previously dominated Korea's approach to questions of popular housing. The Koreans appeared increasingly to be opting for the kinds of housing provided in Bank projects as a matter of national policy. In Jamaica the Bank may have been successful in persuading the government to adopt an approach to low-income housing that would entail the construction of 14,000 one-bedroom, inexpensive shells as an alternative to three-bedroom, contractor-built models.

These and other examples seemed to give substance to a Bank report which claimed that "the basic approach incorporated in the Bank's program has been increasingly adopted by developing countries as an alternative to slum clearance and 'low-cost' housing schemes which, because of the heavy subsidies involved, could not possibly meet even a fraction of the needs of the urban poor. In this change of attitudes, the World Bank's program has played a leading role. Moreover in almost all the countries with Bank-assisted projects the initial projects are now leading to much larger-scale programs on a multicity regional or national scale."

Yet, despite these claims, numerous Bank initiatives were not as readily embraced as those of Indonesia and the Philippines. In Morocco, for example, while there appeared to be a desire on the part of the government to replicate projects similar to the Rabat project in secondary cities, it was not disposed toward introducing new concepts desired by the Bank, such as moving toward a more comprehensive policy of urban land use, seeking to identify the urban poor not resident in the squatter settlements, or undertaking projects that would result in a net addition to the housing stock. Apparently, the king decided that he would buy the sites-and-services and slum-upgrading projects for some existing settlements throughout Morocco, but he did not want things to get out of hand.

Similarly, in Brazil there was some movement toward low-income housing under the regime of General Ernesto Geisel. Terms and conditions of low-income housing loans were redesigned in 1974. A whole new program of lending for low-income housing was created. Still, it was not enough; it did not really reach the urban poor in Brazil. In this context much was made of a Bank project for sites and services in three large Brazilian cities. The sheer size of the project and its multicity nature seemed to give the appearance that Brazil was going national with sites and services, that there had been a significant redirection in Brazilian low-income housing policy. Nevertheless, a project officer working on urban projects in Brazil cautioned against taking the project as evidence of a "wholesale reorientation of Brazilian housing policy." It was, in his words, "far from that."

The evidence for such a wholesale change of approach was limited in the Ivory Coast as well. There the concept of sites and services was nothing new. It dated back to 1915, or thereabouts. Slum upgrading, however, was a new concept. On this, according to Bank project officers, the Ivorians were "very reluctant." They refused to upgrade certain areas of Abidjan, and a compromise was struck with the Bank. They complained about the cost of upgrading, about what they saw as the worthlessness of existing structures, and—worst of all in their view— about the fact that the upgraded areas would not look modernized even after they were done. For these and other reasons there apparently was no great enthusiasm for replication of slum-upgrading projects in the country.

There was a mixed bag in Thailand as well. On the one hand, there was a clear desire on the part of the Thais to replicate the sites-and-services aspect of the pilot project in Bangkok. This they wished to do unambiguously. But there was no such clear desire regarding the upgrading component. The apparent cost-recovery problems into which the pilot project ran raised questions for the Thai government about the replicability of the project. Similarly, the extension of the sites-and-services and upgrading projects in Tanzania ran into difficulty as a result of conflicts with the Bank about cost recovery and related issues. In El Salvador there was a problem with the high-standard building codes in effect. Project officers stated that in the preparation work for a third urban project in El Salvador the Bank was in effect "rewriting the codes." But whether these lower-standard codes would be accepted by the Salvadoran government, and therefore become the basis for a whole new approach to low-income housing policy in that country, "remained to be seen."

New Trends in Urban Lending? The Bank's Own Critique

As did the analysis of the implementation experience regarding the Bank's rural development projects, the record of that experience in

the urban sector reveals a mixed bag of problems, obstacles, potentialities, and successes. The problems and obstacles were attributable
to both conditions within recipient countries and some failings in the
Bank's own designs for urban development. In effecting some kind
of balance sheet of the Bank's poverty-oriented urban work, it was
particularly useful to obtain the impressions of the Bank staffers responsible for its implementation.

The Bank's urban poverty work discussed here was continuously
evolving over the last several years. In their own assessments of that
work, many Bank staff offered observations about the past and suggestions for the future. These emerged from a wide-ranging round
of interviews with staff at all levels of urban work. They showed a
realization that the Bank can make its own mistakes, that by no means
can all of the problems with its urban poverty program be attributed
to the recipient countries.

Many staff, for example, raised the question of whether a housing-
based approach really went to the core of the urban poverty problem.
Many were not sure that housing was the main issue. The skepticism
was frequently voiced in graphic terms. One project officer wanted
to know: "After you do all this [sites and services and slum upgrading],
what's the guy got? Nothing." The questions also extended to some
of the community facilities provided in urban projects. A project officer
working on Colombia questioned the feasibility of training people in
Bank urban projects for the kinds of jobs for which there is little
demand in that country. "What happens if you train people for jobs
that don't exist? Isn't this dangerous, socially and politically?"

Housing was fine as far as it went. Housing was a necessary but
by no means sufficient element in a strategy to alleviate urban poverty.
These seemed to be the views of many in the Bank's urban poverty
program.

Those who expressed these views were sharply critical of the Bank's
own work on employment. One officer offered the candid opinion
that "the Bank has not done a damn thing about employment." Another
argued that "the Bank has no approach whatsoever to questions of
employment." Still another argued that "welfare is one thing; income
and employment are quite another. The long-term approach must be
on the side of income and employment." Another made the distinction
between a shelter-based and an income-based approach in the Bank's
urban work, claimed that the shelter-based approach had been trium-
phant thus far, but that it was definitely necessary to move in the
direction of an income-based approach.

Several members of the urban staff extended the argument to offer insightful observations of a more general nature. According to one, the Bank "has very low productivity in what might be called its policy work." According to another, "the big problem is that nobody, in the Bank or elsewhere, knows about the intersectoral allocation of the marginal dollar. On manufacturing and employment generation versus housing, for example, who knows where the marginal dollar should go?"

While it seemed true that no one knew precisely what the "intersectoral allocation of the marginal dollar" was or should be, many Bank urban project officers offered some suggestions. These suggestions had different labels, but they all tended in roughly the same direction.

The City Strategy

According to a Bank officer working on Indonesia, "there should be more focus on the whole city as a productive entity. How, for example, do you make a city function better? This might mean water supply in some circumstances; in others, it might mean something else again." He advised more multisectoral lending and more multidisciplinary work.

An officer working on Colombia also subscribed to the need for a city strategy. "What is the tax base of the city? What is the real economic potentiality of the city? What are the realistic employment opportunities in the city? These are the kinds of questions we should be asking."

A project officer with a long history of involvement with the Bank's work in Calcutta subscribed to what he called the "city strategy game." The city strategy was what the Bank had in fact adopted in Calcutta. As he put it, "It was like taking on New York City!" The irony, of course, was that plunging into the kinds of work the Bank was doing in Calcutta was what many in the Bank would like to do—but it was done in probably the most intractable place of all. This was the "city strategy game," to be sure, but what a city to do it in!

Regional Development

This was another label for the redirections of urban work implied as necessary by many Bank staff. The common denominator here, as it was phrased by several project officers working on Korea, was "the search for projects that had high economic benefits and that fit together in a systematic regional context." The Bank's urban projects in Korea did have somewhat of a regional development flavor. In the first project, approved in 1974, there was a mixture of components. There were the usual serviced residential plots, but they were in three secondary cities instead of Seoul. There was also, however, a market in one city. There was a fisheries port with an on-shore market and cold storage facilities. There were two access roads in two cities. What looked on the surface like a hodgepodge was justified in the name of regional development. Much was made by Bank project officers of the nonshelter components of this first Korean project because these allegedly indicated a different approach to questions of urban poverty (beyond just housing).

The regional development emphasis was alleged to be even more evident in a second urban project in Korea. This included two large industrial estates, a water supply component, two bridges, fisheries, technical assistance, and 3,750 serviced residential plots.

If it were to be taken to its logical conclusion, the regional development approach would presumably put an end to the arbitrary distinction, prevalent at the Bank during the McNamara years, between rural and urban development, between rural and urban projects.

Sector Program Lending
The logical evolution of the Bank's urban work would be for the isolated urban project to be integrated into a comprehensive urban program. Several loans to Brazil in the housing and transport sectors were seen as already indicative of the approach. According to the director of the Urban Projects Department, something akin to the Brazilian approach would soon be employed in countries like India, Indonesia, and the Philippines. The problem of course was a familiar one: the more advanced of the developing countries tended to be the ones with the institutional and human resource capabilities for implementing these kinds of sector program loans. The poorest countries, who might need them more, might be largely devoid of the capability for implementing them.

In any event virtually all urban project officers interviewed stated that the ultimate aim of Bank urban lending in the country under their supervision was some kind of sector loan. In Morocco, for example, "the Bank's ultimate goal, still clearly very far off, is some kind of a sector loan. But this is clearly contingent upon the adoption by the government of a clear-cut policy involving considerably more than only sites and services in squatter settlements. There is a need on the part of the government to 'broaden out.'" In Jamaica a proposed second urban project would be, in effect, a housing sector project. Such examples could be repeated in other countries.

Return to Trickle-Down?

Several project officers even ventured a bit of heresy. They suggested that greater attention to employment generation, the city strategy, regional development, sector program lending, and the like meant inevitably some departure from an explicit antipoverty orientation in the Bank's urban work. Particularly in regional development it was felt that there was some trickle-down theory implicit in the suggested approach since there would be less emphasis on direct benefits and beneficiaries and more on indirect effects on economies. There would be a search for growth poles. Labor-intensity would not be treated as a panacea and noble arguments about basic human needs would have less attention than the production side of urban work.

The Politics of Poverty-Oriented Projects

As the Bank attempted to move in an antipoverty direction under McNamara, a number of political controversies, tensions, and contradictions were generated within the institution. There were many Bank officers who were not wildly enthusiastic about the poverty-related reorientations of lending, and they came into conflict with those of their colleagues desiring to move more rapidly into antipoverty initiatives. The politics of implementing poverty-oriented development projects therefore largely involved organizational and programmatic conflicts within an institution experiencing some abrupt changes in the definition of its tasks. There were many bureaucratic turf struggles, generational discrepancies, debates between theorists and practitioners, contrasting viewpoints on agricultural development, equally contrasting viewpoints about employment generation, and so forth. These were manifested in many of the case studies discussed here: how the regional chief economists took issue with the poverty-impact guidelines established by urban poverty personnel, how the operating divisions treated the guidelines for assessing the antipoverty impact of rural development projects, how the traditional water supply personnel looked rather condescendingly at the urban poverty upstarts, how country economists questioned the need for explicit discussion of poverty and income distribution issues in country economic reports, or how the antipoverty focus under McNamara generated political disputes over the country allocation of the Bank's lending program.

The politics within the Bank were joined by two other aspects of the politics of poverty-oriented development assistance as practiced by the Bank. These were the nature of the Bank's relations with the countries that were the recipients of its funds and the politics within those recipient countries.

The Bank's involvement in antipoverty projects altered its relations with recipient countries in some discernible ways. The lending process is a process of negotiation. Some of the strategies of both lender and borrower occasioned by the Bank's antipoverty emphasis affected the dynamics of this process. The Bank was brought more directly into the political debate in recipient countries. The interactive process of the Bank and policy makers in these countries became a complicated game. Political development trends within recipient countries did not appear to augur well for the practical realization of the Bank's goals for antipoverty lending under McNamara.

In confronting political considerations more directly in this chapter, it is assumed that macroeconomists can reconcile the competing claims of growth and distribution, producing redistribution with growth. It is also assumed that agricultural economists can design viable strategies for small-scale, subsistence farms; that scientists, engineers, and technicians can develop appropriate technology; and that urban and regional planners can devise ways to make the urban environments in which the poor live more humane and prevent hyperurbanization in ways that are economically efficient (without resorting to simplistic administrative fiats). It is assumed, in short, that livability emphases are both ethical imperatives and economic possibilities.[1] So the World Bank's poverty-oriented development projects are designed to implement them. The real problems are, however, political and pose some formidable obstacles to poverty-oriented development assistance.

Political Trends and Antipoverty Lending

Economic development, though responsible for the emergence of a number of middle-income countries in the developing world, has been far from uniformly associated with democratic political development. In practice the optimistic equation—more economic development contributes to more political democracy—appears to have gone awry.[2]

If the assumption is made (empirically verifiable but not systematically verified in the literature) that polyarchies or democracies distribute social and economic benefits more evenly than various kinds of nonpolyarchies, then the apparent failure of the optimistic equation implies that for the most part political development has been either ignored or at the expense of the poor because there are so few genuine polyarchies among the developing countries.[3]

Many political trends in developing countries during the McNamara years were markedly regressive from the standpoint of the participation of the poor in the benefits of development; examples include Argentina since 1976, Brazil under the generals, and Chile since 1973. As in Chile immediately after the coup that overthrew Allende, sometimes there were efforts to establish political regimes that bordered on totalitarianism. More commonly, however, there were movements toward authoritarian or corporatist regimes. Generally, the ways in which political interests were structured in such regimes gave them a decidedly conservative slant in terms of the meaningful expression of the interests of the poor or the meaningful satisfaction of their demands.

Recent redemocratization in some developing countries has not changed matters as much as might be supposed. Some have argued that the liberalization of the regime in Brazil, the end of military government in Ecuador and Peru, the return to civilian rule in Nigeria, or the reinstallation of an elected regime in India negate arguments about the prevalence of nondemocracies in developing countries. But this misses the point. The insignificance of such superficial redemocratization is underscored by recent observations of some of its principal theoreticians. In a conference on transitions from authoritarian rule in Latin America and Latin Europe, one observer speculated that "a transition to democracy can be made only at the cost of leaving economic relations intact, not only the structure of production but even the distribution of income." In Spain, for example, "the political system has been transformed without affecting economic relations in any discernible manner."[4] Another observer argued that the holders of economic power want assurances that their position in the vanguard of the economy will not be undermined by any redemocratizing or liberalizing forces.[5] These are telling observations of considerable relevance to the politics of poverty-oriented development projects. Redemocratization may alter the form of politics in some developing countries, but it is highly unlikely to alter the substance of public policy output, particularly output on behalf of the poor.

If these propositions about political development in recipient countries are approximately correct, were the Bank's poverty-oriented development strategies under McNamara on a collision course with the most important political trends in these countries? Given the situation described, the undertaking of antipoverty projects by the Bank in many developing countries appeared, on the surface of it, somewhat incongruous. Latin America is a case in point. In Bolivia an agricultural development project was supposed to benefit 3,600 poor rural families. In Brazil a project appeared to incorporate important elements of agrarian reform. The Dominican Republic undertook a rural education project with Bank funds involving the establishment of 200 rural community learning centers. El Salvador began a sites-and-services project and a rural, nonformal education project. Honduras adopted an educational project involving vocational training and the establishment of experimental rural training centers to create rural community leadership. Paraguay engaged in a rural development project intended to benefit about 7,000 low-income families.[6]

From the start these efforts did not seem plausible because the willingness of such countries to undertake antipoverty projects did not appear to square with the nature of the political systems in these countries, being seemingly contrary to their most powerful groups and individuals, their economic development policies, or the kinds of development strategies they were pursuing. Could it really be expected that the Pinochet military regime in Chile would care about its small-scale farmers, the military regime in Brazil about agrarian reform, the regime in El Salvador about rural education, or General Alfredo Stroessner's Paraguay about rural development? The undertaking of poverty-oriented projects in these countries raised the question of why these recipient countries might have been party to these kinds of projects in the first place. At least five hypotheses may be suggested:

1. The regimes were sincere and had genuinely reoriented themselves toward antipoverty concerns. While the regimes might have manifested no ardent desire for a social revolution, they were apparently committed to the implementation of serious reforms.

2. The projects were undertaken in such countries because the tail of foreign assistance wagged the dog of the recipient country. (The dynamics of this process are sketched out below.)

3. For many practical purposes the country was not the recipient. A particular governmental agency within the country was. The agency wanted to undertake the projects. It was permitted to do so for various reasons, not all of which were sanguine.

4. The concern with these kinds of projects was only an example of tokenism, in any case simulated, minimal, and perfunctory. The regimes wished to give a symbolic gesture in the direction of reform and little else. Undertaking a few poverty-oriented projects with money supplied from abroad was an easy way of doing this. In this view the implementation of a few such projects added up to little or nothing. The projects were a useful way of buying off discontent and would have minimal linkage effects. (There is, however, a directly competing hypothesis, and this is considered below.)

5. The projects were undertaken because, somewhat ironically, such projects might actually serve to consolidate authoritarian or corporatist regimes.

Any of these reasons for the recipient country's engaging in development projects shows that the political dimensions of poverty-oriented development assistance go considerably beyond bureaucratic politics at the Bank's headquarters itself. How did the countries' political processes and their relations with the Bank affect the formulation and implementation of antipoverty development assistance strategies?

The Bank Attempts to Measure Sincerity

For regimes that were sincere, their desire or willingness to undertake antipoverty projects was ideally free of dissimulation. But what were the appropriate indicators of this? Sincerity presumably did not mean the professed desire for a social revolution bringing to power poverty-oriented revolutionaries; if this is what was meant, it was not often to be found (or sought by the Bank). Rather, what was needed was some indicator of the antipoverty commitment of nonrevolutionary regimes.

Interviews with Bank officials revealed how a country's commitment to antipoverty objectives was ascertained by the Bank. In Brazil, for example, much was made by the Bank of changes in wage policy under the regime of General Ernesto Geisel after mid-1974. Cost-of-living increments for the lowest-paid laborers were generally seen as more satisfactory than those prevailing under the policies of the previous economy minister. Regarding Colombia, there was frequent reference by the Bank to the national plan of the government of Alfonso López Michelsen, 1974 to 1978, which was geared toward improvements in the income levels of the poorest 50 percent of the population. Regarding Mexico, the Bank placed considerable emphasis upon the agrarian policies of the administration of Luís Echeverría, 1970 to 1976. These were seen as reversing a long-standing neglect of the *ejidatarios* and poor private farmers in Mexico.

For these and other countries, there was a tendency to employ discrete measures of sincerity or commitment. The Bank generally avoided arguments about overall changes or goals in political regimes and emphasized instead such microlevel measures as providing more dynamic planners, or more developmentally inclined bureaucratic agencies, or new development-specific laws (rather than a whole new mentality). More commonly, there emerged a tautology of sorts: the mere willingness of a country to engage in a poverty-oriented development project was itself taken as an indicator of sincerity. Geisel represented a change from the previous Brazilian government as evidenced by his willingness to begin several microregional rural development projects in the northeast; Echeverría represented a change from the previous Mexican government as evidenced by his willingness to undertake the PIDER project; and so forth.

Given the recent history of Latin American reformism, and of such reformism in other parts of the developing world, it is necessary to be skeptical about the sincerity hypothesis. In Brazil it was debatable whether the changes in wage policy taken by the Bank as a positive indicator of the regime's antipoverty commitment were more important than the negative indicator stemming from the conclusion of a Bank study of rural development in the northeast: "in Brazil today there is no strong political commitment to agrarian reform." Similarly, in Colombia, it was debatable whether the new plan would fare better than its predecessor of 1962 which for years was the major domestic document analyzing Colombian economic problems. One observer concluded that "neither had it been designed to be implemented nor had any real attempt been made to implement it. The Colombian General [or Ten-Year] Plan [of 1962] was nothing more than a generally well-organized preliminary attempt at quantifying and coordinating possible goals for economic policy."[7] As for Mexico one assessment openly disputed the alleged commitment to poverty alleviation of the agrarian policies of the Echeverría administration. It concluded: "The peasants' desperation, stimulated by the Echeverría government's revolutionary rhetoric, has brought their patience to an end. The Mexican political system has two irreconcilable, but fundamental, features. Its raison d'etre requires that revolutionary land reform slogans continue, encouraging the have-nots, but offending the haves. But the whole political structure ensures that officialdom, including the army and police, are on the side of the haves."[8]

The examples indicate that efforts to determine the sincere or committed government were not easy. They were akin to attempting to identify the sincere lover or politician. It would clearly have been preferable for the World Bank to be able to identify countries engaging in poverty-oriented projects free of dissimulation, but in practice this was a difficult task. Like the apparently sincere lover or politician apparently sincere countries have numerous motivations for engaging in their actions. Among country motivations the desire really to benefit the poor as an integral part of a larger development strategy may be only one among many priorities—and not necessarily the most important one at all.

The Tail Wags the Dog

Another reason a country might implement a poverty-oriented project has to do with the pronounced historical faddism among the dispensers of foreign assistance. John White's study of the politics of foreign aid has captured this argument best: "The pressures that condition the behavior of multilateral agencies give rise to a situation in which the inherent danger is that developing countries will be required to produce problems to fit the solutions currently advocated, rather than seek solutions to problems as they arise."[9]

There was some of this flavor in the history of antipoverty efforts at the Bank. When in 1973, McNamara proclaimed that the institution was explicitly and urgently interested in problems of rural poverty in developing countries, some lower-level functionaries in the Bank and some policy makers in a number of developing countries decided that they had better get interested, too.

The result was more or less the production of problems. In Brazil, for example, some state governments seized upon the occasion to present for approval some high-cost (therefore nonreplicable) agricultural development projects in the northeast (it should be noted these projects were rejected by the Bank). In Colombia, the authorities dressed up one of sixteen leftover projects of the agrarian reform agency, called it a "rural development project," and presented it to the Bank for approval. Within the Bank itself some loan officers and division chiefs, reading the cues from McNamara, correctly concluded that points were to be won by including rural development projects in country-programming papers. There ensued a scramble to identify potentially fundable projects, "to produce problems to fit the solutions currently advocated." To a large extent this procedure turned the traditional project cycle upside down. Instead of countries coming to the Bank with identifiable projects perceived as possible solutions to existing problems, the Bank went to countries with solutions and requested the identification of problems for potential funding. (Academicians accustomed to the politics of grantsmanship and to dealing with research-supporting foundations will no doubt see clear parallels with this process.)

So much for rural poverty. But what about urban poverty? McNamara's 1975 address to the Board of Governors on reducing poverty in the cities of the developing world led to a replication of the rural process. Countries brought in projects deficient in various ways, and within the Bank a scramble occurred to identify urban antipoverty projects. The Bank identified itself as explicitly and urgently concerned with problems of urban poverty, and solutions (and Bank funding) were declared to exist. So housing and small-industry problems were produced, generating projects to deal with these problems.

The responses of many countries to this situation seemed eminently rational. A country may have submitted poverty-oriented projects to the Bank and agreed to finance its share of them because it believed, or was led to believe, that this accommodation to current Bank emphases might get it what it really wanted from the Bank. It is not difficult to imagine the arguments of the Brazilians: "We have demonstrated our interest in the problems of rural poverty—just look at our rural development projects in the northeast! Now let's talk about our steel mill!" In this instance, the reasons for engaging in the poverty-oriented project had little or nothing to do with sincerity and a lot to do with appeasement of the World Bank.

The recipient country's response to the cues coming from the Bank may have led to what White calls "a growing disparity between the language used by the recipient to make his case for aid and the uses to which he actually puts it."[10] In White's opinion, "Concessions to the donor's developmental objectives may be only apparent concessions. He [the recipient] pursues a presentational strategy of stating policies of which the donor will approve, although he does not intend to implement them, or of emphasizing trends of which the donor may approve, although these trends are not the most significant ones, and may even be presented on the basis of false data."[11] The situation is not always or even mainly one of overt prevarication. It is, rather, a bargaining or exchange situation that appears to give rise to some roughly agreed upon set of rules; "the one who wins is the one who is most skillful in breaking the rules."[12] Who won when a poverty-oriented project was approved? The Bank? The country? Both? Neither? Like questions about sincerity, these were not easy questions to answer.

There was another way in which the tail of foreign aid may have wagged the dog of the country. This had to do not with the necessity of accommodation, appeasement, or presentation but with conditions of extreme underdevelopment in many countries. In such cases any net addition to resources—no matter what it financed—was likely to be welcome. In one scenario the provision of World Bank resources could free recipient-country resources for the pursuit of other projects to which the country attached priority. A case could be made on behalf of the argument that something, however meager, had to be done to attempt to alleviate at least the worst aspects of absolute poverty among the poor farmers and urban slum dwellers of the Brazilian northeast. Perhaps this had to be done not because it was sincerely desired to assist the poor, or because it fit into some larger development strategy, but because, if something was not done to alleviate the plight of the poor, they might have begun to cause trouble. (For the moment the question of whether social turbulence was really likely is left aside.)

By not having to finance $23 million for a rural development project in the Lower São Francisco River valley (the sum of a Bank loan for that purpose), or $23.5 million for educational development in the northeast (the sum of a Bank loan for that purpose), the Brazilian government had $46.5 million to spend on other, including nondevelopmental, concerns. Seen in this light, Bank resources financed not only the projects that had been appraised and approved but also projects, perhaps perverse ones, that had not. Even the approved projects may have entailed side benefits going not to the poor but to those allied with the political regime, such as rural contractors. This is why "it is not enough to prove, as donor agencies try to prove when commending the aid programme to parliament or public, that aid has done what the donor intended it to do. One must always pose the question: 'What else did it do?' "[13] The hope that these additional things would be done may have been the principal reason for the country's undertaking the poverty-oriented project in the first place.

Disaggregating the Recipient
There is a sense in which poverty-oriented foreign assistance supplied by the Bank was provided not to a country but to specific agencies within it. For a more complete understanding of the recipient's reasons for undertaking poverty-oriented projects, one needs to know something (frequently a great deal) about bureaucratic politics in the particular country under consideration. Some agencies within the country may have had antipoverty objectives; others, even some specifically intended for these purposes, may have not. Much depended on who within the recipient country was conducting the negotiations with the Bank.

The case of the Mexican PIDER rural development projects illustrates the point. Among the Mexican federal institutions participating in the projects were the Ministry of Agriculture, the Ministry of Finance, the Ministry of Public Works, the Ministry of Water Resources, the Ministry of Health, the Agrarian Reform Commission, the Federal Electricity Commission, the National Corporation for Basic Marketing, the Committee for Administration of the Federal School Construction Program, the National Arid Zones Commission, the National Indigenous Institute, the National Institute for Rural Community Development and Low Cost Housing, and the Ejidal Bank. Each of these institutions possessed its own operational style—the product of different role orientations, different clientele groups each served, different resources, different bureaucratic strategies, and different interactive patterns with other agencies. The particular manner in which project funds were allocated to these different agencies, and the ways in which project tasks were divided among them, had discernible effects upon project outcomes. Another example of such organizational issues concerns conflicts between finance ministries and sectoral ministries in developing countries. These are the subject of a considerable literature in the field of development administration, and the manner in which these conflicts are resolved has much to do with the pattern of implementation of specific projects.

These considerations mean that once again the willingness of a recipient country to engage in a poverty-oriented project could not be taken as evidence of a regime-level commitment to antipoverty concerns. It might simply have meant that a particular bureaucratic agency triumphed over some other agency, perhaps for essentially idiosyncratic reasons. It might have meant that the important wielders of power in the regime permitted an agency to engage in an antipoverty project in exchange for that agency's support on some matter crucial to the powerful groups, or simply to give the agency something to do or to keep it quiet.

Even the willingness to establish an autonomous agency to oversee the implementation of a poverty-oriented project may have been deceptive. For, as Hirschman has pointed out, "a number of autonomous agencies that were set up to infiltrate the old order by a new spirit have in fact been infiltrated in turn. In a number of cases . . . the 'autonomous agency' has shown a worse performance in this respect than the national government and its direct subdivisions."[14] Moreover the insulation from politics that is a frequent justification for establishing the autonomous agency can also mean insulation from political power: "this loss may be crippling, especially for agencies engaging in highly controversial social . . . innovation."[15] The willingness to implement a poverty-oriented project, and to effect certain organizational changes in connection with it, did not necessarily mean a disturbance of the bureaucratic status quo. A new institution might indeed have been created, but the impact of the institution might have been quite minimal.

Other analysts of the developmental role of the World Bank have called attention to the necessity of disaggregating the recipient. The study by Mason and Asher concluded that "in the typical case . . . the Bank is likely to find itself supporting the executive branch of the government against opposition elements in the parliament, or the prime minister and minister of finance against spending ministries, or even the interests of a particular ministry against the rest of the government. How much influence the Bank can exercise depends largely on the amount and character of the political support behind proposed projects."[16]

Another study shows how bureaucratic entrepreneurs in developing countries—many of whom hitched their star to antipoverty concerns in the McNamara years, because poverty was a fashionable cause— may use the World Bank in their bureaucratic struggles at home. Planning commissions, for example, may often act this way.[17]

The subject provides considerable room for additional research. There are unsettled questions concerning which implementing agencies are favored by the Bank in specific countries and contexts, how they are encouraged instead of agencies that have fallen into disfavor, and what political processes are involved in the formation of entirely new institutions. If the Superintendency for the Development of the Northeast (SUDENE) seems to have atrophied, what would be the Bank's organizational vehicle for the pursuit of rural development in Brazil? Why was the implementation of a Bank-financed sites-and-services project in El Salvador entrusted to a private foundation? Why did the Caja Agraria instead of the official agrarian reform agency oversee the implementation of the Bank's rural development projects in Colombia? These are not trivial matters; within them lie clues to the origins and evolution of poverty-oriented projects. Bureaucratic politics in the recipient country, and the relationships of bureaucratic agencies with the World Bank, are an important part of the politics of poverty-oriented development projects.

Tokenism and Related Issues

The small enclave nature of many of the Bank's antipoverty projects might have reflected the assumption on the part of elites in developing countries that the projects' implementation would not seriously affect the basic structure of political, social, or economic relations in the countries. The willingness to implement poverty-oriented projects might thus have been a cheap way of simulating a concern with poverty, a token, a symbolic gesture and little more.

The subject is, however, more complicated than the mere tokenism hypothesis appears to make it at first glance, for it gives rise to alternative conflicting hypotheses about the subsequent effects of projects. It raises the issue of whether the effects of poverty-oriented projects can be contained.

If it is possible for the elites in recipient countries to use the projects to buy off discontent and for symbolic purposes, a poverty-oriented project may actually assist in the avoidance of the root or structural causes of a country's economic ailments. It may serve as an instrument of political quiescence and symbolic reassurance, thereby immobilizing potentially troublesome individuals and groups.

Under these circumstances the high-cost, nonreplicable pilot project may have a functional role to play. It demonstrates what a wonderfully successful job is being done with assistance for the peasants in a given locality; at the same time, however, its very high cost assures that not too many such wonderful jobs will be undertaken. In this way the undertaking of antipoverty projects in developing countries is analogous to missionary work. The task of missionaries, it may be argued, is not to change the structure that produces benighted souls; it is enough that a few such souls be saved. With this sort of orientation the primary question for elites in developing countries is how the sociopolitical spread effects of poverty-oriented projects can be contained, and this may influence where projects are located, who administers them, which groups they benefit, or how they are described in public pro-nouncements. A case in point would be a Bank project designed to provide agricultural credit for 22,000 small farmers in Chile. The project was probably intended to show that the economic policies of the military regime in Chile were not really retrograde, but the effects of the project were presumed by the Chilean authorities to be thoroughly containable.

While the successfully tokenistic nature of poverty-oriented projects may mask the real issues, there is a counterpossibility that entails lack of containment, excessive spread effects, and the coming into play of theories of relative deprivation. A project might set in motion forces difficult to control. Peasants in nonadvantaged regions might want projects like those benefiting peasants in other regions. Urban dwellers untouched by sites-and-services projects might begin to demand such projects for themselves.

More generally, the implementation of poverty-oriented projects benefiting a few of the poverty groups might heighten the consciousness of those not included. They might begin to make invidious comparisons not only with other poor people but with the position of the elite itself. The possibility of some change opened up by the project suggests the possibility of even greater change. Antagonisms and instabilities ("contradictions" is perhaps the most currently fashionable word) may be created by the implementation of a few poverty-oriented projects, swamping the symbolic and buying-off-discontent effects. (Since the resources for effecting wholesale structural changes are unlikely to exist, the problem may be particularly acute. This may be the classical reformer's dilemma.)

A number of historical experiences have illustrated this sequence of events and shed light on some aspects of poverty-oriented politics. A particularly relevant example was provided by the experience of the Chilean agrarian reform under the administration of the Christian Democrat Eduardo Frei from 1964 to 1970. With the benefit of hindsight, certain features of the Chilean reform were suggestive of political dimensions of the Bank's rural development projects.

The Chilean reform provided that expropriated properties would be distributed primarily to those who previously worked them. The land redistribution features of the reform did not extend to landless laborers or migrant workers. (Recall the primary beneficiaries of World Bank rural development projects.)

Figures differ on the extent of the reform under the Frei administration, but virtually all observers agree that it did not go as far as originally intended. Residents of the cooperative settlements formed after expropriation numbered only 12.7 percent of the total number of resident and nonresident rural wage-workers.[18] Another calculation indicated that fewer than 10 percent of the poor rural families in Chile were beneficiaries of the land redistribution process under the Frei regime.[19] (Recall that World Bank rural development projects generally benefit only a small proportion of the poor population in project areas, and a much smaller proportion of the poor in the entire recipient country.)

An important corollary of the reform, however, was the process of social and political mobilization in the countryside. Agricultural unions increased dramatically from 1964 to 1970, as did other rural associational groups. This was "a classic case of mobilization outrunning capabilities."[20] (The question of whether substantial mobilization has occurred in areas where World Bank rural development projects have been undertaken is a subject for empirical inquiry.)

The reform produced some unanticipated consequences and possibly counterproductive effects. It appeared to increase rivalries between social classes, heighten antagonisms within the peasant class in rural areas, and redound to the electoral disadvantage of its chief protagonists (the Christian Democrats). One observer concluded that workers excluded from the agrarian reform process, "not seeing why they should be excluded and others included for apparently arbitrary or even political reasons, seemed highly discontented."[21] He concluded that "the integration of some rural workers involved increasing estrangement between them and the vast majority of peasants and rural workers who did not gain access to land."[22] Figures indicate that the income levels of the members of cooperatives were between two and five times higher than those of noncooperative peasants.[23] (Recall the substantial incremental income gains expected from World Bank rural development projects.) It was concluded that competition between cooperative members and excluded peasants was an important source of political conflict in the land reform process.[24] These conflicts appeared to lead to a boomerang effect working against those Christian Democrats who had hoped that the reform would provide a new clientele for the party and would guarantee political stability as well. The principal electoral implication of the agrarian reform seems to have been polarization, with both the left and the right gaining at the expense of the centrist Christian Democrats. A further indication of the boomerang effect was the process of illegal land seizures during 1971, the first year of the administration of Salvador Allende.

These experiences of Chilean agrarian reform will not necessarily be replicated whenever and wherever World Bank rural development projects are undertaken. The Chilean example, however, demonstrates how symbolic effects may be overwhelmed by the failure to contain spread effects. Although the Bank's rural development projects seldom entail the overt redistribution of existing assets such as land, they are expected significantly to increase the income levels of their beneficiaries. There is thus a distinct possibility that they may set in motion at least some of the dynamics of relative deprivation processes found in the Chilean case.

Among the Bank rural development projects reviewed for this study, there were many whose characteristics suggested potentialities of replicating (albeit in small regionally specific enclaves) features of the Chilean experience. The Rio Grande do Norte project was an example. The project was undertaken in an area where the economically active rural population was divided into about 35 percent temporary workers, 20 percent sharecroppers, 35 percent small owner-operators, and 10 percent large owner-operators. As noted in chapter 5, however, the main group of project beneficiaries was expected to be the poor farm families owning and operating their own small farms. Sharecroppers and landless laborers were to participate only marginally in the key agricultural credit component of the project. The net income from cotton production of farms under 50 hectares was expected to increase from $210 to $430 in six years and of farms from 50 to 200 hectares, from $590 to $1,200.

Different hypotheses can be entertained about how the nonadvantaged farmers in the project region might respond to this anticipated doubling of the incomes of their small owner-operator neighbors. Perhaps they may conclude that things in the general area are improving, and that they are the next in line. For these reasons they may remain quiescent. But, on the other hand, they may have a more pessimistic view and take matters into their own hands. It is of course difficult to generalize about the response. Most regimes in contemporary developing countries should probably be skillful enough to keep things from going beyond tokenism. But not all rulers are skilled politicians adept at symbolic gratification. Not all seemingly containable projects can in fact be contained. The larger sociopolitical effects of World Bank poverty-oriented projects remain, therefore, to be ascertained.

Problems with Corporatist Regimes
Another possible reason for a country's implementation of a poverty-oriented project concerned the relationship of such projects to a common type of political regime in developing countries. It may be asked how such projects squared with authoritarian or corporatist regimes in the developing world, since such regimes outnumber their democratic competitors by a wide margin. Numerous Latin American regimes, including those of Argentina, Brazil, and Mexico, have frequently been referred to as corporatist. Examples are not confined to Latin America, however. Among other countries where the Bank's work is prominent, Korea, Indonesia, and the Philippines would also fall under the designation.

But what is meant by corporatism? This question has recently been answered in diverse ways, provoking considerable debate about the essential hallmarks of corporatist regimes. Scholarly work, however, reflects an emerging consensus that seeks to limit use of the term to particular features of the system of interest representation. Philippe C. Schmitter has defined corporatism as "a system of interest representation in which the constituent units are organized into a limited number of singular, compulsory, noncompetitive, hierarchically ordered and functionally differentiated categories, recognized or licensed (if not created) by the state and granted a deliberate representational monopoly within their respective categories in exchange for observing certain controls on their selection of leaders and articulation of demands and supports."[25] (The principal competing system of interest representation is pluralism.) Other observers have adopted a somewhat broader definition, using the term corporatism to refer to a certain pattern in the relations between the state and the associational groups of civil society. In this view the state structures, subsidizes, and ultimately controls such groups.[26]

If its definition is limited to various features of the system of interest representation, it is questionable whether corporatism is a regime type at all. Schmitter maintains that corporatism is compatible with many different kinds of regime types, whether characterized by different party systems, ideologies, levels of political mobilization, or public policies. In some policy arenas a corporatist system of interest representation might prevail, and in others a pluralist system—all within the same type of regime.[27]

Corporatism, moreover, is difficult to correlate with any particular kinds of public policy. It appears that regimes customarily considered corporatist may pursue either socially progressive or conservative policies. There appears to be no apparent association between corporatism and the substance of public policies. It has been associated with a wide variety of policy orientations, from right to left. Corporatism has occasionally seemed to favor labor over employers, occasionally exactly the reverse.

Some observers have, however, pretended to find a particular kind of policy-making process in systems called corporatist. In the case of economic policy making in Mexico, Susan Kaufman Purcell shows how some defining characteristics of an authoritarian regime—what she calls "limited political pluralism, low subject mobilization of the population, and the predominance of patrimonial rulership"—present policy makers in Mexico with options and constraints that differ significantly from those found in nonauthoritarian regimes.[28] Among its other features the policy-making process in authoritarian systems appears to provide decision makers with greater autonomy than they might experience in pluralist systems.

What is the import of these features of corporatism for the study of the politics of poverty-oriented development projects? Such Bank projects were implemented by numerous countries whose systems of interest representation may be described as corporatist. Poverty-oriented projects were not ruled out in such systems if they could be integrated into an existing clientelistic network of interest representation. If they could be so integrated, it was possible that the increased mobilization and participation which they presumably would call forth (such as more people participating in the commercial sector of the economy, the establishment of agricultural cooperatives, new community development organizations, and so forth) could be substantially controlled, directed, and moderated. If this was so, then the implementation of poverty-oriented development projects did not need to disturb some of the principal features of corporatist or authoritarian systems—such as limited mobilization, depoliticized and deideologized decision-making processes, and, in general, guided or directed social change (the "revolution from above"). Poverty-oriented projects could even facilitate the consolidation of such regimes by providing symbolic (as well as substantive) payoffs for their "vertical authority structures."[29]

It depended, of course, on the nature of the project and how it was organized. From the standpoint of the authoritarian regime it would have been preferable to provide for nonclass-specific beneficiaries, "something for everybody" in the project and not just poverty groups; to implement the project by an agency in the regular (corporatist) bureaucratic structure rather than create an autonomous agency, although possibilities for penetrating the latter undoubtedly existed; or to design the project with as little an innovative organizational component as possible (a simple agricultural credit project administered by established financial intermediaries may be less upsetting of the interest representation structure than rural community learning centers, or a general nutrition project less upsetting than a project entailing the creation of new rural health organizations, and so forth). Additional hypotheses could be suggested, outlining the various ways in which poverty-oriented projects might be designed to maintain the essential characteristics of the corporatist systems implementing them.

Say a loan to Honduras in 1974 financed a project to "establish experimental rural training centers for farmer training, home economics, and rural community leadership." If rural community leadership could easily be co-opted, if subsequent issues could be compartmentalized within the educational sector so that they did not link up with similar demands from leadership in other sectors, if the leadership were provided with some form of institutionalized access to decision making but always in a dependent fashion vis-à-vis the main policy-making agencies, what would be the sum effect of the poverty-oriented project? How would it really change anything?

Seen in this light, the implementation of an experimental rural education project in Honduras may have about as much larger meaning as the implementation of a poverty-oriented project in some favored ward of Mayor Daley's Chicago, where there was also limited political pluralism, low subject mobilization of the population, and the predominance of patrimonial rulership. In either case the systemic significance of the undertaking could have been legitimately questioned.

National policy makers have broader objectives than those of the World Bank's project officers. Bank officers want to increase production and incomes of the poor through rural development projects and projects of urban employment generation, whereas the policy makers might, in addition (or above all else), wish to broaden political participation in a controlled way, increase political patronage, or further their ideological objectives. Among such objectives may be the "pretense of class symmetry and equality of access" which is likely to be well reinforced by the undertaking of a poverty-oriented project.[30]

The Bank's Contribution to Defensive Modernization

From the World Bank's perspective it frequently seemed more important that its poverty-oriented projects were implemented at all — not why they were implemented. It might have been troubling to some that the projects were implemented even though the regimes implementing them were not committed to antipoverty objectives, or that the tail wagged the dog, or that the Bank might have worked only with one favored little bureaucratic agency and ignored the rest, or that this might have only been tokenism, or that poverty-oriented development projects might actually have served to consolidate and not undermine authoritarian regimes.

The Bank did not, perhaps could not, worry too much about these matters. It was more concerned with the concrete results of its projects — so many beneficiaries here, so many upgraded facilities there. The kinds of considerations raised in this chapter were likely to be seen by the vast majority of World Bankers as the fanciful musings of an idle social scientist.

What needs to be emphasized, however, is the interplay between the process by which public policy is formed and the substance of the resultant output.[31] The substantive characteristics of World Bank poverty-oriented development projects are likely to be much affected by the political processes involved in their design and implementation. This has been pointed out, for example, in the discussion of how a desire to contain spread effects might have influenced where projects were located, how they were administered, and which groups they benefited. This was a point not totally lost on World Bankers, but it is one they by and large chose not to concern themselves with.

Was there an underlying political rationale for the World Bank's poverty-oriented work under McNamara? This question was put to many World Bankers at all levels of the institution. Their collated responses suggested that there was. The underlying political rationale for the Bank's poverty-oriented development projects seemed to be political stability through defensive modernization. Political stability was seen primarily as an outcome of giving people a stake, however minimal, in the system. Defensive modernization aims at forestalling or preempting social and political pressures. If defensive modernization is successful, it results in conservatism among the newly modernized and thus to their contributions to political stability.

Defensive modernization, if successful, will lead to the creation of a modern small-holder sector in the rural areas. Such a small-holder sector will be integrated with the national commercial economy. Its success will be tied up with the success of that economy. It will be co-opted. It will be, to use the words of a Bank project officer, "fiercely individualistic on the production side," reticent toward joining in co-operatives and other forms of group activity, loath to link its interests with those not yet modernized.

Defensive modernization, if successful, will have similar consequences in urban areas of developing countries. There it can be expected to create or fortify a petite bourgeoisie composed of the small-scale industrialists, the small entrepreneurs in the informal sector, and the newly employed. The Salvadoran experience, where the urban development projects noticeably failed to raise the social consciousness of the projects' beneficiaries or to stimulate them toward larger goals and processes of social action, is probably typical of what can be expected in many developing countries in the future.

Whether projects turn out as conceived depends on any number of variables. One is the extent of the destabilizing tendencies that the poverty-oriented projects themselves might set in motion. Another is the sheer extent of the effort. Even if the basic postulates of the theory are accurate, the effort will have to be larger than it is at present. Efforts on the current scale will leave too many out of the newly modernized status quo. Too many latent instabilities will remain. Not to be ignored are countervailing national or international developments. A hideously retrograde regime, such as that in El Salvador today, may condemn any externally induced effort at defensive modernization to total failure. Adverse trends in the political economy of the international system (such as continued exacerbation of some of the financial trends discussed in chapter 3) may contribute to the pauperization of countries and peoples and thwart the apparently desired ends of socioeconomic conservatism and political stability.

How then should the World Bank's efforts to contribute to political stability be evaluated? Radical critics of the Bank's poverty-oriented work are unabashed in their intepretation: the effort is to be severely criticized because it holds back the forces promoting real change. For these critics it would be better to have no Bank projects at all. The now-poor would become even poorer; this would contribute to the heightening of contradictions in the existing socioeconomic structure and presumably bring the system tumbling down. The radical critics seem to be afraid that the effort at defensive modernization might actually succeed. Reformist defenders of the Bank's poverty-oriented projects, on the other hand, value political stability and the sorts of social and economic reforms designed to cultivate it.

The effort here was not to resolve this debate with all its manifold ramifications but to outline some of the principal political considerations and the rationale of the Bank's poverty-oriented work. Only after it is clear what the Bank attempted under McNamara is it possible to debate its utility and worth more intelligently. The analytical and normative orientations that would need to be brought to bear in such a debate were briefly sketched out in the first chapter.

10

The Bank after McNamara

Two events in 1981 — the arrival of the Reagan administration and of
A. W. Clausen to replace McNamara as World Bank president — brought
heightened visibility to the role of the Bank and intensified the debate
about that role. The new American administration, with only a tenuous
commitment to multilateral development assistance, confronted the
Bank with considerable skepticism. It questioned the utility of the Bank
on many grounds, one of which was the poverty-oriented programs
begun under McNamara. Clausen's appointment raised the possibility
of a new agenda for the Bank that would differ to some extent from
that of the outgoing president. Would the future level of Bank programs
aimed at the poorest countries and poorest people in the developing
world be as extensive as they were under McNamara?

Many observers of the Bank were concerned that there might be
a retreat in the 1980s from the poverty alleviation emphasis of the
McNamara years. Clausen, former chief executive officer of the Bank
of America, was seen by some as the Reagan administration's chosen
instrument for implementing its private-sector approach to the development of poor countries. Since Clausen was an eminent commercial
banker, it was presumed he would be more concerned than McNamara
with market-oriented development strategies, more concerned with
expanding the economic pie in developing countries than with carving
it up, more concerned with assuring Wall Street than with meeting
the demands of the Third World.

Other factors also seemed to suggest a retreat from poverty alleviation. The decade of the 1980s is generally not seen as a time for
bold new advances on the antipoverty front worldwide, any more
than it is domestically in the United States. Budgetary stringencies in
both developed and developing countries are thought to argue against
such advances. If this is not the time to rebuild the South Bronx or

restore Watts, then it is not the time to alleviate poverty in Bangladesh or the Sahel. Some of the acknowledged limitations of the Bank's antipoverty projects, discussed throughout this study, have been revealed, and these presumably argue for consolidation rather than expansion. In the dire financial straits in which many developing countries currently find themselves, money moving is held to be more important than poverty alleviation. What is supposedly needed in the steady-state world is a bank that commands resources and transfers large amounts of money.

Illustrative of this concern are the views of Mahbub ul Haq, who resigned as the World Bank's director of policy planning in March 1982, in part because of "major policy differences" with the Bank's new president.[1] According to one report, Haq assumed his new position as Pakistan's minister of planning and development because he was "convinced that he can do nothing in Clausen's new World Bank, subservient as it is to the hardliners in the U.S. administration. The impact of right-wing economics is, he believes, destroying all that the Bank achieved in the McNamara years."[2]

The concern was evidently not limited to those who have left the Bank. In early 1982 an internal task force on the Bank's poverty focus circulated a report whose principal conclusion was that "the poverty focus should remain an integral part of the Bank's overall development and lending strategy." The authors of the report were skeptical, however: "Our discussions [within the Bank] revealed widespread uncertainty about whether the commitment to poverty alleviation has been weakened or abandoned. The current concern with energy and structural adjustment, combined with the transition to a new chief executive, make many staff members question the Bank's commitment to this objective. New signals, real or imagined, are already affecting both policy dialogue and planned lending." Would the Bank turn its back on the world's poor? This is a key question because nowhere else in the international development assistance community exists the magnitude of resources which the Bank can devote to poverty alleviation.

Conservative Critique Confronting Clausen

Clausen's appointment to the Bank's presidency occurred in the context of a mounting conservative attack on the Bank within the United States, the Bank's largest donor. The head of a study team on development assistance formed to advise incoming President Reagan concluded that American taxpayers should not be asked to pay for the "little experiments in so-called social progress" which the Bank was funding and that, therefore, the American role in the Bank as well as other multilateral institutions should be deemphasized.[3] The administration joined the fray shortly after taking office. In the first week of the Reagan presidency, its budget director wrote a memo that argued for the elimination or reduction of American participation "in a range of multilateral organizations that are not responsive to U.S. foreign policy concerns and that in many cases may be ineffective in producing sound economic development."[4] Key congressmen hostile to the Bank contributed to the attack. The administration then began a comprehensive review of American participation in the multilateral development banks, with primary emphasis on the World Bank.

What were the principal elements of the conservative critique of the Bank? The conservatives began with objection to the quantitative growth of the Bank and IDA in the McNamara years. It was pointed out in chapter 1 that lending experienced an approximate twelvefold increase in current dollars from fiscal 1968 to fiscal 1981 — an approximate fivefold increase in constant dollars. The critics did not like this quantitative expansion. They claimed that the Bank had grown too big and too fast, that it had usurped the international development effort at the expense of others (such as the American bilateral assistance program or the programs of the regional development banks like the Inter-American Development Bank), and that its future growth along past lines could not continue to be financed.

The critics were also strident in their objections to the Bank's qualitative reorientations. The conservative line of criticism saw the Bank's poverty-oriented projects begun under McNamara as "giveaways," "welfare" programs, money wasted on projects with marginal rates of return. Budget Director Stockman's memo claimed that IDA "in recent years has placed a major emphasis on programs fostering income redistribution," with the clear assumption that this was bad.[5]

Much of the conservative critique was overtly ideological. Such was the argument, discussed in chapter 1, that the Bank's loans supported socialist schemes in developing countries and thereby undermined capitalist development. A related argument was that the Bank loaned to the wrong countries and was thus not compatible with the goals of American foreign policy.[6] The conservatives desired to focus development assistance on countries with economic and political systems compatible with American interests (or which could supposedly be made compatible through modest doses of such assistance). In general, according to the conservatives, the United States needed more attention to its security interests in developing countries, even if this meant less attention to its interests in development.

The critics also alleged that the United States did not get enough out of the Bank in terms of its concrete economic interests. They maintained that there was insufficient procurement of American goods and services under Bank projects (contracts for the provision of such goods and services are awarded through international competitive bidding), thus there was not enough export promotion for American firms, and thus the World Bank was not a "good buy" for the United States. American participation in the Bank was not perceived as cost-effective.

This conservative attack on the Bank emanating from its most important donor country, taken in conjunction with the adverse international context of development discussed in chapter 3, confronted the Bank's new president with a vastly different tactical situation from that which existed when McNamara took office. For McNamara, the primary task was to educate the world about poverty at a time when there were sufficient financial resources to combat poverty and to stimulate economic growth. For Clausen the task was to convince those with resources (now severely constrained) of the probity of the Bank. Without support in the world's financial and political centers of power the Bank would be unable to continue the poverty-oriented course charted in the McNamara years. It could talk all it wanted about the "poor majority" in the developing world, but it would be unable to act upon its rhetoric.

Retrospective on the McNamara Years

In assessing the future of the Bank's antipoverty efforts, it is first necessary to emphasize some aspects of those efforts under McNamara. Although any effort to ascertain precisely the allocation of lending between traditional projects for infrastructure investments and poverty-oriented projects is fraught with methodological difficulties, it may be estimated that considerably more than one-half and perhaps as much as two-thirds or more of combined Bank and IDA lending remained traditional at the end of the McNamara presidency. McNamara's Bank markedly increased lending for poverty-oriented activities, but it was by no means transformed into an antipoverty agency exclusively. Traditional lending grew significantly in absolute amounts, and even much poverty-oriented lending frequently appeared quite traditional.

Moreover the conservative argument that the Bank operated a vast welfare program under McNamara neglects the basic rationale behind the Bank's poverty-oriented projects. The arguments of chapters 5 and 6 indicated that the Bank's projects designed to alleviate rural poverty were consistent with its long-standing emphasis on economic growth. The rural development projects were designed to raise the output and income of small rural producers, not to keep them on the dole. Other positive features of the projects included the development of new technical packages for small-scale farmers, changes in public sector investment planning for rural development, and the incremental accumulation of new knowledge about assisting the rural poor.

The Bank's urban poverty projects likewise defined their goals in sound business terms such as affordability, cost recovery, and replicability. Mortgage payments, rental fees, and user charges meant that it should be possible to replicate the projects without requiring outright subsidies from the public treasuries of developing countries.

Before McNamara the World Bank saw the main route to growth in projects of basic economic infrastructure — basic roads, dams, ports, steel mills, and telecommunications facilities. Under his presidency that route was widened to include social sector investments, human resource development, assistance for small-scale farmers, aid to small-scale industrial establishments, and the many links of poverty alleviation to growth. But the objectives were the same. The contrast was not between growth-oriented projects before McNamara and "welfare" projects under McNamara but between projects entailing different routes to growth.

Additional support for this argument comes from the fact that poverty-oriented projects do not appear to have sacrificed the Bank's growth objectives. Regarding rural development projects, the evidence indicates acceptable, if not more than adequate, rates of return from completed undertakings. While evidence from the Bank's project performance audit reports is still limited because of the newness of most of the projects, it tends to support the justification of poverty-oriented projects in terms of traditional canons of performance.

Another conclusion is that the Bank's country and sectoral allocations of lending were highly compatible with private sector interests in development as well as the interests of American foreign policy. Appendix B gives the twenty largest cumulative recipients of Bank loans, IDA credits, and Bank/IDA money combined. The table shows that, far from lending to the "wrong" countries in terms of America's geopolitical and geostrategic interests, the Bank and IDA have loaned the vast bulk of their resources to countries highly important to those interests. The list of these Bank/IDA borrowers reads like a who's who of developing countries in terms of their historical and contemporary importance to American foreign policy interests. Judged solely on the basis of where the World Bank under McNamara put its money, the United States was an effective prosecutor of its interests at the Bank. American conservatives have failed to note that there was no new lending by the Bank to Allende's Chile, that there was sharply curtailed lending to Peru following nationalization of the International Petroleum Company, and that there was no lending to Peronist Argentina from 1973 to 1976 (it resumed when the generals returned).

The debate about the economic costs and benefits of American participation in the World Bank tended to focus in the latter McNamara years on the narrow question of how much the United States got out of the Bank and IDA compared to what it put in. There was a tendency to reduce the matter to a comparison between what the United States contributed in Bank capital subscriptions and IDA replenishments versus what American firms obtained in procurement under Bank projects. Such resort to the contribution/procurement ratio as the sole criterion for assessing the benefits and costs of participation was simplistic, since it completely ignored the overall importance of the growth of developing country economies to American private sector trade and investment. Even so, the equation worked in favor of the United States. World Bank procurement figures released in March 1981 show that, while the United States had contributed $935 million to the Bank from its inception, Bank loans to other countries had generated $6.4 billion in contracts to American companies.[7]

While it is true that American contributions to IDA since 1960 have totaled $3.2 billion and American enterprises have obtained only $1.15 billion in contracts under IDA projects, this discrepancy may result from a tendency for contracts in former colonies to go to former colonial powers, or from the absence of an American comparative advantage in providing the goods and services required by IDA projects, or from the relatively high percentage of local procurement by IDA projects, not from an institutional bias against buying American.[8] Even with the inclusion of IDA the ratio of contributions to procurement favored the United States. A Treasury Department assessment concluded that the American current account surplus over the life of all of the multilateral development banks was approximately $11 billion.[9]

Finally, the Bank's country economic and sector work under McNamara (or its work in the "macropolicy dialogue," as it has increasingly come to be called) did not change in a poverty-oriented direction as much as its project work apparently did. This principal conclusion was reiterated in the report of the Bank's task force on its poverty focus. The report observed that manpower allocations for work on poverty, basic needs, and related topics in the Bank's special economic reports were only 11 percent of total allocations for such reports in fiscal year 1982. According to the task force's report, "the evidence . . . suggests that the Bank has been more effective at the project level. The poverty focus has usually not been very significant in the macroeconomic dialogue." Of the twenty-six country programming papers produced in fiscal 1981, "nearly all mention poverty-related issues although the extent of coverage varies widely, and the relation to lending program choices is still often tenuous." When poverty-related issues were raised, moreover, the analysis of the Bank's country economic and sector work revealed a consistent set of institutional preferences that were a long way from adding up to socialist recipes. The Bank's neoliberal ideology is in many ways the antithesis of socialism. Even when the Bank operated in socialist countries under McNamara, it made efforts to orient their economic policies along the lines suggested by the institution's prevalent ideology. It applied various correctives to socialism. This was abundantly apparent in the relations between the Bank and Tanzania over the years of McNamara's leadership.

What may be concluded from this brief review of the activities of the Bank under McNamara? To summarize: the Bank did not throw overboard its traditonal lending for projects of basic economic infrastructure. Its poverty-oriented projects were congruent with its long-standing emphasis on economic growth. The rates of return on poverty-oriented projects were generally satisfactory. The allocation of Bank funds was, broadly speaking, in both the economic and political interests of American foreign policy. Market-oriented systems tended to be encouraged and socialist-oriented ones urged to consider market solutions. The Bank's macroeconomic policy advice was still very much in the neoclassical mode and dealt with poverty alleviation in a largely subsidiary fashion. While the Bank under McNamara was no longer a bastion of developmental traditionalism, it was a long way from adopting the more radical implications of attempting to mount an attack on poverty. The concern that the Bank might desert the poor must depart from a realization that under McNamara it never totally embraced them.

Clausen's Initial Emphases

What are the apparent concerns of the Bank's new president? One is a reiteration of the important role of the private sector in development and the ways in which the World Bank can relate in a more creative fashion to that sector. (Reference is both to the private sector in the developed countries, and the role it might play in investments and exports to the developing countries, and to the private sector within the developing countries themselves, and the role it might play in the domestic development of those countries.) This was a central theme in Clausen's first annual address to the Bank's Board of Governors. In another important address, Clausen expressed his belief that "those countries have demonstrated the best economic performance that have encouraged their private sectors."[10] Shortly before that speech the Bank had released a report on the future development of sub-Saharan Africa. According to Clausen, one of its principal messages was that "the economic growth in these countries can be accelerated by the more effective use of their domestic private sectors."[11]

Clausen also has sought to inter the North–South model of international economic relations. In his view, "the old North–South economic model of the international economy of the 1960s and 1970s is no longer very useful. It . . . has tended to create a bipolar concept of world economic dynamics that glosses over—or completely leaves out—a whole series of other elements of economic activity that just do not fit into a rigid North–South dichotomy."[12] Among these other elements were the emergence of the newly industrializing countries, technological advance in the developed countries, the expanding role of the private sector in meeting the world's capital requirements, and the acceleration in the movement of workers across international frontiers. These developments would mean a qualitatively different world by 1990, and the World Bank would have to understand better this newly emerging international reality. In so doing, however, "the World Bank . . . will remain a bank. And a very sound and prudent bank. It is not in the business of redistributing wealth from one set of countries to another set of countries. It is not the Robin Hood of the international financial set, nor the United Way of the development community. The World Bank is a hardheaded, unsentimental institution that takes a very pragmatic and nonpolitical view of what it is trying to do."[13]

It would be simplistic to conclude, however, that these emphases amount to "betraying the poor." Clausen has given vigorous endorsement to IDA on many occasions after assuming the presidency of the Bank. Almost 90 percent of IDA resources in fiscal 1981 went to countries with per capita incomes below $390. Clausen has stressed that IDA "remains the world's most important single source of concessional assistance for the poorest of the poor developing countries," and that he does not believe that the United States would "turn its back on those hundreds of millions of individuals who only want a chance to improve their own economic performance."[14] He also has placed great emphasis on the problems of sub-Saharan Africa and has urged a doubling of aid to the poorest African countries.[15]

In a lengthy interview with the author, Clausen indicated that he is not uninterested in poverty alleviation. But he approaches the matter quite differently from his predecessor. McNamara emphasized targeting of benefits and beneficiaries. By so doing, he was perhaps somewhat oblivious to the country context in which these targets were located. While Brazilian macroeconomic policies made it extremely difficult to mount a meaningful attack on Brazilian poverty, they did not prevent (in this view) zeroing in on the rural poor in the Brazilian northeast. The Bank-financed rural development projects in the northeast were thus justified despite the adverse country context. But Clausen is very concerned about the context. He emphasizes "macroconditionality" and wants the Bank to design "packages of projects" that could be tied to such conditionality. In this view there can be no meaningful poverty alleviation without the right set of country policies.

A number of additional factors, going beyond simply the views of its new president, are likely to ensure continuation of the Bank's poverty-oriented work. One of these is institutional inertia. Just as earlier it was difficult to steer the World Bank away from a commitment to basic economic infrastructure, it would now be difficult to steer it away from a commitment to poverty alleviation. Hundreds of poverty-oriented projects are under implementation, more are in the pipeline, and large numbers of Bank staff are involved in antipoverty initiatives. All of this would be extremely difficult to reverse. It is also well recognized that poverty-oriented lending has considerable appeal in the eyes of many donor countries. This is particularly the case with some European donors, but even the U.S. Treasury Department's report on the multilateral development banks concluded that the poverty-oriented lending of the Bank and IDA had made a significant contribution to the furtherance of American humanitarian objectives in developing countries.[16] Poverty-oriented lending counteracts the argument that foreign assistance takes money from the American taxpayer of modest means and gives it to the wealthy in poor countries. This is one of the main instrumental purposes for continuing such lending. There is also an awareness that no other institution—bilateral or multilateral, official or nonofficial—can alleviate Third World poverty on the scale on which the Bank has been doing it. A retreat from a concern with poverty alleviation on the part of the World Bank would leave an enormous gap in the total world flow of resources for antipoverty purposes. It is unrealistic to think that this would be compensated by increased flows from other sources.

All of this suggests that the ideological and programmatic differences between "McNamara's Bank" and "Clausen's Bank" have been exaggerated. Much of the emphasis upon the role of the private sector in development has been a tactical device, a partly symbolic response to the context confronting Clausen. It assures the private sector in the major donor countries (particularly the United States) that the Bank can be trusted to be a responsible financial intermediary. While McNamara's Bank had for some a "leftist" image which obscured the real nature of its operations, Clausen's Bank has acquired for others a "rightist" image which likewise obscures what the Bank is really doing.

Future Changes at the Bank

Yet Clausen's agenda for the Bank does entail changes, and it needs to be asked how such changes might affect the antipoverty work.

One such change is the effort to give greater operational relevance to arguments about the role of the private sector in development. This is taking several forms. Cofinancing with private commercial banks is a principal theme. (There can also be cofinancing with other *public* institutions, such as bilateral or multilateral aid agencies.) Increased emphasis on this antedated the arrival of Clausen. From fiscal 1977 to fiscal 1979 World Bank operations providing for cofinancing with private commercial banks averaged ten a year with the private sector contribution amounting to about $400 million a year. In fiscal 1980 and 1981, however, before McNamara's departure, the number of such cofinanced loans had grown to an average of twenty a year, and the private sector contribution to $1.7 billion a year.[17]

Cofinancing is the process through which an official lending institution, like the Bank, joins with private creditors in making a loan. They are coparticipants in the loan. The Bank loan presumably leverages additional money from private lenders, thereby channeling greater total amounts of capital to the developing countries than would be channeled by either lender loaning separately. This allegedly has advantages for the private lenders, offering them more diversified lending opportunities (such as project lending instead of only suppliers' credits or balance-of-payments support) as well as greater information on recipient countries and loan administration services (such as project supervision). It also is alleged to have advantages for the development banks, since it in theory increases the possibility that private bank funds will be directed to some higher-risk countries and used in high-priority development projects. While private cofinancing was involved in only 21 of the Bank's 140 development projects financed in fiscal 1980, an official of the U.S Treasury Department reported that between one-third and two-thirds of Bank projects could be cofinanced with the private sector within the next one to five years.[18]

Another possibility under the rubric of greater encouragement to the private sector is an expansion in the role and lending activities of the International Finance Corporation. As noted in chapter 2, IFC lending in fiscal 1980 represented only about 6 percent of total World Bank Group commitments. In fiscal 1981, however, the IFC approved new investments equal to the total approved in the entire first fifteen years of its history.[19] Clausen has spoken glowingly of the IFC on more than one occasion, including his first annual address to the Board of Governors, and representatives of the Reagan administration have been even firmer in their support for this component of the Bank Group.

There is some Bank interest in a multilateral insurance agency that would provide a kind of political risk insurance to investors wishing to invest in developing countries. A possible model at the national level is the Overseas Private Investment Corporation (OPIC) of the United States. This is a government-owned corporation that provides investment incentives to American business by offering political risk insurance and financial services. OPIC insures against risks of currency inconvertibility, expropriation, and damages resulting from war, revolution, or insurrection. It also provides American business with information about foreign investment opportunities and supplies funds for investment feasibility studies on a cost-sharing basis. Another alternative is that of a "GATT for investment"—what Clausen has referred to as "a general set of agreements on the whole issue of international investment."[20] The Bank is disposed to participate in such an effort so that investment can be "the effective driving force of development that it can become in the 1980s and beyond."[21]

Other changes at the Bank entail some alterations in its lending program. The Bank's lending for energy is on the increase. Planned lending for energy development in fiscal 1982 was approximately $3 billion, a 25 percent increase over the level for fiscal 1981 and an amount that would boost the share of Bank lending for the energy sector to almost a quarter of the Bank's total lending program. This includes lending for electric power generation, the development of coal resources, and oil and gas exploration and development.

There may also be an increase in the Bank's structural adjustment lending because such lending by its very nature facilitates macroconditionality more than the Bank's traditional project lending. The Bank's first two structural adjustment loans to Turkey, for example, covered sixteen separate areas of macropolicy.[22] Of the Bank's first twelve structural adjustment loans negotiated since the policy was approved, ten included provisions on agricultural pricing policy; eleven included measures to increase export incentives; ten called for revision and review of the entire public sector investment programs; and eight were aimed at the ability of the countries to mobilize resources through changes in budgetary policy.[23] These are all areas notoriously difficult to affect through lending for specific sectoral or subsectoral projects. Structural adjustment lending is compatible with Clausen's general approach to the development of low-income countries.

Greater attention to macroconditionality could also affect the country composition of Bank lending. If macroconditionality were to mean the attachment of loan conditions that encourage market-oriented solutions to development problems, and if countries adopting such solutions were to be rewarded with greater Bank lending, then some important country reallocations could be expected. This would seem a logical conclusion of combining an emphasis on macroconditionality with an emphasis on private-sector or market-oriented development models.

Some changes may also be in store for IDA. Maturities of IDA credits may be shortened. An interest rate on IDA credits may be introduced. Clausen has voiced the possibility of some kind of trigger mechanism for repayment of IDA credits, whereby countries would begin repaying the credits upon maturing from IDA to the Bank. A tougher maturation policy might be adopted, with previous IDA recipients moving more quickly into blend and Bank borrowing. Changes in the country allocation of IDA funds may be required, most notably through a reduction in the share going to India. There could be a multitiered IDA with different loan terms and requirements for different countries (according to their level of development and creditworthiness). These and related changes would be designed to mollify some donors who have come to regard IDA as a "global soup kitchen" or "an international entitlement program."[24]

Finally, the Bank will of necessity have to devote greater attention to the financing of its lending program, that is, to Bank borrowing and other sources of funds. A high Bank official told the author that there would have to be "more address of the Bank's funding needs." The Bank will have to "fight for levels of funding." There will be a "necessity of private sources of funding because official development assistance simply isn't going to grow." Also required will be "more money from new sources—such as the Middle East, Norway, and Japan."

What are some of the implications of these financial concerns? Some observers are worried about "crowding out"; they fear that a stagnant or dwindling market for fixed-interest, long-term securities could bring the Bank increasingly into competition with other borrowers on the fixed-interest, long-term market. The Bank might have to consider changes in its lending policies partly out of financial necessity, partly to appease a latent sense of unease among its creditors. Consideration might be given to variable-rate lending of some kind. The Bank has many loans outstanding at low interest rates but must currently borrow in volatile financial markets at high rates. This has not been a major problem to date but could conceivably become one in the future. There might also have to be shorter maturities on future Bank loans. There might have to be differentiation in the interest rates charged and other terms applied to its borrowers; should the Bank continue to apply the same inflexible interest rate to every borrowing country no matter what the project?

Cofinancing of development loans with private commercial banks, an expanded role for the IFC, multilateral investment schemes supported by the Bank, increased lending for energy development and structural adjustment, greater attention to macroconditionality, a certain toughening of IDA and its lending terms, a greater concern with Bank borrowing and the financial side of its lending operations: in principle do any or all of these approaches *necessarily* have to be at the expense of the Bank's concern for poverty alleviation which marked its activities during the McNamara years? While these newer Bank emphases need not ipso facto constitute a threat to the continuation of the Bank's poverty-oriented work, there are dangers that need to be briefly pinpointed.

Limitations of Private-Sector Emphasis

The emphasis on the role of the private sector in development can easily be overdone. The importance attributed to cofinancing is a case in point. Although there has been a high level of recycling of excess liquidity on the international capital markets since the mid-1970s, a large number of developing countries remain with only limited access to capital. Cofinancing in theory could alleviate this problem, but it apparently has not done so. As of the end of 1979 about 80 percent of the Bank's private cofinancing commitments went to Latin American countries, with ten projects in Brazil alone.[25] This indicates that co-financing has been largely limited to the middle-income developing countries, those countries with greater access to the international capital markets through their perceived creditworthiness. It is thus debatable whether cofinancing can significantly speak to the needs of lower-income developing countries.

This also raises the question of whether the much touted additionality of capital flows to developing countries, which supposedly results from increased cofinancing, has actually materialized. In a recent interview the Bank's treasurer offered the opinion that the cofinancing portion supplied by private commercial banks may well be substitutional, not additional capital. Commercial bank resources flowing into cofinancing of a World Bank loan might have flowed to the recipient countries in any event. If this is so, then the leveraging or catalytic role of the Bank in this regard may be exaggerated.

There are also grounds for concern if as many as two-thirds of future Bank loans were to be cofinanced. Despite efforts to effect a better liaison between private banks and the World Bank, the respective lending instrumentalities have some sharply different criteria regarding where loans should go, for what purposes, with what conditions, and so forth. Substantially increased cofinancing could lead to the excessive intrusion of private bankers' criteria into World Bank decision making.

In the case of the International Finance Corporation there is a similar concern about the countries to which its resources have flowed. While the IFC has attempted to expand its operations in the poorest countries in recent years, only 14 percent of its total loan equity and syndication commitments for fiscal 1980 were in countries with per capita incomes below $360.[26] (By way of contrast, 86 percent of IDA commitments for that fiscal year were in countries with incomes below that figure.[27]) One reason for the apparent discrepancy between the IFC's announced objective of increasing its transfers to the poorest countries and its actual ability to do so is the size of IFC-funded projects undertaken in these countries. Light industry, for example, has his-torically been the largest category in terms of the number of IFC operations in the poorest countries. Because of the labor intensiveness and domestically oriented nature of the output of these projects, the average investment per project has been smaller than in other sectors. Transfers of IFC capital to the private sector in the least developed countries generally have been hindered, moreover, by constraints of managerial expertise, technical knowledge, and other factors relating to absorptive capacity. Nevertheless, to be a more effective antipoverty instrument than it has been to date, the IFC would need to increase its activities in the poorest countries and in sectors closely related to the alleviation of poverty. In middle-income developing countries it would need to pay greater attention to employment generation, correcting its apparent historical tendency to assist capital-intensive industrial enterprises in such countries.

A certain skepticism must also be registered regarding the Bank's recently expressed interest in assisting the flow of private direct investment abroad. This proposal immediately confronts the role of the profit motive in a market economy. It may well be that private investment has a role to play in development, but it is also certain that its own set of institutional demands makes it a poor substitute for official development assistance. The need for flattering annual reports and competitive profit margins constrains even the most socially concerned businessman. One of the major development challenges of the future is how private investment could be channeled, by the World Bank or by others, in ways that would make greater contributions toward poverty alleviation, employment creation, and human resource development. The possibilities would seem many and varied, ranging from tax and other incentives within *developing* countries themselves to affect the locational and sectoral investment decisions of foreign investors to programs in *developed* countries that might subsidize investors in various ways for undertaking investment projects with demonstrable employment-creating effects.

Problems Implicit in Lending Program Changes
While too great an emphasis on courting the private sector could adversely affect the Bank's antipoverty activities, so might pronounced changes in the nature of its lending program. The increasing emphasis on structural adjustment lending leads to a concern that the conditionality attached to such lending would resemble too closely the conditionality attached to the stabilization programs of the International Monetary Fund. These have historically been alleged to be at the expense of the poor (as indicated in chapter 2, through contraction in government social programs, wage freezes, reduction or elimination of food subsidies, and the like). Some within the Bank have expressed the concern that its structural adjustment lending might similarly neglect the interests of the poor, that they would be sacrificed on the altar of fiscal and monetary austerity. The concern was most recently voiced in the report of the Bank's task force on the poverty focus, in which one of the principal recommendations was that future structural adjustment lending conditions explicitly take into account the effects of such lending on poverty groups within recipient countries. Such a

concern was not evident, however, in a recent paper on such lending prepared by the Bank official most prominently identified with the structural adjustment concept.[28] It remained to be seen whether there were viable ways of incorporating an explicit concern for the poor into the design of structural adjustment conditionality.

The concern with an increase in the Bank's lending for energy development is related to a somewhat different point. Under McNamara, with the spectacular growth in the aggregate transfer of Bank resources already documented, there could be increased lending in absolute amounts for all sectors (poverty, nonpoverty, traditional, new-style, and so forth). Under Clausen and in the difficult climate for development assistance of the 1980s the aggregate amount of Bank lending is highly unlikely to grow at the rapid rates of the McNamara years. Therefore, if there is to be a substantial increase in the Bank's energy lending program, and if total Bank lending is going to grow by only modest amounts, then a growth in energy lending would necessarily be at the expense of lending to other sectors. What other sectors might these be? There is concern both within and outside the Bank that poverty-oriented lending might suffer as a result of the desired increase in energy lending. There are two responses to this concern: poverty-oriented lending could continue to increase while other, nonpoverty sectors are cut back; or the Bank could make a systematic effort to see to it that its expanded energy lending has a clear, beneficial impact on poverty groups in borrowing countries. Either response would obviate the necessity for excessive misgivings about an increase in the Bank's energy lending program somehow hurting the poor.

Limitations of Financial Emphasis
Too great a concern with toughening the terms of its lending would also threaten the Bank's poverty-oriented work. In an interview with the author, McNamara openly questioned whether countries like India (and others much poorer) could really afford to borrow on the harder terms being proposed. Although the Bank's treasurer might have been able to say that in his first eleven years at the Bank he had found no concern on Wall Street about its poverty-oriented lending, it is questionable whether he will be able to say that as unequivocally in the future. In parlous financial times banks find it difficult to lend to poor people. That is obviously the case in the United States today, and it could be the case in the World Bank as well. The kinds of financial changes under consideration would doubtlessly reduce the concessionality of Bank/IDA lending. This may be unavoidable, but its impact

on poor recipients—countries and peoples—cannot be seen as anything but unfavorable. The Bank therefore will have to exercise care in designing the terms of its future lending program to reduce to the maximum extent possible any adverse impact on its poorest borrowers.

At the extreme, then, all of the changes now under consideration at the World Bank run the danger of converting it into little more than an underwriter of the schemes of commercial banks, multinational corporations, and the supply-side theories of the more committed capitalist ideologues. But the danger is not, it is argued here, an excessive one. The Bank under Clausen remains aware of the complementary nature of the private and public sectors in the development of poor countries. There is a realization that equating macroconditionality with IMF stabilization programs would seriously jeopardize the unique role of the Bank as a development institution. There is widespread awareness within the institution of the potentially disastrous results that would accompany the crippling of IDA. Financial authorities at the Bank do not maintain that the legitimate concern with borrowing needs and lending terms mean that it should become just another bank among many. For these reasons the changed emphases discussed here are incorrectly interpreted if they are seen as efforts to undo the principal accomplishments of the Bank under McNamara, particularly its accomplishments in the area of poverty alleviation.

Future Effectiveness of Poverty-Oriented Work

Poverty-oriented lending of the World Bank is highly likely to continue for an even more fundamental reason. This is because of the central datum about development over the next two decades: continued poverty in the developing world. It is highly likely that more than one billion people will be living in absolute poverty in the year 2000, given current trends of economic growth and distribution in developing countries—a condition that McNamara referred to in his final annual address as "life so limited by malnutrition, illiteracy, disease, high infant mortality, and low life expectancy as to be beneath any rational definition of human decency."[29]

The Bank and its major donor countries must care about this projection for a number of reasons. They must care on moral or ethical grounds, for the notion that the rich should assist the poor is, as McNamara himself phrased it, "the foundation of every great religion and every democratic society."[30] The Bank also cares for straightforward economic reasons. A significant amelioration of the plight of the Third World's poor would greatly expand world markets for the Bank's principal shareholders and would expand investment opportunities for private investors within its principal donor countries. Finally, the World Bank's caring about poverty in poor countries is important to the United States and other developed countries for political and strategic reasons. One billion people living in absolute poverty is a reality very likely to lead to intolerable political instability in many poor countries of great importance to rich countries. A greater Bank effort to overcome absolute poverty would be eminently compatible with the interests of the developed countries in political stability, reform, and peaceful change. The real question confronting the World Bank and the developed countries which are the main donors of development assistance therefore is not whether they can afford to care about world poverty; it is how to act upon their valid concern about poverty.

Many of the answers to this question have to do with the future effectiveness of the Bank's antipoverty work. In its recent report on the Bank's poverty focus under McNamara, the Bank task force included among its recommendations "expanding and improving the effectiveness of poverty-oriented project work." It had, however, very little to say about how this should be done. The present study of the Bank's poverty-oriented work begun in the McNamara years suggests a number of ways in which the question of the Bank's effectiveness might be addressed. Most of these presume that the essential parameters of the Bank's operations are likely to remain much the same in the future, that the Bank is unlikely to be transformed into something highly or totally different from what it is at present (it will not, for example, become the organizational vehicle for the redistribution of the world's income).

A number of changes, varying in degree of feasibility, could conceivably improve the Bank's future effectiveness as an antipoverty instrumentality. Some of these concern the Bank's relations with other organizations devoted to the alleviation of poverty in the developing world. For example, the Bank might want to consider joint venture funding with other development assistance agencies, particularly those largely or completely devoted to antipoverty work. An example might be the Inter-American Foundation (IAF). The IAF, a creation of the U.S. Congress, was established to grant small credits to nongovernmental intermediaries in Latin America. Extending its first funds in 1971, it has emphasized bottom-up development, self-help, participatory development strategies, collective self-reliance, distribution-oriented projects, and the like. In the interviewing for this study, many observers (both inside and outside the World Bank) held up the IAF as an organizational model of what a real poverty-oriented development assistance agency should look like.[31] Whether this is the case or not, mechanisms could be sought whereby the large amounts of funds available from the Bank for poverty-oriented work would be joined with the experience, established relations, and knowledge of the poverty sector of such agencies. In one variant these agencies would provide seed capital for poverty-oriented organizations and projects in recipient countries, and the Bank would then enter with much more substantial amounts of funding. In a proposed Bank urban project in Guatemala, for example, an effort was made to involve organizations previously funded by IAF as the recipients of the proposed loan. (The effort unfortunately failed because of political difficulties within Guatemala.)

There is likewise considerable room for expanding and coordinating the activities of private voluntary organizations (PVOs) in developing countries. These organizations operate their own development programs in the Third World. In the United States alone, there are approximately 500 to 600 such organizations.[32] They tend to be nonprofit, tax-exempt organizations heavily dependent on private contributions for revenue. There would seem to be considerable room for expanding and coordinating the activities of these organizations. Because of their direct focus upon recipients, many PVOs tend to have greater grassroots experience within a particular sector or country than the larger bilateral or multilateral institutions. By virtue of their typically small size many are also less bureaucratically constrained. Yet size can be a double-edged sword. The PVOs cannot compare with the bilateral and multilateral agencies in the quantitative transfer of capital and resources. The total commitments of all PVOs registered with the Agency for International Development (AID, the U.S. development assistance agency) in fiscal 1979 was $1.2 billion, compared with World Bank and IDA commitments in that year of $10 billion.[33] Given more financial resources, many PVOs could probably double or triple the extent of their operations without a problem. A recent amendment to U.S. foreign assistance legislation stipulates that AID earmark 16 percent of its total program to such private voluntary organizations.[34]

It might be useful to pursue the question of whether the World Bank could have a similar role to play in liaison with these kinds of organizations for antipoverty purposes. The effort would be to overcome the tension that seems to exist between resources and expertise in the provision of development assistance. It frequently seems as if those who have the local-level knowledge and expertise to combat rural and urban poverty (such as private voluntary organizations, nonprofit foundations, local activist groups of the poor themselves, and various other nongovernmental intermediaries) lack the resources required by the sheer magnitude of the task. It would remain to be seen whether such organizations would embrace some form of Bank assistance, even if ways could be devised to facilitate it. While expansion of the impact of private voluntary organizations could come about through expansion of their capital bases, closer association with the American government or the World Bank could present a threat to those factors that have apparently made the organizations effective in the past.

However it is done, an intensified effort needs to be made to explore the feasibility of utilizing nongovernmental intermediaries as recipients of the transfer of Bank resources. They may be more effective vehicles for the address of poverty alleviation than the governmental inter-mediaries through which the Bank now almost exclusively lends. This will not be an easy task, however; attempts to smuggle in change through nongovernmental intermediaries may soon run into the op-position of wary governments, as the Inter-American Foundation learned when it was requested by the government of Brazil to cease its activities in that country.

Another possibility that deserves exploration would have the Bank serve as project officer for the implementation of projects by other functional agencies in the UN system, such as UNICEF. Perhaps the Bank could fund projects whose implementation would be supervised by such other agencies. Attention could also be given to a more effective relationship between the Bank and the regional development banks, particularly the Inter-American Development Bank, which is easily the largest of these. The Bank presently has some cooperative programs, but it has serious doubts about the technical competence of some of the UN agencies, as well as doubts about what it sees as the politicization of these agencies and the regional banks. Nevertheless, the Bank and these other agencies could devote more thought to ways of harmonizing their programs.

Some other changes that might improve the Bank's effectiveness as an antipoverty instrumentality are not related to other organizations; rather they concern the Bank's own operations. For example, the Bank might become more of a wholesaler of antipoverty funds; the recipient country more of a retailer. The Bank might make more sector program loans instead of lending for a multiplicity of miniprojects. It could cultivate poverty-oriented analogues to the development finance com-panies (DFCs) which it has long supported in industrial development. The traditional approach has been to make relatively large loans to DFCs, which then lend the funds to industrial undertakings within recipient countries.

Something similar is perhaps required to transfer resources for poverty alleviation. The difficulty, however, is that the creation of such intermediaries in developing countries implies heroic institutional capacities (to say nothing of the political will) which is seemingly beyond most of them at present. Nevertheless, such an organizational framework in the long run seems to make more sense than the Bank's current practice of disbursing relatively small amounts of funds directly from Washington.

There is another reason for the recommended approach. The Bank's antipoverty projects begun under McNamara were very staff-intensive; they consumed large amounts of staff time but yielded relatively small loans. In the first full fiscal year after approval of a typical Bank-funded urban project in a recipient country, supervision averaged as high as 38.5 staff weeks per project per year. Study of data for fiscal years 1975 to 1978 revealed that urban projects consistently required more supervisory input than any other kind of Bank project, with the single exception of population and nutrition projects (themselves antipoverty projects of course). Rural development projects required an average of 13.3 staff weeks in fiscal 1978. By contrast, Bank projects in the traditional power sector required an average of only 9.3 staff weeks of supervision per project per year in fiscal 1978. Poverty-oriented projects caused the productivity of staff, crudely measured, to decline. It was doubtful at the end of McNamara's tenure whether the Bank could continue to process an ever-increasing number of such relatively small projects; the staffing implications appeared too severe.

The tendency under McNamara was to diversify lending within countries. As a result, by the end of his presidency, the Bank was lending in some countries (such as Brazil) for rural development, basic urbanization, basic education, nutrition, and for other poverty-related purposes (as well as for various traditional purposes). There was a legitimate concern that not enough of any one thing was being financed, with a consequent dissipation of impact in all sectors. In the future the Bank might consider limiting its antipoverty involvement in a recipient country to only one or two sectors instead of attempting to do just a little bit of everything.

A related suggestion is that the Bank should do simple things first and more complex ones later if ever. Its new-style rural development projects often appeared to contain too many multisectoral components. As was demonstrated, these created many difficulties of coordination and frequently slowed down the implementation of projects. Poverty-oriented projects should perhaps aim to do one good thing and to do it well. One way out of some of these dilemmas would be for the

Bank to undertake parallel poverty-oriented projects in different sectors, perhaps within the same region of a recipient country. Linkages and complementarities might eventually be exploited automatically without slowing entire projects down.

World Bank resources in the future are highly unlikely to grow at the expansionary rates of the 1970s. Resources will remain stagnant in real terms or will grow only moderately. This means that new Bank president Clausen will be obliged to consider ways in which the Bank can exploit its existing resources more effectively. There needs to be much greater attention to the Bank's nonproject work, to the other elements of its tasks discussed in chapter 2. The Bank's institution building and other technical assistance activities in developing countries should take on added importance. Frequently, these will be found to be of substantially greater significance than the aggregate transfer of financial resources by the Bank. They can build up the retailers of antipoverty funds in recipient countries. Another internal task awaiting the Bank's attention is substantially greater coordination of its project work with its country economic and poverty-oriented research work. Such coordination would speak to several of the difficulties discussed by urban poverty staff in chapter 8: it would, for example, improve decisions about the intersectoral allocation of the marginal dollar.

 ˙ The Bank's antipoverty expertise would be improved by some degree of decentralization. There appears to be a necessity for more (and more fully staffed) regional or country resident missions. The centralized-in-Washington, traveling-mission oriented approach does not seem particularly well suited to reaching the poor. They are not likely to be found in one- or two-shot missions to developing countries. Decentralization should assist in the Bank's accumulation of greater local knowledge of the contexts of poverty-oriented development projects, knowledge that would also be facilitated by the more substantial encouragement of project monitoring and evaluation units staffed by nationals from the recipient countries themselves.

In a sense therefore a poverty-oriented World Bank in the future would need to become a more political institution and require greater awareness of the sociopolitical contexts of its operations at the local level. One observer reached this conclusion about the Bank's work in Indonesia: "The newer projects have embroiled the Bank in the cultural and political crosscurrents of a host of small Indonesian communities. The background needed to understand these forces is more than the Bank has managed to muster so far. Many observers consider the Bank's clumsy performance in these and other projects the result of ignorance about the way things work in Indonesia."[35]

The Bank's approach under McNamara was an overtly technocratic one. It was thought possible to develop basically similar projects to reach basically similar poverty groups and solve basically similar problems—wherever they existed. There was some limited evidence that the Bank at the conclusion of McNamara's presidency was beginning to give somewhat more attention to other considerations—such as the local political situation, the tribal context, peculiarities of local socioeconomic structure—but there did not yet seem to be a major effort in this regard. The balance between the Bank's professed apolitical role and the political awareness that is required for effective poverty alleviation will be an issue in the future, as it has been in the past.

There is another sense in which the Bank would need to become more political if it wished to improve its work as an antipoverty instrumentality. It would have to exercise greater leverage on behalf of poverty-oriented activites in the countries that are the recipients of its resources. Among the variables influencing the possibility of the Bank's employing such leverage might be the size of the Bank's lending program as a percentage of the country's total external capital requirements (the greater this percentage, the greater might be the leverage), the current economic condition of the country (the worse off the country, the more it might need the Bank, the better might be the possibility of leverage), or the history of the country's past involvement with the Bank (the more harmonious, the greater might be the leverage almost by definition). When all is said and done, however, very little evidence could be unearthed in this study that pointed in the direction of the Bank's consistently and systematically exercising leverage on recipient countries in order to persuade, cajole, manipulate, or compel them into undertaking poverty-oriented projects and into assigning greater weight to the distributional aspects of development strategies. There appears to have been much too little of this kind of leverage. No doubt the objection will be that the exercising of such leverage on behalf of antipoverty concerns is not feasible or practical. This may well be, but it is difficult to know until a greater effort is made.

These are some of the changes that Clausen's Bank might wish to consider if, as has been argued here, it does not wish to abandon the antipoverty initiatives of the McNamara years. Those Bank staff members committed to the antipoverty approach no doubt have their own agenda for change. Some of the changes given consideration here are undoubtedly more feasible than others, but none would appear to be totally outside the reach of the Bank as it is today. They would markedly change but would not totally transform the institution. They have the potential for improving its capabilities in the field of poverty alleviation. They would better harmonize the Bank's roles as bank and development agency, mover of money, and antipoverty instrumentality.

A Need for More Fundamental Changes?

If the conservative critique of the Bank holds sway, and if the Bank accommodates to it excessively by reverting totally to a traditional banking role, then few if any of these kinds of changes will even be considered. Even if the conservative attack on the Bank is successfully blunted, however, the financial stringencies inherent in the contemporary international context of development will constitute a threat to a continuation or extension of its poverty-oriented role. In either case what would be left behind in the future is any response to the structural (or radical) critique of the Bank. Excessive accommodation to the policy implications of the conservative critique would leave the Bank wide open to attacks from the left.

In thinking about the Bank's future, the structural critique is of relevance on two levels. One is the level of the international system and its relationship to what has come to be called North–South relations. The other level is that of the domestic systems within the countries of the South. The argument in this volume has been that the Bank has tended to accommodate itself to the prevailing structure of North–South relations and the prevailing socioeconomic and political structures within developing countries. In so doing, it has adopted a practical approach to its activities which has resulted in certain constraints on its effectiveness. Given international and national realities, the Bank has on the whole performed well.

Such a conclusion does not satisfy the structuralists, however. They believe the Bank is captive to the dominant forces within the international system, such as the moneylenders of the large private banks and the chieftains of the multinational corporations. They believe it is also captive to the economic and political elites within the countries that receive Bank money. With this perspective, thinking about the future of the World Bank makes little or no sense without thinking about a virtual transformation in these structures of dependency.

One can be far from adopting this whole argument and still see its salience at a time when conservative forces are, if anything, seeking to reinforce and intensify the very structures to which the radical critics are vigorously objecting. While the times may not appear appropriate for thinking about more than relatively modest changes in the role and operations of the World Bank, it must be admitted that the future of the Bank under Clausen and beyond cannot be discussed totally in isolation from the future of North–South relations more generally. What kind of World Bank does the world want in the future? A complete answer to the question would depend upon answering the more fundamental question: What kinds of North–South relations does the world want in the future? Different answers to that question would affect matters such as the future financing of the Bank, its power structure, its organization, its nonproject functions, the balance between its traditional and poverty-oriented activities, and the like.

Many of the issues in contemporary North–South relations were addressed by the Independent Commission on International Development Issues, popularly known as the Brandt Commission because it was chaired by Willy Brandt, former Chancellor of the Federal Republic of Germany. The suggestion of creating such a commission was first advanced by McNamara in a speech in Boston early in 1977, and he reverted to it in his address to the Annual Meeting of the Board of Governors in Washington in September of that year. The commission was composed of eighteen representatives, including ten from developing countries. It released its report early in 1980, approximately two years after commencing deliberations. The report dealt with the entire range of issues confronting the countries of the North and South: the world food situation, population, commodity trade, energy, industrialization, world monetary order, investment, and so forth.[36]

The commission proposed initiatives and reforms in a great variety of areas, including some dramatic initiatives concerning the sources of development assistance. It proposed, for example, "an international system of universal revenue mobilization based on a sliding scale related to national income, in which East European and developing countries—except the poorest countries—would participate."[37] It also recommended "introduction of automatic revenue transfers through international levies on some of the following: international trade; arms production or exports; international travel; [and] the global commons, expecially seabed minerals."[38]

In the area of institutional innovations the commission urged consideration of a new international financial institution to be called a World Development Fund. The Fund would have universal membership, and decision making within it would be "more evenly shared between lenders and borrowers." According to the commission, the Fund "would supplement existing institutions and diversify lending policies and practices"; "it would seek to satisfy the unmet needs in the financing structure, in particular that of program lending"; and "ultimately it could serve as a channel for such resources as may be raised on a universal and automatic basis."[39]

The analysis and recommendations of the Brandt Commission were not thoroughgoing enough to satisfy the more radical among the structuralist critics of the contemporary international order.[40] The view here, however, is that the Brandt Commission's concrete recommendations were less important than the spirit that animated them. That spirit assumed the reality of dramatically increased interdependence among nations, the mutuality of interests between North and South, and the necessity for going beyond the present structure of North–South relations to a significantly different paradigm. Taking this spirit seriously would oblige going beyond Bretton Woods, to some kind of fundamental transformation of the procedures and institutions negotiated at this conference which in large measure outlined the world order for the post-1945 era.

The McNamara years at the Bank will be remembered in large part as an effort to rectify some of the omissions in the formation of the Bank. As McNamara departed and Clausen entered, the Bank seemed to be approaching the limits of trying to be both the institution it was created to be and the institution into which McNamara attempted to convert it.

Ultimately at issue is nothing less than the appropriate institutional format for the address of poverty alleviation over the next several decades. Despite the substantial and generally promising efforts of the Bank, the problems remain and are reaching alarming proportions. The solution, however, is not to dismantle the World Bank or convert it into a passive underwriter of the flows of private capital but to examine the whole range of international institutions with an eye to using them more effectively. This examination would include an assessment of the respective roles of the World Bank, the UN specialized agencies, the regional development banks, bilateral assistance programs, private voluntary organizations, private investment, the need for entirely new institutions, and the like.

There is need for a serious look at the role of the private sector in poverty-oriented development strategies. There is need for an equally searching examination of the respective comparative advantages of bilateral and multilateral institutions for providing development finance on behalf of poverty alleviation. The relationship of the World Bank to the regional development banks needs to be explored. The question of appropriate new institutions calls for analysis. Consideration might even be given to creation of an IDA administratively and financially separate from the Bank. IDA might become the world's preeminent development agency. It could engage in poverty-oriented projects in all developing countries, including middle-income countries. The Bank could become the world's preeminent multilateral bank, lending on near-commercial terms to middle-income countries and perhaps for projects of basic economic infrastructure in the poorest countries as well.

This is but a sampling of the kinds of institutional issues that would require consideration in a meaningful discussion of ways to combat world poverty in the future. Although the outlines of a future World Bank within the context of a significantly restructured international order can be only dimly perceived at present, it is difficult to see the Bank—under Clausen or anyone else—not playing a central role.

What may ultimately be required, but to which the conservative critics of the Bank seem remarkably oblivious, is a structure of North–South relations that would be more facilitative of the Bank's operations. Some of the current debate about the effectiveness of the Bank in reaching the world's poor would be resolved if adverse international and national constraints on development were reduced and parameters conducive to effectiveness significantly expanded.

This means that those who are urging the World Bank to become more effective as an alleviator of world poverty, including the conservatives who are demanding its effectiveness, are unaware of what this would entail. Greater effectiveness would require profound changes in the patterns of relations between rich and poor countries—and in the patterns of relations between rich and poor people *within* poor countries. If there is any betrayal of the poor on the part of the Bank, now or in the future, it is seen by this study to have its roots in the international and national conditions under which it must operate, not in the policy designs of McNamara's successor.

Appendix A Organization of the World Bank under McNamara

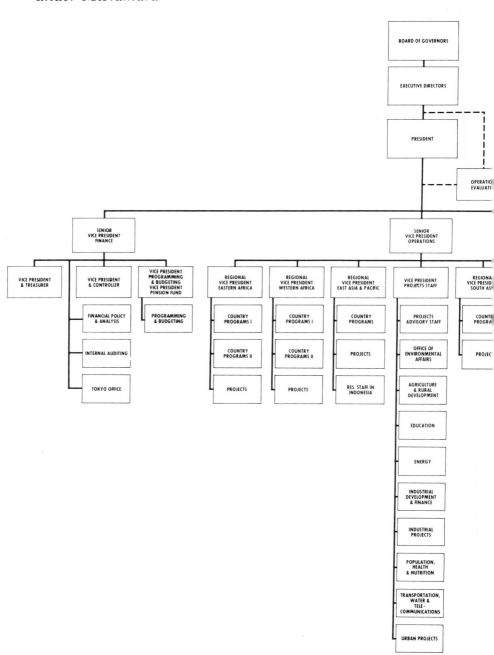

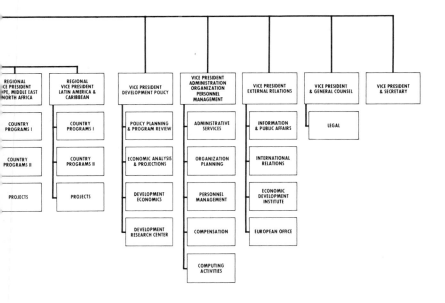

REGIONAL VICE PRESIDENT PE, MIDDLE EAST NORTH AFRICA	REGIONAL VICE PRESIDENT LATIN AMERICA & CARIBBEAN	VICE PRESIDENT DEVELOPMENT POLICY	VICE PRESIDENT ADMINISTRATION ORGANIZATION PERSONNEL MANAGEMENT	VICE PRESIDENT EXTERNAL RELATIONS	VICE PRESIDENT & GENERAL COUNSEL	VICE PRESIDENT & SECRETARY
COUNTRY PROGRAMS I	COUNTRY PROGRAMS I	POLICY PLANNING & PROGRAM REVIEW	ADMINISTRATIVE SERVICES	INFORMATION & PUBLIC AFFAIRS	LEGAL	
COUNTRY PROGRAMS II	COUNTRY PROGRAMS II	ECONOMIC ANALYSIS & PROJECTIONS	ORGANIZATION PLANNING	INTERNATIONAL RELATIONS		
PROJECTS	PROJECTS	DEVELOPMENT ECONOMICS	PERSONNEL MANAGEMENT	ECONOMIC DEVELOPMENT INSTITUTE		
		DEVELOPMENT RESEARCH CENTER	COMPENSATION	EUROPEAN OFFICE		
			COMPUTING ACTIVITIES			

Twenty Largest Recipients of Bank Loans, IDA Credits, and Bank/IDA Resources Combined, Cumulative, 1948 to 1980

Bank		IDA		Bank/IDA	
Brazil	5,313.7	India	8,285.2	India	11,055.8
Mexico	4,113.6	Bangladesh	1,454.2	Brazil	5,313.7
Indonesia	3,056.0	Pakistan	1,244.9	Mexico	4,113.6
South Korea	2,948.5	Indonesia	931.8	Indonesia	3,987.8
India	2,770.6	Egypt	783.6	South Korea	3,059.3
Colombia	2,761.4	Tanzania	538.7	Colombia	2,780.9
Yugoslavia	2,684.1	Sudan	522.5	Yugoslavia	2,684.1
Turkey	2,407.4	Kenya	408.3	Turkey	2,585.9
Philippines	2,389.9	Sri Lanka	369.6	Philippines	2,512.1
Thailand	1,960.4	Ethiopia	368.1	Pakistan	2,128.9
Romania	1,502.8	Burma	363.0	Thailand	2,089.9
Morocco	1,437.3	Zaire	277.0	Egypt	1,908.6
Nigeria	1,380.7	Madagascar	255.2	Romania	1,502.8
Argentina	1,350.3	Nepal	235.7	Bangladesh	1,500.3
Iran	1,210.7	Cameroon	230.5	Morocco	1,488.1
Malaysia	1,132.6	Yemen Arab Republic	208.3	Nigeria	1,416.2
Egypt	1,129.0	Senegal	187.7	Argentina	1,350.3
Algeria	1,091.0	Ghana	179.0	Iran	1,210.7
Pakistan	884.0	Turkey	178.5	Kenya	1,197.6
Japan	862.9	Mali	173.2	Malaysia	1,132.6

Note: Bank lending commenced in 1948; IDA lending commenced in 1961.

Appendix C   Rural Poverty Projects with Documentary and/or Interview Work

Algeria	Technical Assistance for Rural Development
Benin	Hinvi Agricultural Project
Benin	Zou-Borgou Cotton Project
Bangladesh	Rural Development Project I
Bangladesh	Barisal Irrigation Project
Bolivia	Ingavi Rural Development Project
Bolivia	Ulla Ulla Rural Development Project
Brazil	Lower São Francisco Polders Project
Brazil	Rio Grande do Norte Rural Development Project
Brazil	Bahia Rural Development Project (Paraguacu)
Brazil	Alto Turi Land Settlement Project
Brazil	Paraiba Rural Development Project (Brejo)
Brazil	Ceara Rural Development Project (IBIAPABA)
Burma	Irrigation I
Cameroon	Integral Rural Development Project (ZAPI)
Cameroon	Semry Rice Project
Colombia	Integrated Rural Development Project
Colombia	Córdoba 2 Agricultural Development Project
Colombia	Caquetá Rural Settlement Project Phase II
Colombia	Atlántico Irrigation Project
Colombia	First Agricultural Credit Project
Ecuador	First Livestock Development Project
Ecuador	Second Livestock Development Project
Ethiopia	Agricultural Minimum Package Project
Guyana	Tapakuma Irrigation Project
Haiti	Rural Development Project in the Northern Department
India	Rajasthan Dairy Development Project
Indonesia	Review of the Bank's entire agricultural program
Ivory Coast	First Cocoa Project
Korea	Rural Infrastructure Project
Liberia	Lofa County Agricultural Development Project

Madagascar	Village Livestock and Rural Development Project
Malawi	Lilongwe Land Development Program Phase I
Malawi	Shire Valley Agricultural Development Project Phase I
Malaysia	Jengka Forestry Project
Malaysia	Jengka Triangle Project I
Malaysia	Johore Land Settlement Project
Mali	Mali-Sud Agricultural Project
Mexico	Fifth Agricultural and Livestock Credit Project
Mexico	PIDER I Integrated Rural Development Project
Mexico	PIDER II Integrated Rural Development Project
Mexico	Third Irrigation Project
Mexico	Integrated Rural Development Project I (Papaloapan Basin)
Mexico	Third Livestock and Agricultural Development Project
Morocco	Meknes Agricultural Development Project
Nepal	Rasuwa-Nuwakot Development Project
Niger	Agricultural Credit Project
Nigeria	Funtua Agricultural Development Project
Nigeria	Lafia Agricultural Development Project
Nigeria	Western State Cocoa Project
Nigeria	Gombe Agricultural Development Project
Nigeria	Gusau Agricultural Development Project
Pakistan	Hill Farming Technical Development Project
Paraguay	Small Farmer Credit and Rural Development Project
Paraguay	Second Rural Development Project
Philippines	Rural Development (Land Settlement) Project
Philippines	Eleven irrigation projects
Rwanda	Cinchona Project
Senegal	Casamance Rice Project
Senegal	Eastern Senegal Livestock Development Project
Sierra Leone	Integrated Agricultural Development Project
Tanzania	Kigoma Rural Development Project
Tanzania	Tabora Rural Development Project
Tanzania	Mwanza-Shinyanga Rural Development Project
Thailand	Northeast Irrigation Development Project
Tunisia	Cooperative Farms Project
Turkey	Corum-Cankiri Rural Development Project
Upper Volta	Agricultural Development Project
Yemen Arab Republic	Southern Upland Rural Development Project

Appendix D Urban Poverty Projects with Documentary and/or Interview Work

Bolivia	Urban Development Project (La Paz)
Brazil	Sites-and-Services and Low-Cost Housing Project
Colombia	Urban Development Project
Colombia	Cartagena Urban Development Project
Egypt	Urban Development Project
El Salvador	Second Urban Development Project
El Salvador	Sites-and-Services Project
Guatemala	Earthquake Reconstruction Project
India	Madras Urban Development Project
India	Calcutta Urban Development Project
India	Second Calcutta Urban Development Project
Indonesia	Second Urban Development Project
Indonesia	Jakarta Urban Development Project
Ivory Coast	Urban Development Project (Abidjan)
Jamaica	Sites-and-Services Project (Four Cities)
Kenya	Second Urban Project
Kenya	Sites-and-Services Project
Korea	Gwangju Urban Development
Morocco	Rabat Urban Development Project
Peru	Urban Sites-and-Services Development Project
Philippines	Manila Urban Development Project
Senegal	Dakar Sites-and-Services Project
Tanzania	Second National Sites-and-Services Project
Thailand	Bangkok Sites-and-Services and Slum Improvement Project
Zambia	Lusaka Squatter Upgrading and Sites-and-Services Project

Notes

Chapter 1

1. Edward S. Mason and Robert E. Asher, *The World Bank Since Bretton Woods* (Washington, D.C.: The Brookings Institution, 1973), pp. 189, 190, 151, 152.

2. Ibid., p. 833.

3. Ibid., pp. 842, 844.

4. Ibid., p. 227.

5. Ibid., p. 226.

6. Ibid., p. 186.

7. Ibid., p. 125.

8. *World Bank Annual Report 1968*, pp. 8–9; *World Bank Annual Report 1981*, p. 10.

9. *World Bank Annual Report 1981*, p. 187.

10. The data on total staff in 1968 are from the *Report of the Task Force on Forms of Association* (a report of the World Bank Staff Association; Washington, D.C., July 27, 1978), p. 4. The data on total staff in 1981 are from the Information and Public Affairs Department of the Bank. The data on professional staff in 1968 are also from this department. The data on professional staff in 1981 are from *World Bank Annual Report 1981*, p. 10.

11. Robert S. McNamara, *Address to the Board of Governors* (Nairobi, Kenya: September 24, 1973).

12. Hollis Chenery et al., *Redistribution with Growth* (London: Oxford University Press, 1974).

13. *World Bank Annual Report 1968*, p. 8; *World Bank Annual Report 1981*, pp. 12–13.

14. Computed from data contained in *World Bank Annual Report 1981*, p. 12.

15. *World Bank Annual Report 1978*, p. 18.

16. Ibid.

17. These data were provided by the Urban Projects Department of the Bank.

18. These estimates were provided by the Education Department of the Bank.

19. These data were provided by the Population, Health, and Nutrition Department of the Bank.

20. These data were provided by the Population, Health, and Nutrition Department of the Bank.

21. This percentage was computed from data contained in *World Bank Annual Report 1968*, pp. 8–9.

22. This percentage was computed from data contained in *World Bank Annual Report 1980*, pp. 124–125.

23. *World Bank Annual Report 1980*, p. 11.

24. *Report of the Task Force on Forms of Association*, p. 9.

25. On this subject, see James P. Grant, "Development: The End of Trickle Down?" *Foreign Policy*, no. 12 (Fall 1973), pp. 43–65.

26. McNamara defined absolute poverty as "a condition of life so degraded by disease, illiteracy, malnutrition, and squalor as to deny its victims basic human necessities." See *Address to the Board of Governors*, September 24, 1973, pp. 6–7.

27. For an excellent general survey of the relationships between distribution and developmental concerns, see William R. Cline, "Distribution and Development: A Survey of Literature," *Journal of Development Economics*, 1 (1975), pp. 359–400.

28. For a general survey of this issue, see David Turnham, assisted by I. Jaeger, *The Employment Problem in Less Developed Countries: A Review of Evidence* (Paris: Organization for Economic Cooperation and Development, 1971).

29. Paul Bairoch, *The Economic Development of the Third World Since 1900* (Berkeley: University of California Press, 1975), p. 31.

30. These are discussed in T. N. Srinivasan and P. K. Bardhan, eds., *Poverty and Income Distribution in India* (Calcutta: Statistical Publishing Society, 1974).

31. Cited in John A. Mathieson, *Basic Needs and the New International Economic Order: An Opening for North–South Collaboration in the 1980's* (Washington, D.C.: Overseas Development Council, May 1981), pp. 22–24; ILO, *Employment, Growth and Basic Needs: A One-World Problem* (New York: Praeger, 1977); Jan Tinbergen, coordinator, *Reshaping the International Order: A Report to the Club of Rome* (New York: E.P. Dutton, 1976).

32. Jerome Levinson and Juan de Onis, *The Alliance that Lost Its Way* (Chicago: Quadrangle Books, 1970), p. 5.

33. Ibid., p. 8.

34. Mathieson, p. 21.

35. Ibid.

36. Ibid., p. 22.

37. Ibid.

38. Eugene H. Rotberg, *The World Bank: A Financial Appraisal* (Washington, D.C.: World Bank, May 1976), p. 21.

39. "Foreign Aid Retrenchment," "B List" (Office of Management and Budget, January 27, 1981), p. 3.

40. The critic is Edwin J. Feulner, president of the Heritage Foundation, cited in "Foreign Aid: Debating the Uses and Abuses," *New York Times*, March 1, 1981, p. E5.

41. Teresa Hayter, *Aid as Imperialism* (London: Penguin, 1971), p. 9.

42. Mason and Asher, *Since Bretton Woods*, p. 648.

43. "The First Mistake," *The Wall Street Journal*, November 7, 1980, p. 26.

44. Albert O. Hirschman, *Journeys toward Progress: Studies of Economic Policy-Making in Latin America* (New York: The Twentieth Century Fund, 1963), p. 255.

45. Thomas E. Weisskopf, "Capitalism, Underdevelopment, and the Future of the Poor Countries," *The Review of Radical Political Economics*, 4 (Spring 1972), p. 28. Also found in Jagdish Bhagwati, ed., *Economics and World Order* (New York: Free Press, 1972), p. 65.

Chapter 2

1. *International Finance Corporation Annual Report 1980*, p. 2.

2. The Bank's lending rate is adjusted one or more times per year. The new guidelines approved in July 1979 allow for a spread of one-half of one percent over the cost of borrowing, which is estimated for a twelve-month period using the actual cost of borrowing for the previous six months and the estimated cost for the following six months. See *World Bank Annual Report 1980*, p. 884.

3. *World Bank Annual Report 1981*, p. 10.

4. *World Bank Annual Report 1978*, p. 17.

5. Ibid., p. 10.

6. It does not, however, refer to the IFC.

7. *World Bank Annual Report 1981*, p. 190.

8. *Annual Address to the Board of Governors 1977*, p. 32.

9. *Annual Address to the Board of Governors 1976*, pp. 22–23.

10. *Annual Address to the Board of Governors 1977*, p. 11.

11. World Bank, *Health Sector Policy Paper* (Washington, D.C.: February 1980) and World Bank, *Education Sector Policy Paper* (Washington, D.C.: April 1980).

12. This goal was first stated in *Education Sector Working Paper* (Washington, D.C.: December 1974), p. 7. It was elaborated upon in *Education Sector Policy Paper* (April 1980).

13. World Bank, *World Development Report 1978* (Washington, D.C.: 1978), p. 33.

14. *The Research Program of the World Bank* (June 1981), p. 6. This formal research is to be distinguished from the Bank's economic and sector work and from what the Bank calls its operational review and policy work. The latter exceed research in expenditures, representing outlays of $34.7 and $21.8 million, respectively, in fiscal 1980. *The Research Program of the World Bank*, p. 6.

15. Ibid., p. 4.

16. Ibid., p. 8.

17. Ibid., p. 47.

18. Ibid., p. 48.

19. Ibid.

20. Ibid., p. 49.

21. Ibid.

22. Ibid., p. 47.

23. Ibid.

24. Ibid., p. 48.

25. Ibid.

26. Ibid., p. 21.

27. Ibid., pp. 21–22.

28. Ibid., p. 22.

29. Albert O. Hirschman, *Journeys toward Progress: Studies of Economic Policy-Making in Latin America* (New York: The Twentieth Century Fund, 1963), pp. 235–238.

30. Bernard Chadenet and John A. King, Jr., "What Is 'A World Bank Project'?" *Finance and Development*, 9 (September 1972), pp. 4, 5.

31. Mason and Asher, *Since Bretton Woods*, p. 269.

32. Ibid., p. 264.

33. *World Bank Annual Report 1980*, p. 68.

34. Ibid.

35. Ibid.

36. *World Bank Annual Report 1981*, p. 70.

37. *World Bank Annual Report 1980*, p. 124.

38. *World Bank Annual Report 1981*, p. 70.

39. Warren C. Baum, "The Project Cycle," *Finance and Development*, 7 (March 1970), p. 6.

Chapter 3

1. Robert S. McNamara, *Address to the Board of Governors* (Washington, D.C.: September 30, 1980), p. 4.

2. *World Development Report 1981*, p. 49.

3. Ibid.

4. *Address to the Board of Governors 1980*, p. 15.

5. Willy Brandt et al., *North–South: A Program for Survival* (Cambridge, Mass.: The MIT Press, 1980), p. 239.

6. See Michael Lafferty, "Focus on High Risk Areas," *Financial Times* (May 11, 1981, Section III), p. I.

7. *World Development Report 1981*, p. 97.

8. Ibid., p. 58.

9. Ibid., p. 59.

10. Brandt, *North–South*, pp. 228–229.

11. It was a large part of the focus of a conference on IMF conditionality sponsored by the Institute for International Economics in Washington, D.C., in March 1982.

12. Multilateral flows as a percentage of total gross foreign flows are highest, however, in relatively low-income countries such as India (41 percent), Tanzania (33 percent), Bangladesh (29 percent), and Kenya (25 percent). Private flows predominate in such middle-income countries as Mexico (93 percent), Brazil (91 percent), Argentina (89 percent), and Malaysia (86 percent). See U.S. Treasury Department, *U.S. Participation in the Multilateral Development Banks in the 1980s* (Washington, D.C.: February 1982), p. 3.

13. Mason and Asher, *Since Bretton Woods*, p. 711.

14. Ibid.

15. Brandt, *North–South*, p. 230.

16. Mason and Asher, *Since Bretton Woods*, p. 707.

17. Robert S. McNamara, *Address to the Board of Governors* (Washington, D.C.: September 30, 1974), p. 23.

18. Robert A. Packenham, *Liberal America and the Third World* (Princeton, N.J.: Princeton University Press, 1973), p. 41.

19. Dorothy Seavey, "Basic Economic and Political Rights, Developing Countries and U.S. Foreign Policy" (Washington, D.C.: Overseas Development Council, draft, January 23, 1978), p. 17.

20. Escott Reid, "McNamara's World Bank," *Foreign Affairs*, 51 (July 1973), p. 795.

21. World Bank, *Questions and Answers—World Bank and IDA* (Washington, D.C.: January 1974), p. 3. Also see Eugene H. Rotberg, *The World Bank: A Financial Appraisal* (Washington, D.C.: World Bank, January 1981), pp. 21–26.

22. Rotberg, *A Financial Appraisal*, 1981, p. 12.

23. *World Bank Annual Report 1980*, p. 86.

24. *World Bank Annual Report 1970*, p. 35.

25. *World Bank Annual Report 1980*, pp. 158–159.

26. Ibid., p. 88.

27. Rotberg, *A Financial Appraisal*, 1981, p. 21.

28. Ibid., p. 23.

29. Ibid., pp. 12, 35.

30. *World Bank Annual Report 1975*, p. 76.

31. For the article in question, see V. H. Oppenheim, "Whose World Bank?" *Foreign Policy*, no. 19 (Summer 1975), pp. 99–108.

32. Rotberg, *A Financial Appraisal*, 1981, p. 18.

33. *World Bank Annual Report 1980*, p. 159.

34. John A. Holsen, "World Bank Techniques for Country Evaluation," Paper prepared for delivery at a symposium on the Outlook on Private Market Financing and Risk in Developing Countries, organized by the Export-Import Bank of the United States (Washington, D.C.: April 21, 1977), p. 2.

35. The data were furnished by the Information and Public Affairs Department of the Bank.

36. *Report of the Task Force on Forms of Association*, p. 3.

37. The mere fact that no project was turned down by the directors does not necessarily mean that they have little or no influence. As in other agencies, directors planning to turn a project down might get in touch with the staff first to make sure that the project never reaches the directors' level. This is a plausible hypothesis, but little evidence could be found to sustain it.

38. Escott Reid, *Strengthening the World Bank* (Chicago: University of Chicago Press, 1976), p. 199.

39. *New York Times*, December 22, 1976, p. 3.

40. However, seven of these countries later resumed borrowing from IDA, and IDA lending continues to four of them. See U.S. Treasury Department, *U.S. Participation in the Multilateral Development Banks in the 1980s*, p. 70.

41. Ibid., p. 72.

42. Ibid., p. 71.

Chapter 4

1. Chenery et al., *Redistribution with Growth*, p. 12.

2. Ibid., pp. 11–13.

3. Robert S. McNamara, *Address to the Board of Governors* (Nairobi, Kenya: September 24, 1973), p. 6.

4. Chenery et al., *Redistribution with Growth*, p. 38.

5. Irma Adelman and Cynthia Taft Morris, *Economic Growth and Social Equity in Developing Countries* (Stanford, Calif.: Stanford University Press, 1973), p. 189.

6. David Morawetz, *Twenty-five Years of Economic Development—1950 to 1975* (Washington, D.C.: World Bank, 1977), p. 41.

7. Ibid., p. 43.

8. For a summary of some of the leading simulation studies, see Cline, "Distribution and Development," pp. 378–387.

9. Chenery et al., *Redistribution with Growth*, p. 17.

10. Ibid., p. 47.

11. Ibid., p. 48.

12. Ibid.

13. Ibid.

14. Ibid., p. 49.

15. Oscar Altimir, "The Extent of Poverty in Latin America," Paper prepared for the Economic Commission for Latin America (ECLA), July 1978, pp. 3, 4, 8, 9.

16. Chenery et al., *Redistribution with Growth*, p. 56.

17. Ibid., p. 72.

18. Robert S. McNamara, *Address to the Board of Governors* (Washington, D.C.: September 25, 1978), p. 35.

19. Ibid., especially pp. 6–20.

20. Morawetz, *Twenty-Five Years of Economic Development*, p. 26.

21. Ibid., pp. 28–30.

22. Robert S. McNamara, *Address to the Board of Governors* (Washington, D.C.: September 26, 1977), p. 7.

23. John A. Mathieson, *Basic Needs and the New International Economic Order: An Opening for North–South Collaboration in the 1980's*, (Washington, D.C.: Overseas Development Council, May 1981), p. 28.

24. Ibid., p. 30.

25. See Morris D. Morris and Florizelle B. Liser, "The PQLI: Measuring Progress in Meeting Human Needs," Communique no. 32 (Washington, D.C.: Overseas Development Council, 1977). Also see John W. Sewell and the Staff of the Overseas Development Council, *The United States and World Development: Agenda 1977* (Washington, D.C.: Overseas Development Council, 1977), pp. 147–152.

26. James P. Grant, *Disparity Reduction Rates: A Proposal for Meeting and Targetting Progress in Meeting Basic Needs*, Monograph no. 11 (Washington, D.C.: Overseas Development Council, September 1978).

27. John W. Sewell and the Staff of the Overseas Development Council, *The United States and World Development: Agenda 1980* (Washington, D.C.: Overseas Development Council, 1980), pp. 152–164.

28. Ibid.

29. T. N. Srinivasan, "Development Policies and Levels of Living of the Poor: Some Issues," Report on the Workshop on Analysis of Distributional Issues in Development Planning, Bellagio, April 22–27, 1977, p. 42.

30. See, for example, Robert A. Dahl, *A Preface to Democratic Theory* (Chicago: University of Chicago Press, 1956).

31. Again it could be argued that the Bank had no business theorizing about such political complexity given its primary task of economic development and the political constraints upon it. It is likely, however, that more attention to the politics of poverty-oriented work would have facilitated the Bank's work on development. As will be apparent in subsequent chapters, many of the implementation difficulties in poverty-oriented projects stemmed from a lack of appreciation of political constraints existing at the time of project inception.

Chapter 5

1. Robert S. McNamara, *Address to the Board of Governors* (Nairobi, Kenya: September 24, 1973), p. 16.

2. Ibid., p. 15.

3. World Bank, *Rural Development Sector Policy Paper* (Washington, D.C.: February 1975), p. 19.

4. World Bank, *The Task Ahead for the Cities of the Developing Countries* (Washington, D.C.: July 1975), p. 15.

5. World Health Organization, *Community Water Supply and Excreta Disposal in Developing Countries, Review of Progress*, Statistical report, 29 (1976).

6. *Rural Development Sector Policy Paper*, pp. 12–13.

7. Ibid., p. 13.

8. Albert Waterston, "A Viable Model for Rural Development," *Finance and Development*, 11 (December 1974), p. 22.

9. See, for example, Comité Interamericano de Desarrollo Agrícola (CIDA), *Chile: Tenencia de la tierra y desarrollo socio-económico del sector agrícola* (Santiago, 1966), pp. 19–20.

10. Erik Eckholm, "The Dispossessed of the Earth: Land Reform and Sustainable Development," *Worldwatch Paper 30* (Washington, D.C.: Worldwatch, June 1979), p. 17.

11. R. Albert Berry and William R. Cline, *Farm Size, Factor Productivity and Technical Change in Developing Countries*, draft, June 1976, summarized in Schlomo Eckstein et al., *Land Reform in Latin America: Bolivia, Chile, Mexico, Peru, and Venezuela*, World Bank Staff working paper no. 275 (Washington, D.C.: April 1978).

12. Subcommittee of the Committee on Appropriations, House of Representatives, Ninety-fifth Congress, Second Session, *An Assessment of the Effectiveness of the World Bank and the Inter-American Development Bank in Aiding the Poor* (Washington, D.C.: 1978), p. 85.

13. James W. Wilkie, *Statistical Abstract of Latin America* (Los Angeles: UCLA Latin American Center, 1978), vol. 19, pp. 50–51.

14. International Labor Office, *Poverty and Landlessness in Rural Asia* (Geneva: ILO, 1977), p. 11.

15. Ibid.

16. I am indebted to James P. Grant for this analogy.

Chapter 6

1. Two main sources of evidence are used here. The first is comprised of documentary materials available and accessible at the Bank. These include the relevant project supervision reports, special assessments which the Bank has carried out on a limited number of projects, annual reports prepared by the geographical divisions of the Bank analyzing the status of all projects under their supervision, and project profiles prepared for 28 projects by the Agriculture and Rural Development Department within the Bank's Central Projects Staff. Given the relatively limited amount of documentary material, however, it was necessary to have extensive recourse to detailed interviews with individual project officers at the bank. These are officers charged with the supervision of projects. They are intimately acquainted with the projects through repeated visits to project sites, frequent dealings with project officials in recipient countries, and access to all documentation on projects. Detailed interviews with such officers were second-best alternatives to visiting the projects themselves and talking with local officials and the intended beneficiary populations, but they were still extraordinarily useful for learning about project behavior.

Interviews were conducted for several months during 1978, 1979, and 1980. They covered projects in Bolivia, Brazil, Colombia, Guyana, Haiti, Indonesia, Korea, Malaysia, Mexico, Nepal, Nigeria, Paraguay, the Philippines, and Tanzania. It is difficult to be precise about the exact number of projects covered in these interviews because some interviews ranged across numerous projects in one country (such as 6 land settlement projects in Malaysia and 11 irrigation projects in the Philippines); other interviews covered only a single project (such as in Haiti). At least 25 separate projects were the subjects of interviews; if to these are added the number of projects discussed in interviews which ranged across numerous projects in a single country, the total comes to at least 50.

2. The sociology of agricultural extension is always interesting, the more so in an ostensibly socialist system. This is because, ordinarily, progressive farmers would be selected as the focus of the extension effort, but this cannot be done here; it would be "un-Tanzanian."

3. The project was a highly unusual and in many ways atypical Bank project. It was rushed through appraisal after it became apparent that the Bank-financed dam upstream from the project area would alter the flow of the São Francisco River in ways that would be disastrous for rice cultivation in the project area.

4. *The Wall Street Journal*, November 10, 1977, p. 26.

5. *World Bank Annual Report 1978*, p. 8.

6. Ibid., p. 9.

7. Ibid.

8. Frances Moore Lappe and Joseph Collins, *Food First* (Boston: Houghton Mifflin, 1977), p. 347.

9. Ernest Feder, *McNamara's Little Green Revolution: The World Bank Scheme for the Self-Liquidation of the Third World Peasantry* (The Hague: Institute of Social Studies, undated), pp. 19–20.

10. Aart J. M. Van de Laar, "The World Bank and the World's Poor," *World Development*, 4 (October–November 1976), p. 849.

Chapter 7

1. World Bank, *The Task Ahead for the Cities of the Developing Countries*, p. 7.

2. The data contained in this paragraph are from the relevant project appraisal reports for each country.

3. World Bank, *The Task Ahead for the Cities of the Developing Countries*, p. 15.

4. World Bank, *Housing Sector Policy Paper*, p. 14.

5. Ibid., p. 15.

6. These data were provided by the Urban Projects Department of the Bank.

7. Bairoch, *Economic Development*, p. 164.

8. Raúl Prebisch, *Change and Development — Latin America's Great Task*, Report submitted to the Inter-American Development Bank (New York: Praeger, 1971), p. 30.

Chapter 9

1. See Robert L. Ayres, "Development Policy and the Possibility of a 'Livable' Future for Latin America," *The American Political Science Review*, 69 (June 1975), pp. 507–525.

2. See Guillermo A. O'Donnell, *Modernization and Bureaucratic — Authoritarianism* (Berkeley: University of California Press, 1973).

3. For a discussion of polyarchy, see Dahl, *A Preface to Democratic Theory*.

4. Adam Przeworski, "Some Problems in the Study of the Transition to Democracy," revision of a paper presented at a workshop on Prospects for Democracy: Transitions from Authoritarian Rule in Latin America and Latin Europe, sponsored by the Latin American Program of the Woodrow Wilson International Center for Scholars, Smithsonian Institution, Washington, D.C., September 25–26, 1979, pp. 18–19.

5. Guillermo A. O'Donnell, "Notes for the Study of Processes of Democratization from the Bureaucratic-Authoritarian State," Paper presented at the workshop on Prospects for Democracy, Woodrow Wilson International Center for Scholars, Smithsonian Institution, Washington, D.C., September 25–26, 1979, p. 15.

6. General project descriptions are from various Bank annual reports relating to the years in which the projects were undertaken.

7. Richard M. Bird, *Taxation and Development — Lessons from Colombian Experience* (Cambridge, Mass.: Harvard University Press, 1970), p. 7.

8. *Latin America Newsletter*, 9 (November 28, 1975), p. 375.

9. John White, *The Politics of Foreign Aid* (New York: St. Martin's Press, 1974), p. 56.

10. Ibid., p. 96.

11. Ibid.

12. Ibid., p. 97.

13. Ibid.

14. Albert O. Hirschman, *Development Projects Observed* (Washington, D.C.: The Brookings Institution, 1967), p. 156.

15. Ibid.

16. Mason and Asher, *Since Bretton Woods*, p. 431.

17. Naomi Caiden and Aaron B. Wildavsky, *Planning and Budgeting in Poor Countries* (New York: John Wiley & Sons, 1974), p. 149.

18. David Lehmann, "Political Incorporation Versus Political Stability: The Case of the Chilean Agrarian Reform, 1965–70," *The Journal of Development Studies*, 7 (July 1971), p. 374.

19. Robert L. Ayres, "Economic Stagnation and the Emergence of the Political Ideology of Chilean Underdevelopment," *World Politics*, 25 (October 1972), p. 41.

20. Robert L. Ayres, "Political History, Institutional Structure, and Prospects for Socialism in Chile," *Comparative Politics*, 5 (July 1973), p. 505.

21. Lehmann, "Political Incorporation," p. 383.

22. Ibid.

23. Robert R. Kaufman, *The Politics of Land Reform in Chile* (Cambridge, Mass.: Harvard University Press, 1972), p. 118.

24. Ibid., p. 120.

25. Philippe C. Schmitter, "Still the Century of Corporatism?" in Fredrick B. Pike and Thomas Stritch, eds., *The New Corporatism* (Notre Dame, Ind.: University of Notre Dame Press, 1974), pp. 93–94.

26. See, for example, David Collier and Ruth Berins Collier, "Who Does What, to Whom, and How: Toward a Comparative Analysis of Latin American Corporatism," in James M. Malloy, ed., *Authoritarianism and Corporatism in Latin America* (Pittsburgh: University of Pittsburgh Press, 1976).

27. Schmitter, "Still the Century of Corporatism?" p. 124.

28. Susan Kaufman Purcell, "Decision-Making in an Authoritarian Regime: Theoretical Implications from a Mexican Case Study", *World Politics*, 26 (October 1973), pp. 28–54.

29. For a discussion of vertical groups with particular application to Brazilian politics, see Douglas A. Chalmers, "Political Groups and Authority in Brazil: Some Continuities in a Decade of Confusion and Change," in Riordan Roett, ed., *Brazil in the Sixties* (Nashville, Tenn.: Vanderbilt University Press, 1972).

30. Schmitter, "Still the Century of Corporatism?" p. 124.

31. On this issue, see Robert L. Ayres, "Political Regimes, Explanatory Variables, and Public Policy in Latin America," *Journal of Developing Areas*, 10 (October 1975), p. 29.

Chapter 10

1. *The Sunday Times* (London), March 7, 1982, p. 10.

2. Ibid.

3. "Foreign Aid: Debating the Uses and Abuses," *The New York Times*, March 1, 1981, p. E5.

4. "Foreign Aid Retrenchment," "B List" (Office of Management and Budget, January 27, 1981), p. 3.

5. Ibid., p. 7.

6. See James P. O'Leary, "Rethinking Foreign Aid," *The New York Times*, March 10, 1981, p. A19.

7. "World Bank Contracts: Does the U.S. Get Its Share?", *The Interdependent*, 7 (March 1981), p. 4.

8. The data on IDA contributions and contracts are found in ibid.

9. International Development Cooperation Agency, "Congressional Presentation Fiscal Year 1982" (Washington, D.C.: IDCA, 1981), p. 8.

10. A. W. Clausen, *Address to the Brookings Institution Seminar on the Future Role of the World Bank* (Washington, D.C.: January 7, 1982), p. 4.

11. Ibid., p. 5.

12. Clausen, *Global Interdependence in the 1980s, Address to the Yomiuri International Economic Society* (Tokyo: January 13, 1982), p. 2.

13. Ibid., p. 23.

14. Clausen, *Brookings Address*, p. 19.

15. Clausen, *Yomiuri Address*, p. 14.

16. U.S. Treasury Department, *U.S. Participation in the Multilateral Development Banks in the 1980s* (Washington, D.C.: February 1982), p. 55.

17. Clausen, *Brookings Address*, p. 5.

18. See the remarks by R. T. McNamar, Deputy Secretary of the Treasury, before the Brookings Institution Seminar on the Future Role of the World Bank (Washington, D.C.: January 7, 1982), p. 9.

19. Clausen, *Brookings Address*, p. 4.

20. Ibid., p. 8.

21. Ibid.

22. Ernest Stern, "World Bank Financing of Structural Adjustment," Paper prepared for the Conference on IMF Conditionality, organized by the Institute for International Economics, Airlie House, Virginia, March 24–26, 198⁻, p. 6.

23. Ibid.

24. Clausen, *Brookings Address*, pp. 19, 21.

25. Roger S. Leeds, "Co-financing for Development, Why Not More?" Overseas Development Council Development Paper no. 29 (Washington, D.C.: Overseas Development Council, April 1980), p. 22.

26. Data from the Information Office of the International Finance Corporation and the *IFC Annual Report 1980* (Washington, D.C.: 1980), pp. 16–17.

27. *World Bank Annual Report 1980*, p. 9.

28. Stern, "World Bank Financing."

29. Robert S. McNamara, *Address to the Board of Governors 1980* (Washington D.C., September 30, 1980), p. 17.

30. "Robert McNamara and the World Bank," Transcript of a *Communique* program broadcast on June 19, 1981 by National Public Radio.

31. There is of course an obvious problem in attempting to argue that the World Bank should become like the IAF. The IAF has been successful in large measure because of its small size; its credits to its Latin American recipients in fiscal 1980 totaled only about $24 million. Proposals to convert the World Bank into something resembling a mammoth IAF do not make sense. It would be difficult, if not impossible, to commit $2.7 billion to Latin America and the Caribbean (the size of Bank commitments in that fiscal year) as compared to $24 million annually and still preserve organizational identity.

32. See Wynta Boynes, ed., *U.S. Non-Profit Organizations in Development Assistance Abroad: TAICH Directory 1978* (New York: Technical Assistance Information Clearing House, 1978). Also see Supplement I, TAICH Directory, August 1980.

33. This information is from the Advisory Committee on Voluntary Foreign Aid of the Agency for International Development, fiscal year 1979.

34. Biden-Pell Amendment to the International Security and Development Cooperation Act of 1981, Report of the Committee on Foreign Relations on S.1196 (Washington, D.C.: Government Printing Office, no. 97–83, 1981), p. 54.

35. *The Wall Street Journal*, November 10, 1977, pp. 1, 26.

36. Willy Brandt et al., *North–South: A Program for Survival* (Cambridge, Mass.: The MIT Press, 1980), pp. 282–292.

37. Ibid., p. 291.

38. Ibid.

39. Ibid.

40. Teresa Hayter, *The Creation of World Poverty: An Alternative View to the Brandt Report* (London: Pluto Press, 1981).

Index